FOND MEMORIES OF PLAYING FOR THE BLACK & GOLD

I well remember my dear friend Dick LeBeau saying to me not long ago, "The Steelers Nation makes me proud to be a Pittsburgh Steeler." Our son, David, is a 1989 West Point graduate and recently retired as a Lieutenant Colonel from the Army after serving 24 years in the Army as an Infantry officer. He said that during his 24-year career at his stateside and foreign country duty Posts, including four tours in Iraq, "I marveled and was amazed with the support and enthusiasm for the Steelers Nation and the Terrible Towel, not only from Pittsburgh native troops but from all around our country and people from other countries. It was heart-warming.

Bill Priatko
Steelers 1957

As a rookie in 1969, we played our games at Pitt Stadium, as Three Rivers was not yet completed. That year, Chuck Noll's first year in his 23-year run, and we were a measly 1-13. The fans were used to mediocre Steelers teams, and the fan base was not user friendly, to say the least. It seems like the 13 games we lost were almost expected from the fans. Then, the magic started. In 1970, we went 5-9, in 1971 ... 6-8, and by then, the Steelers fans were watching an evolution take place. They were not disappointed in 1972, as we went 11-3, and nearly went to the Super Bowl, only to be beaten by the Dolphins in their famous 17-0 season. The tide had turned. The black and gold colors began to appear in huge numbers, the Steel Curtain was established, and the rest is history. The Chuck Noll era created a dynasty and rewarded all the Steeler faithful for the years of mediocre football. Although no team can stay on top forever, the Steelers and the fans are a force to be dealt with.

Warren Bankston
Steelers 1969-1972

My first experience with Steelers Nation came in April 1993, when I arrived to play for the Black & Gold. On the night before my first day of offseason workouts at Three Rivers, I tuned into a local sports talk show while driving around getting to know the city, and I came across a weird sounding man with a raspy voice, using all these slang words I never heard of prior to my arrival. As it turned out, he was the Leader, Cheerleader and Homer play-by-play announcer for the Steelers, that set this frenzy Steelers Nation into motion for decades. Good old Myron Cope, the man who probably had something to do with all the Steelers bars throughout the country, in one way or another. A TRUE FAN.

Mike Tomczak
Steelers 1993-1999

During the 1970s Pittsburgh and Western Pennsylvania were going through a real rough patch economically. Many in the fan base were adversely affected. The team helped in a big way, to get them through it. It made them feel good about themselves, Pittsburgh and Western Pennsylvania. They were more than miners and steelworkers, they were part of the "Steelers Nation." We the players felt that they were a big part of the reason we were winning. Our identity...our work ethic...what we felt about ourselves, was more than a little fueled by our fans.

John Stallworth
Steelers 1974-1987

As a Pittsburgh Steeler, I experienced the greatest feeling a player can have. I was always surprised with some gifts or encouraging words as I battled through injuries. Just to know that I hadn't been given up on was great motivation and a confidence booster! I remember when a loyal fan gave me a mustard seed. It was so awesome to get something that meant "Faith." God said, "All you need is faith the size of a mustard seed and you can do anything!" I had already believed this, but to receive one from a fan that I didn't know, hit home for me. I love Steelers fans! Steelers fans are the best in the world!

William Blackwell
Steelers 1997-2001

I only played two years – 1964 & 1965. I started a few games at safety and was a back up defensive back for most of my career. One story from those years stands out in my memory bank. It was the last game of the season (1965) and we were playing the Cowboys in Dallas. I was coming off an ankle injury and I hadn't practiced any of our defensive schemes for the week and was just going to be on the special teams (punt and kickoff teams) for the game. We certainly weren't a factor in our division, so we all went out and partied until the wee hours. Well, the next morning I discovered I had lost my contacts, and my vision was 20/300 without them. I thought I had nothing to worry about because even though I could hardly see I could see the movement of the players. Well, 10 minutes before the start of the game, Buster Ramsey (Head Defensive Coach) came to me and said, "You are going to have to start at free safety because Jim Bradshaw pulled a muscle in pre-game warm-ups. Needless to say, it was an adrenaline rush – knowing we were going against Don Meredith, Bob Hayes & Company without even practicing any of our defensive schemes. It ended up being one of the best games of my brief career – intercepted a pass (my only NFL interception) for a 35-yard return and made 8 tackles without hardly being able to see.

I have very fond memories of my years with the Steelers and am very proud I had an opportunity to play for them. At that time Art and all the Rooneys were down on the field for most practices and knew everyone by first name – it was a real family.

Bob Sherman
Steelers 1964-1965

Always a Home Game

OUR JOURNEY THROUGH STEELERS COUNTRY IN 140 DAYS

Always a Home Game

OUR JOURNEY THROUGH STEELERS COUNTRY IN 140 DAYS

JOSH MILLER AND SHAWN ALLEN

st. lynn's press

PITTSBURGH

Always a Home Game
Our Journey Through Steelers Country in 140 Days

ISBN-13: 978-0-9892688-2-0

Library of Congress Control Number: 2013941491
CIP information available upon request

First Edition, 2014

St. Lynn's Press . POB 18680 . Pittsburgh, PA 15236
412.466.0790 . www.stlynnspress.com

Book design – Holly Rosborough
Editor – Catherine Dees

Photo Credits:
The photos in this book came from friends and supporters of *Always a Home Game:*
Shawn Allen, Josh Miller, George Dykeman, Abbey Way and Domenic Mantella
– and all the great Steelers fan clubs and bar owners across Steelers Nation
who contributed their personal and memorabilia photos.
Football Graphic, pgs 4, 37, 203: © Carlos Santa Maria - Fotolia.com

Printed in Canada
On certified FSC recycled paper using soy-based inks

This title and all of St. Lynn's Press books may be purchased for educational, business or sales promotional use. For information please write:
Special Markets Department . St. Lynn's Press . POB 18680 . Pittsburgh, PA 15236

10 9 8 7 6 5 4 3 2 1

JOSH:

To my father, Richard Miller, who was my biggest fan. He lost his battle with cancer during the course of this Journey. I hope my son looks up to me the way I looked up to him. Yes, he was a huge Steelers fan as well.

To Angie, Olivia, Caleb and Ava: thank you for letting me do this book. I know it wasn't easy.

SHAWN:

To the love of my life, Carolyn, with your support and wisdom ever-present, your beauty everlasting, and the best days of our lives ahead of us...Prost! And to Lauren and Mac, who are all that a father could ever wish for.

Restrooms

TABLE OF CONTENTS

TABLE OF CONTENTS

ABOUT THE BOOK

✦ ✦ ✦

What possessed us to visit 32 NFL markets in one season? Well, not surprisingly, it all started over a couple of beers and talk about the Steelers. We were hanging out at a neighborhood get together and Josh was telling me how cool it was to run onto the field at the Arizona Cardinals stadium to a sea of Terrible Towels. He said something along the lines of, "I swear it was like being at a Steelers home game." I posited the question, "I wonder whether it's like that anywhere else?"

Well that got the ball rolling. We started making plans to visit all the stadiums and see whether there were more Steelers fans than home team fans. Our plans evolved into visiting Steelers hangouts in the shadows of the other 31 NFL stadiums over the course of the season. Then somebody issued a 100 bar challenge: one hundred bars in the course of a season. How hard could that be? Everyone started throwing out the names of places they had been to on vacation or business trips where Steelers fans gathered. We pictured a book of our Journey. A book of 100 cool Steelers hangouts in Steelers Nation.

Our wives were laughing, no doubt thinking that we would never pull this off. Admittedly, Josh and I come up with crazy schemes on a pretty regular basis. They said they were "in" if we could convince the Steelers that this was a good idea.

Well, it helps that Josh is a former player. Make that an outstanding former player. And one that has always been respectful of the Steelers and the Rooneys. He got us a meeting with the Rooneys and we told them of our plan. Eventually, they gave us their blessing.

A trip to a Super Bowl XLVII party in New Orleans on another business deal eventually put us in touch with a publisher, Paul of St. Lynn's Press. As karma would have it, St. Lynn's is located right next door to the Steelers' practice facility and Paul eats at the Steelers' cafeteria a couple of times a week.

Now which 100 Steelers hangouts to visit? We knew Steelers fans would know of the best places to watch a game in each NFL market. So we started a website. www.alwaysahomegame.com. We put it all out there. We told fans where we were headed each week and asked them where we should show up. Between their feedback and our own research, we came up with our list and we were off and running, driving, flying … The following pages tell the story of the Journey and what we found. ✦

SHAWN: I was not born in the 'Burgh and did not grow up worshiping the Black & Gold. I was born and raised in sunny Southern California and developed an un-American passion for fútbol, rather than football. My first NFL memory is of my younger brother taunting me with a Terrible Towel as the Steelers won another Super Bowl. Why was my punk little brother a Pittsburgh Steelers fan? What was he doing with a Terrible Towel? I didn't know it, but that moment was actually like looking into a crystal ball, and years later I would be a longtime Pittsburgh resident...and still be taunted by the Terrible Towel!

Somehow, I left sunny California for college in Western Pennsylvania. There I fell for a girl who, like me, played soccer. I thought I was home free until she invited me to her family house for a Sunday meal. There is no way I could have prepared for what happened next. I was sitting in a beautiful house in a nice suburb of Pittsburgh, surrounded by an extremely well-educated family. But they all had Terrible Towels tucked into the pocket of their jeans. We sat down to watch a Steelers game, and on one of the first plays I hear "NICE BLOCK!" screamed as Bubby Brister connects on a long pass to Louie Lipps. Nice block...what block? I am thinking nice pass, or great catch, but the conversation is surrounding the pancake block from the fullback. Who are these crazy fans? My introduction to the warped mentality of the Pittsburgh Steelers fan continues. (Author's note: Of course I married the girl, so even though I was not a Steelers fan at the time, I am not a complete idiot!)

If you do not count the hazing from my kid brother or a few wild Sunday afternoons with my in-laws, my personal journey into the psyche of the Pittsburgh Steelers fan started in 2000 when my company was contracted to auction off the memorabilia from Three Rivers Stadium. I knew from experience that this was going to be a tremendous event. However, at the time I did not fully appreciate the passion of a Pittsburgh Steelers fan.

As I toured the multi-purpose stadium for the first time, I expected to see a stadium without an identity. I was thinking, What makes this stadium any different than the one in Cincinnati, or St. Louis? This relic from the 1960s and its multi-purpose design were going away, and the faster the better, in my opinion. I could not have been more wrong and was immediately overwhelmed by the historic significance of the

Steelers organization. From the public concourses to the private offices, everything I experienced was homage to the team, the players and the Rooney family. And it was all genuine. What I saw was a true passion for the city, a team and a community of fans.

Creating memorabilia is a big part of stadium auctions. The artificial turf in Three Rivers Stadium was an excellent opportunity. We decided that the turf would be cut into 4-inch squares and sold in the auction. During the demolition large segments of the turf were saved for this purpose. As we were beginning this process, we were shocked one morning to see we had a visitor. A mountain of a man standing well over 6' 5" and weighing 300+ pounds came walking over to the sections of turf. He was dressed in Black & Gold from head to toe. Without saying a word, he reached into his pocket and pulled out a hunting knife (think Paul Hogan in Crocodile Dundee and the knife he pulled on the street thugs). The auction crew froze with stunned silence. He proceeded to cut a piece of the turf. When we told him that he was not allowed to take the turf, he responded simply, "This stadium will always be a part of my life. Which one of you is going to stop me?" We cowered back to our tasks.

And then there were the fans who wanted to purchase their own seat from us. With over 59,000 seats such an endeavor was an operational nightmare. The decision was made not to allow specific seat purchases, but rather to give each season ticket holder a seat of the same color. This was not received well, and a few ingenious Steelers fans found a way around such clearly irrational decisions.

One such fan, aware of the impending sale took action into his own hands. During the final game

of the 2000 NFL Season he wrote his initials on the bottom of his seat with a Sharpie. He then went to the stadium as the auction crew was accumulating items to be sold in the auction and the demolition crew was simultaneously preparing for the implosion of the stadium in a few short weeks. This fan made a cash donation to the nightly "Iron City Beer fund", and instructed the worker on the seat's location. To insure he received his seats (Section 613, Row F, Seat 12 recalled precisely over 12 years later as if it were his daughter's birthday) he did not tell the workers what was written on the bottom of the seat. A few hours later he received a call correctly identifying the initials on the seat, and he was driving home with a seat from the historic stadium. In speaking with this individual, it is more than a plastic stadium seat. The passion in which he remembers watching games is, for him, embodied in a sun-faded plastic seat. This is not normal; it is fanaticism. Actually, it is pretty normal. It is the life of a Pittsburgh Steelers fan. ✦

JOSH: THE EX-PUNTER

JOSH: People often ask me how cool it is to have played for the Steelers. How do you really answer what it is like to have been lucky enough to play for an organization that has the greatest fan base in all of sports? For me, it is like having a childhood dream come true. Like probably many of you reading this book, I remember first becoming a Steelers fan in the 1970s. The Steel Curtain, Mean Joe Greene, LC Greenwood, Lynn Swan, Terry Bradshaw, Chuck Noll, Mike Webster, Franco Harris, Louis Lipps and the 20 other guys I knew by name by the time that I was 14 years old growing up in New Jersey. I was part of Steelers Nation. How cool is it to be able to call myself a fan and a former player? Beyond cool.

I've been on other teams. I've played on those teams with some really amazing players and I've had a lot of success on those teams. But there is a reason I'm writing a book about the Steelers and their fans. There is just a different feeling you get playing for the Steelers. Part of that, of course, comes from the Rooney family. I know that I was so excited to be signed by the Steelers, that when my first contract came through, I bought them champagne, steaks and lobsters as a way of saying "thank you." Somehow, that personal connection is just there.

Admittedly, the NFL is a business and winning is everything – it puts money in the owners' pockets, and in turn, the players' pockets. But the Rooneys never made us feel like that. They always made us feel as though we were part of a bigger picture – like we were part of Pittsburgh, part of the Steelers legacy and that, whatever our contributions may be, we would never be forgotten. At the end of each game, win or lose, we could count on Mr. Rooney coming down to shake our hands and say "nice game" or "go get 'em next week." During the holidays, Mr. Rooney would always slip a little envelope into the players' lockers as a present. And even though it's been a long time since I've worn a Steelers uniform, any time I see either Mr. Art Rooney or Mr. Dan Rooney, each stops to ask me about my wife Angie and my kids Olivia, Cal (did I mention that his middle name is Steel?), and Ava. Their kindness, generosity and personal connection with players is really amazing.

Of course, the Steelers would be nothing without their fans. The Rooneys know it, and the players know it. Again, I can tell you from playing for other teams; there is just a different vibe that comes from Steelers fans. I remember landing at airports on Saturday nights for Sunday away games. Mr. Rooney would have buses waiting for us on the tarmac so that we wouldn't have to trek through the airport (again, that personal and caring Rooney touch!). We would show up to the hotel in the evening, only to be greeted by cheering fans. Who hangs out at the hotel? How did they even find us? Who does that? It was like being rock stars. The fans would start chanting Steelers songs. This wasn't just in one or two places. This was all over the country. This was every away game.

I was talking about this weird phenomenon with my friend Shawn not too long ago. I was trying to explain how it felt to be a player for the Steelers and be at an away game and feel like the home team. Steelers Nation is big. They travel well. They are loud and they love their damn Steelers. I can't tell you how many times I ran out of the tunnel in an opponent's back yard and felt like I was at Three Rivers Stadium or at Heinz Field. The home team would get booed when they emerged. Ouch! Can you imagine that? Coming out of the tunnel in your own backyard and getting booed. Yet that's exactly what happened on a weekly basis when the Steelers hit the road. No matter how hard they tried, the home team always lost out to the traveling Steelers fans. Black & Gold took over every stadium and made it a home game.

We thought it would be fun to capture this idea in a book. I also wanted to give back to those heroes of my youth. The guys that played in

the early days didn't sign for millions of dollars. There were no retirement plans or health care contracts to take care of them while they aged. They didn't have the specialized equipment that is available now.

I was a punter. I know that I left the game with some scars and pains, but I didn't put my body through what most of those guys did. I've heard it said that every single snap of the ball is like a bar brawl. That's 60 bar brawls every Sunday, 16 Sundays a year. That's 960 bar brawls a season. And that doesn't include practice. Those guys put it on the line for Steelers Nation every single weekend and they are paying the price today. So Shawn and I decided we would give a portion of the proceeds from the Always a Home Game venture to Steelers charities to directly benefit former Steelers players. Not surprisingly, when we tell the fans we run into on our Journey what we are doing, they get right on board. This book doesn't happen if I played for another team. This book only happens because I played for the Steelers. ✦

RATING THE BARS

We visited 100 bars on our Journey through the NFL cities. All kinds of bars, from Steelers bars 24/7/365 to regular sports bars. We rated each one according to the following hypocycloid system:

If you see	✦ ✦ ✦	it's a Steelers bar 24/7/365
If you see	✦ ✦	it's a Steelers bar on Game Days
If you see	✦	it's a sports bar

SHAWN'S BEER-RATING NOTE

In those 100 bars I tasted a lot of beers, local and otherwise, sublime and godawful.

For many years it has been my practice to rate every beer I drink. At one point in my "drinking" life, I used social media to share my insightful ratings. Then my wife pointed out that I had rated over 400 different beers in one 10-month period. She, I mean I, decided that perhaps that was not the best image to project when someone else was paying my salary. Now that I am writing a book about drinking with Steelers fans across the country (I love my job!), not only is it acceptable to talk about beer ratings, it is a job requirement.

I developed this rating system as a way to communicate with friends about beer. It is much like a bell curve – a lot of 3s and very few 1s or 5s. For reference, here is the scale that I will use:

"1"   **So bad that I could not finish the beer** (Michelob Ultra)

"2"   **Did not suck** (Yuengling Lager)

"3"   **Good** (Fat Tire)

"4"   **If you see this beer, I recommend ordering a pint** (Two Hearted Ale)

"5"   **Go out of your way to find it** (Pliny the Elder)

Washington, D.C.
Home of the Redskins

Shawn's Two Cents

It's August 19th as we roll out of the 'Burgh for the first time, and we try to get comfortable for the four-hour trip to the Nation's capital. Running through the list of things we need to capture on this experience, and worrying that we have forgotten something, we remind ourselves that this is a pre-season game for the Steelers as well as the *Always a Home Game* crew.

Our excitement begins to build as we cruise down the Pennsylvania Turnpike and we see the Steelers fans converging on D.C. – at least a dozen cars headed east packed with Steelers jerseys. In the rearview mirror we see an older model American sub-compact. It looks like the only way this vehicle will pass inspection is if the owner "accidentally" leaves a $100 bill under the screw of the air filter. But this bucket of rust flies by us and we're laughing, and then we notice the Steelers flag mounted to the window. Guess he was in a hurry to get to the game and tailgate! Even better, we see a Ben Roethlisberger jersey on a hanger in the back seat.

It doesn't look as though this guy has washed his car since the Steelers played at Three Rivers, but there's nary a wrinkle in that jersey!

Just as we begin to realize that we've underestimated the D.C. traffic (this makes the Parkway East on a Friday afternoon look like an HOV lane), Gooz checks in to make sure that "we are okay." A Washington local, Gooz is a hard-core Steelers fan that Josh knows from Steelers Fantasy Camp. Fans travel from all over the world to attend each summer and Gooz is a 10-year veteran of this St. Vincent tradition. Lore has it that Gooz works for "the Government" in a "top secret" department. So the future of our country is in the hands of Steelers fans (remember – the word "fan" is short for "fanatic"). Steelers Nation will sleep better tonight.

So we give Gooz our location and he guides us with precision into Alexandria, avoiding the worst of the congestion, and we roll up to Southside 815 only fashionably late.

It was good to see a nice selection of craft beer available. One of us ordered a pint of Fat Tire (from New Belgium Brewing Company, a great company that also makes a fine beer) and one of us made a completely uninspired selection (inspired by his last name?) – Miller Lite. We then sought out Greg, the owner, to find out how Southside 815 became a place where Steelers fans hang out.

Not knowing what to expect from the first bar on our Journey, we walk through the door with trepidation, only to be greeted by Steelers fans waving Terrible Towels. It was awesome – here we were in Alexandria, Virginia, for a pre-season game and the Black & Gold are out waving their colors.

Parched from our trek across Pennsylvania, I was excited to evaluate the beer selection, so we bellied up to the bar. The first thing that caught our attention was an Iron City Beer can commemorating Super Bowl X.

Greg, a lifelong Steelers fan, said the intent was to create an environment that was more like Western Pennsylvania than a typical D.C. bar. He placed the Iron City can on the shelf behind the bar and did not think much of it. Then a patron noticed the can and started to show up to watch the Steelers games. As weeks passed, word got around. Now, forget about getting a table on Steelers Sunday, unless you arrive early. If you do, we highly recommend ordering Pittsburgh Benedict, a special meal prepared only on Sundays and especially for the fans of the Black & Gold.

rooms, corn, jalapenos, pepper jack cheese and fresh salsa). Awesome, especially when paired with the fine craft beer selection.

Beer Note: I was immediately drawn to the local brewery, D.C. Brau. Mike suggested "The Public," an IPA with a citrus aroma and a smooth finish. The perfect pairing for the spicy pierogie. A solid "4" on my rating scale. Needless to say, Mr. Miller ordered his namesake, again! Mike told me that they have special arrangements with their beer distributors to allow them to serve Yuengling, Iron City and IC light on Game Days.

Full of good food and good drink, we made our way through the crowd to ask Mike and Meredith how The Mighty Pint became a mecca for Steelers fans. Before opening in 2010, there were more than 16 different bars in the D.C. area where Steelers fans hung out to watch games. Undeterred, Mike and Meredith opened their doors. Apparently, if you build it, they really will come. Questioning how there can be so many Steelers fans in the shadow of FedEx Field, Mike and Meredith responded that the "deadskins" can't compare to the Steelers and their proud tradition.

◆ ◆ ◆
THE MIGHTY PINT
1831 M St. NW
Washington, DC 20036
(202) 466-3010
www.themightypint.com

On to The Mighty Pint. We wove through the monuments on our way downtown (where are the monuments to Franco Harris and Art Rooney, Sr.?). It was surprisingly easy to find parking and get to the bar. There is no doubt that this is a Steelers hangout. There were black and gold balloons and streamers throughout the bar and memorabilia on every wall. Thinking we had made pretty good time getting here, we were shocked to see Gooz sitting at a table already, with a plate of appetizers and a cold brew!

Owners Mike and Meredith welcomed us with a menu that was pure Black & Gold. The variety of "Pumped Up Pierogies" was incredible – there must be little babushka mamas making them in the back. We tried the Old West Pierogies (sautéed with roasted mush-

Two former Steelers players, Keith Gary and Mike Collier, joined us at The Mighty Pint, and they had some great stories about their experiences as players on the road.

Keith Gary – Defensive End, 1983-1988

Keith was a first round draft pick out of the University of Oklahoma in the 1981 NFL Draft. However, he did not immediately sign with the Steelers. After playing two years in the CFL, he came to Pittsburgh where he spent six seasons terrorizing the opposition. In one memorable play, he brought down Bengals quarterback Ken Anderson by the facemask, ripping the whole facemask off in the process.

Keith has been retired for 25 years, but is still recognized as a member of the Steelers family.

As the visit wound down, Keith asked if we'd noticed his scooter on the way in. We wandered outside, looking for some type of cool, vintage Vespa, but didn't see anything. Instead, Keith walks over to a "mobility scooter." He tells us that one of his business ventures involved the renting of scooters. Then this mountain of a man hopped on his mobility scooter, saying it is the best way to get around D.C. With a beep of his horn, he was off.

Mike Collier – RB Super Bowl X

In 1974, Mike was a 14th round draft choice out of Morgan State. Although his career in Pittsburgh was brief, he left Steelers fans with some tremendous memories. Not only did he score a touchdown in his first game, but he also returned a kickoff 94 yards for a touchdown against the Green Bay Packers, helping the Steelers win their second of six Super Bowls.

Even though Mike played in the '70s, when the main rivals for greatness were the Cowboys and the Raiders, his most vivid memories of Steelers fans were in Dallas and Oakland – arguably the most hostile environment for Steelers players and fans alike. He said that hearing fans cheer at these rival stadiums would push the players to give even more.

Keith had similar stories about the loyalty of Steelers fans.

✦ ✦ ✦
POUR HOUSE
319 Pennsylvania Ave SE
Washington, D.C.
(202) 546-0779
www.pourhouse.com

Leaving The Mighty Pint, we head for our third and final stop – the Pour House. The huge Steelers flag flies proudly from the sign out front and there's a group huddling around the door. We've found the right spot. As we approached, one of the guys who has clearly enjoyed his drink that day engaged Josh in conversation, informing him that the Pour House is the place to be. Not only are the Steelers going to be on TV, but a former player, Josh Miller, was going to show up. Josh deadpanned, "I am Josh Miller." The guy was ecstatic. Steelers fans are the greatest. Forget that we were in the Nation's capital, blocks away from the leader of the Free World. The action tonight is at the Pour House because Steelers Nation is in the house!

We finally made our way inside the bar and, just

for fun, we glanced around looking for Gooz. He does not disappoint. There, in a booth along the wall, he sat with his daughter and a delicious-looking plate of soft pretzels.

Moving towards the bar, we catch sight of...Myron Cope? Yoi! No wait; this might be a Double Yoi! Behind the bar is a mirror with Myron Cope's face from 1994, celebrating Myron and his 25th year as the voice of the Pittsburgh Steelers.

Beer Note: After the phenomenal recommendation at The Mighty Pint, I ask about the draft selection and learn that a special keg was tapped for us – Brooklyn Sorachi Ace. I have heard of these special hops developed in Japan, but never had the opportunity to sample them. The folks at Brooklyn Brewery created an incredible farmhouse saison with just a hint of lemon. A solid "4."

We then met Ryan, the bartender and legendary Steelers fan, for a tour of the other floors. For this early pre-season game, the crowd was a bit subdued. Only the main, street-level floor was open that day. Ryan explained that for regular season games, the

Pour House packs three floors with more than 400 Steelers fans. Memorabilia lined the wall. It was easy to picture fans singing the Pittsburgh Polka here on Game Days. The

tour continued and got a bit more interesting. Ryan introduced us to, well, himself. The story goes that as the Steelers prepared for their ill-fated trip to Super Bowl XLV, Ryan was lucky enough to have secured tickets to the game.

Unfortunately, his employer knew how important it was to have his #1 manager working for the big game. Under threat of bodily harm, Ryan promised he would be "behind the bar." But there was no way he would was going to miss out on the chance to see the Steelers win another Super Bowl ring. The elegant solution was to create a miniature full body cardboard cutout of himself (which is now known as "Little Ryan" and is propped up downstairs at the bar). On Game Day, Little Ryan was behind the bar...fulfilling the promise and creating a new legend. "Little Ryan" is routinely taken on road trips and vacations by fans and patrons of the Pour House.

Then he took us to the storage room to give us some D.C. Steelers Fan Club shirts. We noticed the interesting domed shape of the ceiling. Ryan told us that the bar was haunted! In a previous life, the Pour House was the first African American crematorium in D.C. Ryan pointed out that we were then under Pennsylvania Avenue, and that we were standing in the actual furnace. We moved out of that room quicker than Fast Willie Parker when we saw the skull behind the bar.

We finished the trip with a four-hour drive back to the 'Burgh. Wonder if I will see Gooz sitting at my kitchen table drinking a beer when I get back home.

Josh's Extra Points

Rolling back out of D.C., I thought about each of the three bars we had visited. Sure, they were all filled with crazy Steelers fans and great memorabilia. Somebody could have done a genealogy study of Steelers fans at Southside 815. I was taking pictures with fans, with their children, and with their children's children. The Mighty Pint had fantastic fish tacos. The Pour House was like walking into a bar on the North Shore.

The trip to D.C. also taught me something about Shawn, who would be my traveling companion for the next six months. Our sons are best friends, our daughters and wives are close, and I enjoy hanging out with him. So we've got that going for us. But traveling on the road with someone this much is getting to know somebody on a whole different level. He's kind of like a "big brother" I never had. He's smart and is organized and comes off as a bit antisocial. My kind of guy for sure! What I hadn't noticed before this trip was his laugh. Let's just say you would never forget it.

Kansas City
Home of the Chiefs

Shawn's Two Cents

One of the coolest aspects of this journey is that when the Steelers play at home, the Always a Home Game team is featured on the scoreboard at Heinz Field. You may learn, as we did, NOT to call the scoreboard at Heinz Field a "Jumbotron" in front of Steelers bigwigs. "Jumbotron" is a brand name and is a type of board manufactured by Sony. The Steelers use a "Daksboard". That doesn't really roll off the tongue so we are going to go with the "Big Board." Kansas City was the first road trip where we were going to be on the Big Board. Things did not start smoothly. We scrambled to find a replacement for our video guy who flaked out on us after his child was born. But, we found "Georgie Boy" instead, and headed for the land of BBQ.

As we approached Kansas City, we felt it only appropriate to stop at a roadside BBQ. We found Biffle's Smoke House Bar-B-Que. With a name like that how could we go wrong? We were immediately tagged as foreigners. (Could it have been the "Yinz got some BBQ?") The gracious staff helped us to order from one of the most confusing menus we'd ever come across. The combination of entrees, sides, lunch specials and sauces was enough to make heads spin. After ordering the brisket, we settled in to enjoy some excellent KC BBQ. We scarfed down our food with minimal conversation and no table manners worth mentioning. When we finished, we looked over and noticed that Georgie Boy's plate had barely been touched. We panicked for a moment. Had we made a critical error? How were we going to last on a long road trip with a guy who used a napkin and expected to talk during a meal? What was more, he had hoarded all of the stuffed mushroom caps! Fortunately, we gave Georgie Boy a second chance. We knew that, with time, we would drag him down to our Neanderthal ways.

✦ ✦
JOHNNY'S TAVERN

6765 W. 119th Street
Overland Park, KS 66209
(913) 451-4542
www.johnnystavern.com

We arrived at Johnny's Tavern around 2 p.m., a good four hours before kickoff. Of course, most Steelers fans would likely consider this a reasonable amount of time to tailgate before a game. When we entered, the bartender said the "crazy Steelers fans" met in the backroom. We walked into the back room and, much to our surprise, it was nothing special. We started to get nervous for the Big Board filming. About 2½ hours before kick-off, however, the cavalry came riding in.

Ed is the President of the KC Steelers Fan Club. They've been around since 1993 and have over 370 members. They've created their own version of the Terrible Towel, which they use as "membership cards" at events. They give back to local charities too. The 2013 charity of choice is the Kansas City Steelers

Youth Football Program. This is an impressive group. Ed and the fan club came in and transformed Johnny's Tavern before our eyes. It reminded me of the grounds crew at a Pirates game. They worked with precision to transform an average bar into a phenomenal Steelers hangout. Long banquet tables replaced the small high-top tables, the pool table was moved out of the way, and Steelers posters, banners and memorabilia replaced the innocuous beer paraphernalia. Those with the "membership cards" were allowed access to the seating area one hour before kickoff. All others have to wait until 30 minutes before. Considering that the crowd is standing room only for every game, this policy makes sense.

Now it was time to film the segment for the Big Board, but there was a problem. We forgot to bring the LED lights and the bar was too dark. Being the creative little elves that we are, we quickly realized that there was a large light that hung where the pool table had been. Standing on a bar stool, we held the pool light on Josh and Ed for the filming – disaster averted. (all video segments can be found on our website www.alwaysahomegame.com)

Immediately following our segment for the Big Board, one of the local TV stations interviewed us for the five o'clock news. As it turned out, the reporter was from Pittsburgh and convinced his producer that *Always a Home Game* was a story...he was right! About 5:45 p.m., another local news van pulled into the parking lot. The rival station came in and asked for a live segment to be aired on the six o'clock news. We could only imagine that this crew had seen the piece on the other station and did not want to be out-scooped on the story of the century: that there are so many Steelers fans around the country that wherever the Steelers play it always feels like a home game!

After the craziness of filming, it was time to sit back and enjoy the game. A waitress wearing a Hines Ward jersey came to our table carrying a full serving tray of shots. It's a KC Steelers Fan Club ritual – shots before each game. This concoction of Red Bull and flavored vodka was bright yellow and went down smooth. Then all of the sudden somebody yelled, "Who set the river

on fire?" Tony, one of the original KC Steelers Fan Club members, notoriously screamed a similar phrase at a game in Cleveland a few years back when the fan club took a road trip to Cleveland. Now's it's tradition and part of the weekly ritual. Everyone cheered and laughed in response (nobody actually told us who set the river on fire; it seemed to be a rhetorical question).

We met a lot of cool people at Johnny's and heard some interesting stories, but there was one couple in particular, a husband and wife with matching Steelers tattoos on their calves. We went over to find out the story behind the tattoo, but got sidetracked by a Terrible Towel they had with them – really old and somewhat tattered. The husband told us that he and his father had been estranged for a number of years, not speaking. Then, a son was born. The now grandfather reached out with a peace offering – the Terrible Towel he had kept through the years. The reports are that they now have a good relationship. I think Myron would give that a "Double Yoi!"

◆

DANNY'S BAR AND GRILL

13350 College Blvd.
Lenexa, KS 66210
(913) 345-9717
www.dannysbarandgrill.com

Our KC adventure then took an interesting turn. We approached our next stop, Danny's Bar and Grill, in high spirits, feeling great about our experience with the KC Steelers Fan Club. So our expectations were equally high for Danny's.

Danny's is a nice enough establishment and a few Steelers fans do gather there on Sundays, but it doesn't shout "Steelers hangout" when you're here. No Steelers or Pittsburgh memorabilia; no Pittsburgh-related food (c'mon, just put a few fries on top of that sandwich/salad/whatever!); no signs of Iron City or IC Light. And we didn't hear "Yinz" or "Jagoff" once while we were there. The good part of our visit was that some fans of Always a Home Game did show

up, so we decided to have dinner with them and we thoroughly enjoyed our time with them.

Beer Note: Even though Danny's wasn't much of a dedicated Steelers bar, it did have terrific beer serendipity. The featured local beer was Boulevard Pop-Up IPA. In addition to referring to myself (in the third person when I want to sound like a modern-day professional athlete) as a beer sommelier, I am also a hophead – a fancy way of saying that I like IPAs. Not everyone knows the story of the IPA, so I will use this opportunity to tell my own version. (This has not been fact-checked by the librarians at the Carnegie). IPA stands for India Pale Ale. This beer style was first brewed in England in the 19th century. At this time, England ruled the world (or so it believed), and it wanted to bring its beers to the ex-pats living in India. The problem was that traditional English beers could not survive the long voyage by ship. The solution: brew a higher alcohol beverage to fight the rigors of sea travel. But the taste wasn't quite right so the brewers decided to increase the hop content to balance the beer. The result was a very hoppy beer that ages quite well. As with most things, the Europeans got it started, but the Americans made it great! As the craft beer movement gained steam in the '90s, the Pacific Northwest brewers exploited the availability of American hops (Cascade, Centennial, Chinook, Simcoe, et cetera) and pushed the limits of the IPA. By adding even more alcohol and hops, new categories of beer were created. We started to see Double IPAs, Imperial IPAs, and even Triple IPAs (these techniques all refer to the brewing process and the various additions of hops in the brewing process). Now the best IPAs in the world, in my self-appointed beer sommelier opinion, are all brewed in the United States, and the European brewers are traveling here to learn how to make beer.

Back to the beer at Danny's. The Pop-Up IPA brings together two of my favorite things, hops and a session beer. Oh crap, here we go again! The history of a session beer (again, not fact-checked) also goes back to the U.K. It is believed that the term originated during World War I and the extremely long manufacturing shifts (mostly producing shells for the large guns) employed during wartime. The workers were allowed two "sessions" where they could drink beer. They needed a beer that would not get them too slammed so that they could return to work after 6-8 pints (!) – a traditional drinking session in those days. The original session beers were mostly cask-conditioned mild or bitter beers, but the key element was that the alcohol content was around 4% ABV (alcohol by volume). Many U.S. breweries have adopted this tradition in recent years. The modern standard for a session beer is any beer with ABV less than 5%. My personal favorite sessions are Guinness Draft (which is also my favorite light beer – yes, light beer! A 12 oz. glass contains 125 calories. By comparison, a Budweiser has 145 calories and a Blue Moon

has 228 calories!) and Yards Brawler – I cannot wait for our trip to Philly to get a fresh one.

Returning now to the Pop-Up IPA, Boulevard Brewing is a Kansas City institution, established in 1988 on historic Southwest Boulevard. The Pop-UP IPA is a very big citrus IPA with tremendous hop aroma and very little bitterness on the back of the tongue. The Pop-Up at 4.2% ABV is a flagship for the brewery, and means, as compared to other IPAs (average 7% ABV) or Double/Imperial IPAs (average 9% ABV), you can enjoy twice as many! So in this case, I need to modify my rating system. This beer is a "4" – meaning if you see it, order one. But because this is a session beer, it takes on a slightly different meaning. If you see this beer, ORDER TWO!]

11

Oh yes, our first Big Board experience. And, as mentioned above, this was also the birth of Georgie Boy, a truly wonderful human being, but probably the slowest eater on Planet Earth. Let's face it; he was an audible, a "Plan B" if you will. But it worked out unbelievably well and we are happy to have him. As they say, everything works out for a reason.

Now, about our first Big Board show, which was coming live to Heinz Field. I was kind of nervous. Not sure why, given that I make a living talking to people. Maybe it was because Georgie Boy was telling me we had to be clean for 45 seconds straight with no mess-ups, no starting over and no editing. In other words, I have to be perfect in front of the 150 Steelers fans at Johnny's Tavern who are staring at me and yelling, "Here we go, Steelers!"

It's kind of funny, looking back now. We did so many things wrong that day. The lighting was a little off, unless you consider using a pool table light held on an angle by two guys "professional." Ed, the President of the K.C. Steelers Fan Club, and I looked like we were standing in a basement closet. But hey, with all that being said, I thought we did a great job. It was our first Big Board show and you'll always remember your first. Mine was with Ed and Georgie Boy.

I've got to mention how cool Ed and the fan club are. They've been doing this for years and they have it down to a science. I remember walking into Johnny's Tavern and thinking, "This is a Steelers bar? This is going to be a waste of time." But we were there and we were out of options. I was kind of mad that our first Big Board show was going to be in a place that didn't look like a Steelers hangout. I remember going to change into my Steelers attire and coming back into a different place. Johnny's Tavern looked like a bar on the North Shore. It was as if all of Willy Wonka's oompa loompas came in and re-did the joint. Just an absolute Steelers makeover. Needless to say, this put me in great spirits. Not sure how many beers I had that night but I do recall that it was just enough. Again, you always remember your first, and Kansas City will never be forgotten.

Denver
Home of the Broncos

As Josh and I leave for the airport at 3:15 a.m., we know that the 30-hour trip to Denver and back is going to test our endurance – or our ability to sleep on an airplane. Trying to balance visiting 100 bars in 140 days does not lend itself to "quality family time" (Hey kids, who wants to help Dad make travel plans on Expedia?). The trip to Denver does not include a hotel room, but rather a red-eye back to Pittsburgh. That said, when we arrived in Denver, we decided that the best cure for jet lag and altitude sickness was a breakfast burrito!

We quickly located a Big City Burrito joint and ordered what has been voted "best breakfast burrito" in Denver. It came covered in habañero-jalapeño sauce. Tossing aside fears of any repercussions to our intestinal tracts, we gobbled down the burritos. They were delicious. Rejuvenated, we hopped in our rental car and headed off to our first destination.

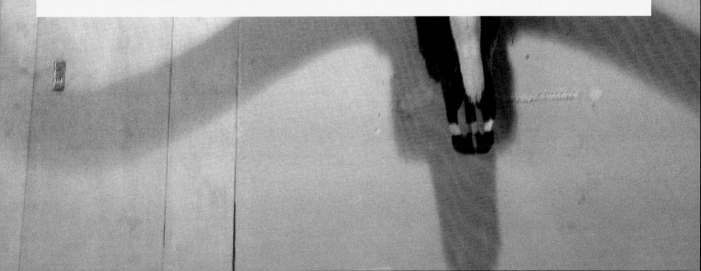

♦ ♦ ♦
THE RUSTY BUCKET BAR & GRILL
3355 Wadsworth Blvd; Ste G-101
Lakewood, CO 80227
(303)980-6200
www.the-rusty-bucket.com

Lynette, the general manager of The Rusty Bucket, greets us with open arms. She immediately apologizes for the Broncos banners and explains that The Rusty Bucket is required to display them to maintain pricing levels or something. We can't even be offended by the banners – the Steelers memorabilia here is incredible. One piece deserves particular mention because it's something they created all on their own. It's known affectionately as "The Steelers Hammer." It's an actual hammer mounted on the wall and, when we arrive, it has a Cleveland Browns helmet set just below it, ready

to be nailed. We were told that the helmet changes each week to represent the opponent. Of course the Browns have earned the right to be "crushed" each off-season.

Beer Note: Because we were north of Denver, I could feel the magnetic pull of the Oskar Blues brewery a short distance away in Longmont, CO. I ordered a Dale's Pale Ale. It was served at the perfect temperature, not too cold. Forget this cold-brewed-Rockies stuff where the beer is so cold it numbs your taste buds. The Rusty Bucket knows how to pour a great pint!

The Rusty Bucket and the Steelers Hammer draws the fans. Lynette tells us that it is "all hands on deck" for the Steelers games. In fact, new hires are even told during the interview process that they will be working on Steelers Sundays. The fans keep coming, so The Rusty Bucket keeps expanding. It now includes two bar areas and an outside seating area as well. All are packed on game days.

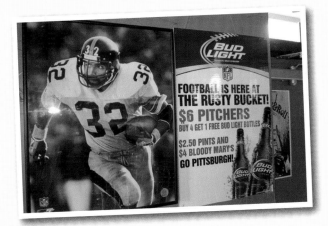

On Game Days, the kitchen cooks up pierogies and Primanti's-style sandwiches for the Steelers faithful. It is not uncommon to see fans line up outside before the bar opens at 9:30, rushing in to claim their favorite seats. These fans come from all over Denver to be together on Game Day.

Ron told us of a story from the prior season opener when the Steelers played. The Rusty Bucket worked with the Steel City Mafia to throw a huge party. Former players Andy Russell and John "Frenchy" Fuqua were in attendance. Ron's marketing savvy was apparent on that day – he bought a fish tank and placed a few goldfish in the tank to honor Frenchy and Frenchy's famous shoes from the glory days in the 1970s.

We then track down Ron, the owner. This guy is a dedicated Steelers fan. Apparently Ron was part of a contingent of fans that used to watch games at another Denver bar, the Hofbrau House. When that closed, the fans had no place to go. Always wanting to open a bar, Ron threw caution to the wind and opened the doors of The Rusty Bucket. Lynette jokes that on Game Days Ron is so nervous everyone is afraid to talk to him – though she isn't sure how much of the nerves relate to the score of the game and how much relates to the fear that the crowds at The Bucket exceed the maximum allowed by the fire code!

Frenchy signed the fish tank for the Rusty Bucket and it holds a place of prominence (needless to say, the fish have not survived!)

As we wound up our visit, we asked Ron about other places Steelers fans hang out in Denver. He tells us

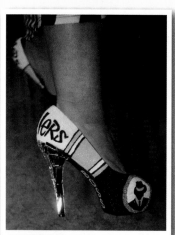

that we need to make the trip to JJ Madwell's. There are Steelers fans who don't want to make the trek into Denver and they apparently head to JJ Madwell's. Given that we still had a few hours before the red-eye was scheduled to take off, we headed up into the Rockies.

Frenchy was an 11th round pick for the New York Football Giants in 1969 out of Morgan State. Little did he know that a trade to the Pittsburgh Steelers for the following season would make him a significant part in one of the most famous plays in NFL history. (The NFL network has chosen this play not only as the greatest play in NFL history, but also the most controversial!). On December 23, 1972, the mighty Steelers lined up against the hated Oakland Raiders for the AFC Divisional playoff game. One fateful pass from Terry Bradshaw, intended for Frenchy, one tremendous hit by Jack "The Assassin" Tatum, and the rest is history... Frenchy ended up playing in 100 games, rushing for over 3,000 yards and scoring 24 touchdowns. Yet, he is still arguably remembered most fondly by Steelers fans for the intended pass he didn't catch. Beyond his athletic abilities, Frenchy was "fashionably" ahead of his time. He gave himself the nickname "The French Count." He was known around the country as one of the flashiest dressers in the NFL. Frenchy's platform shoes featured prominently in this reputation. His shoes were actually miniature fish tanks. Frenchy would choose different tropical fish each day to match his outlandish outfits!

journey out to Conifer, Colorado, to enjoy the fine Italian cuisine and check out this cool Steelers place.

Steelers fans are tight. Even when you think that there might be competition, you find that a love for "them Steelers" overpowers all. Denver was a perfect example. We never would have met Tony or stopped by JJ Madwell's if Ron from The Rusty Bucket hadn't told us about him. The businesses are less than an hour apart in the shadow of Bronco's Stadium. They've got to be competing for the same market. Yet instead of seeing each other as rivals, they see each other as part of Steelers Nation – all supporting the Black & Gold. The camaraderie was fantastic to see.

◆ ◆ ◆
BUCCELLI'S JJ MADWELL'S

26412 Main Street
Conifer, CO 80433
(303) 838-1440
www.jjmadwells.net

We seemed to be heading straight up the mountains. It was late and the stars were unbelievable. Then, like a beacon out of the darkness, we saw an enormous Steelers flag flying beside a small restaurant on the side of the road.

An Elwood City transplant, Tony greeted us at the door wearing his Steelers jersey. This place was packed with Steelers memorabilia. Tony explained that he started in 2008 with just a few items that he had from being a lifelong Steelers fan. As they tend to do, patrons soon started bringing in donations and Tony put them on the wall. Now Steelers fans will make the

What a wonderful trip to Denver. It brought back a lot of great memories of playing football. Of all the stadiums in the NFL, I always seemed to have my best games out here. Maybe it's just the altitude or maybe I'm a head case. But it was probably that the Steelers crew from The Rusty Bucket and JJ Madwell's were at Mile High Stadium making it feel like a home game. Those places sure lived up to the hype.

Weird things I noticed on this trip: Shawn ordered a Dale's Pale Ale immediately upon entering The Rusty Bucket. I made a mental note of the time. It did seem to be very early to be ordering a beer, but he told me that he was using East Coast time, so it was okay. I also noticed that Shawn likes burritos almost as much as he likes beer. Of course, his constant cracking of the knuckles is also starting to get on my last nerve. Maybe it's just that we got up at 3:30 a.m. to get here, but it's making me a little cranky! This should be a fun, fun Journey.

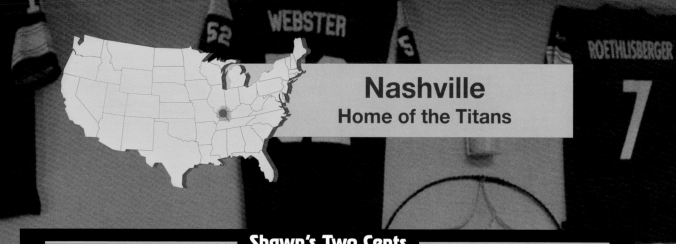

Nashville
Home of the Titans

Shawn's Two Cents

After the 8-hour drive from Pittsburgh to Nashville, we arrived around 2 a.m. and crashed at our hotel. Because Nashville is in the Central Time Zone, the Steelers game started one hour early and we needed to arrive at the bar no later than 10 a.m. In an effort to get as much sleep as possible, we ate breakfast in the hotel. As we followed our server to our table (in a semi-conscious, sleep-deprived state), we commented about her friendly attitude and suggested that management give her a raise. She promptly responded that she had been paid less than minimum wage for her 33 years on the job. We looked at each other – "33" is one of those mysterious numbers not only associated with the Steelers (founded in 1933) but also another Western Pennsylvania original, Rolling Rock beer. Carol told us that her husband was a huge Steelers fan, but had passed away last year. She then informed us that she keeps his Steelers jersey and hat hanging in the closet; that is how she remembers him. The coincidence was amazing. Of all the servers in the restaurant, we got the Steelers fan. This was only a hint of things to come. (By the way, it was only fitting that we left a 33% tip.)

After a great breakfast, we headed for Spanky's Sports Bar, not realizing that the bar did not open until 11:00. This was going to be a problem. For the Titans game, played at Heinz Field, we needed to produce a video for the Big Board. We decided to head to downtown Nashville to capture local footage. The first stop: the Grand Ole Opry. We decorated the large guitar statues in the courtyard with Terrible Towels and got some fine footage of us hopping over the closed gates. Our elation was short lived as we noticed security guards entering the parking lot. Shots of us being hauled away in handcuffs with Terrible Towels probably wouldn't be the best thing to show on the Big Board. So, we ran! Luckily, other tourists occupied the security guards and we lived to document Steelers Nation another day!

♦ ♦ ♦
SPANKY'S SPORTS BAR

330 Welch Rd.
Nashville, TN 37211
(615) 837-3450
www.spankyssportsbar.com

We made it to Spanky's and felt a little better when the Steelers fans also started to arrive before the place opened. Jim and Judy, both from Atlanta but who happened to be in Nashville on business, pulled into the parking lot in head-to-toe Steelers gear. As we told them about our Journey, Jim pulled out his wallet and began to show us his membership cards for a number of Steelers Fan clubs (there were at least five that we could see). Since he travels a lot for his job, he joins fan clubs around the country so he knows where to watch the game each week. We shot some video outside of Spanky's, but because we really needed to send the video off to the Steelers, we had to be content with having most of it be our "tour" around the city.

We soon realized that Spanky's didn't have a kitchen. Of course, that didn't stop the Steelers fans; they were bringing in plates of nachos and crock-pots – all the comforts of home cooking to share with their friends. These fans know how to watch the game in style. We were told that there has been some difficulty getting Iron City in recent years, so the resourceful group has developed a taste for a different beverage – the Black & Gold Margarita. The recipe is a closely guarded secret and we could not pry it from the owner. You will have to visit to try one. This is the number-one seller during games.

As we settled in to talk to the owner, Lundy, we learned that he was a Nashville native. The obvious question – why then open a bar that caters to Steelers fans? Lundy explained that he grew up in the '70s, a time when Nashville did not have a team. As a kid, he loved the Pittsburgh Steelers uniforms and began following them. He has followed them religiously ever since. He showed us all of the memorabilia he has collected over the years. Lundy even modeled a few of the pieces himself.

As the game approached half time, we headed for the door. We had heard of Spanky's traditions and wanted to avoid the Steelers "half time shot specials." Lundy hadn't revealed the secret recipe, but a regular described the shots as "mostly tequila." As much fun as it would have been to hang with the crowd at Spanky's, we had another establishment to visit!

Beer Note: Spanky's is more of a hard liquor bar than a beer bar. So I reached for what most beer drinkers look for when they want a reliable beer – a Yuengling. D.G. Yuengling & Son is the oldest continuously operating brewing company in the United

States, headquartered in Pottsville, Pennsylvania, and one of the largest breweries by volume in the country. That might be more Eagles territory but Steelers fans drink it anyway. In my opinion, Yuengling made some tremendously intelligent marketing decisions in the late '80s. This started with the re-introduction of "pre-prohibition" lager, their number-one selling beer today. This took advantage of the country's interest in darker beers. They then pushed this beer into many college communities. At the time, this was a revolutionary move. Selling a quality beer at a price point equal to the "watered down lagers" most other companies were selling created a very strong customer base that allowed Yuengling to achieve the success it still experiences today.

♦ ♦ ♦
PIRANHA'S BAR AND GRILL

113 2nd Avenue N
Nashville, TN 37201
(615) 248-4375
www.piranhasbar.com

Cruising back into downtown Nashville, we found Piranha's Bar and Grill. They are famous for the 10-lb. Cheesesteak Challenge. The goal is to eat the entire 10 lbs. in 60 minutes. To date, only two individuals have successfully completed the challenge. It is our hope that one of our readers will make the trip to Piranha's and successfully represent Always a Home Game. We didn't have the stomach for the challenge.

We noticed the Pittsburgh influence on their menu, including the option of adding fries and slaw to their sandwich offerings. Then we saw the gut buster of all burgers – the Donut Burger. Something Homer Simpson would love. Instead of buns, the huge cheeseburger patty is wedged between two glazed donuts. Delicious...and highly recommended by the AHG crew (as well as a follow-up EKG).

Beer Note: We approached the bar, looking for some good local beer. To complement the sweet and savory flavors of the Donut Burger, I selected a Dos Perros from Yazoo Brewing. This is a great amber ale with a hint of caramel and a nice hop finish. This is a "3" on its own, but a "4" with the Donut Burger. Yazoo Brewing is a local Nashville craft brewery that opened its doors in 2003. They were quickly identified as a major player in the Nashville market when they won their first Gold Medal at the Great American Beer Festival in 2004.

Rolling out of Nashville, I spotted a familiar sign from my time living in Austin. Chuy's is a Tex-Mex restaurant and one of my favorites. Now, Austin is a health-crazed city, everyone is exercising all the time and nobody is fat. Yet I proudly managed to gain weight while I lived there because of the fantastic food. I went to Chuy's way too often. I felt the pull of the sign in Nashville. The problem was, Chuy's was also one of my wife's favorites. If I convinced Josh and the crew to go, I would be guilty of "infoodelity." I was ready to forgo the Chuychanga when I saw it – the green chile. At the front door there was a six-foot-tall chile announcing the Hatch Chile Festival. My resistance was broken. Besides, I was pretty sure my wife would have pulled in, too, if the situation were reversed.

Most people don't remember, but I played my last NFL game in a Tennessee Titans uniform. I spent about six months in Nashville and must say it is a beautiful place to live, visit and just hang out. I truly couldn't wait to hang out with Steelers fans in Tennessee. This was also a Big Board game and we felt we should do something special for this one. We wanted to jazz up our 44 seconds of Big Board time, so we decided to show Pittsburgh some of the cool spots that Nashville is known for – even if those cool spots were closed or had signs that said, "No Trespassing" or "Do Not Enter." The Grand Ole Opry, a life-like Elvis... we hit them all before we went to Spanky's.

Out of all the Steelers establishments we've gone to so far, the Spanky's experience was the most stressful. Asking people to show up at 10 a.m. to a bar that doesn't open for another hour, just so we can have time to finish our Big Board filming is a big ask. Just being in a bar at 10 a.m. is a call for help. Well, silly me for being that stressed. After all, we are talking about Steelers fans. Of course they're going to be here

two hours before the game because that's what they do. Sure enough, 20 minutes before we needed to finish the film, the parking lot started to fill up. Steelers fans wearing all different kinds of Steelers jerseys came rolling in with their crock-pots, trays of foods and the most amazing Steelers cake and cookies you could ever ask for. I love Steelers fans! The filming went off without a hitch. Georgie Boy was able to put together our Big Board movie in the nick of time.

Off to Piranha's – the home of the Donut Burger. The gigantic burger lives between two glazed donuts. It's brilliant and I wish I had thought of it. It's right up there with the hot dog that lives in a

Twinkie. Yes, this is a great Steelers hangout, wall-to-wall Black & Gold. I also came across one of the most laid-back, coolest guys I've ever met. No joke, I took a picture with him and told him I'd put him in the book. He is over there to the right with the arrow pointed at him.

As if this Tennessee trip weren't already amazing, Shawn introduced us to Chuy's. The Tex-Mex restaurant has the best chips and salsa one man/woman could ever want.

Eight hours and we were back in Pittsburgh. I've finally met a person who can be fully recharged after three hours of sleep. That would be Shawn. He is a machine.

Charlotte
Home of the Panthers

Shawn's Two Cents

We hit Charlotte on the way back from Nash-ville. It had been a long ride in the rental car, but somehow, rolling into Charlotte we felt a little closer to home.

Charlotte almost feels like Pittsburgh to the south. It seems as though many from the Steel Town have ended up in the Queen City. Maybe it's because the climate is milder, or because US Airways relocated jobs here, or because, like Pitts-burgh, Charlotte has a strong banking presence.

There is just something familiar about Charlotte. It's not surprising then that there were a lot of Steeler's hangouts around the area.

Sadly, we had to call an audible partway through our visit when Josh got called away due to his father's declining health. He headed to the airport, but Always a Home Game forged onward! Dom and Abbey were still with me from Nashville, so thankfully I wasn't drinking alone.

was the "Al" part, short for Alexandra, I think, and not the "Big" part!). Even more interesting, Paul, who grew up in Buffalo in Bills' territory, has been a lifelong Steelers fan. Now, here he is in Charlotte, in Panthers' territory, providing a haven for the Black & Gold supporters. Paul opened Big Al's in 1996 and now has establishments in Mooresville, Charlotte and Albemarle. All three support the Steelers, but word has it that the Mooresville location is the best.

On the wall we noticed that Paul had stadium seats from the Three Rivers auction. We had a good laugh when we told him that Shawn ran the auction for the seats. He didn't have a favorite piece of memorabilia, but he did have a favorite story. Above the bar is a photograph from Super Bowl XL signed

by Big Ben. It seems one of Paul's customers left it at the bar for him shortly after the epic victory in Detroit and told the server to deliver it. No note inside. He is still looking to thank whoever gave him such a special piece of Steelers' history. There is probably an Iron City waiting for you at Big Al's.

Big Al's menu deserves a particular call out. There was a great twist on the classic sandwich, the "Pitts-doggie." It is a half-pound hot dog served with fries and cole slaw. Delicious.

✦ ✦ ✦
BIG AL'S PUB & GRUBBERIA

631 Blawley School Rd
Mooresville, NC 28117
(704) 567-2333
www.bigalspubandgrubberia.com

Big Al's Pub & Grubberia is 100% Steelers 24/7/365. The vast array of Steelers memorabilia is mindbog-gling. From Jack Lambert to Ben Roethlisberger, every possible generation of Steelers is represented.

We went looking for "Big Al," but couldn't find him. Apparently Paul, the owner, has confounded many a salesperson over the years who has come into the bar looking for "Big Al." Paul explained that he named the bar after his daughter. (For the record, I think it

♦ ♦ ♦
THE LOCKER ROOM
4809 South Tryon St.
Charlotte, NC 28217
(704) 523-1050
no online presence

The next scheduled stop was The Locker Room. Josh had to take off unexpectedly to make an emergency flight back to Florida. His dad's health was failing so he would miss the remainder of our visit to Charlotte. I was feeling for Josh and his wife, Angie, and every-thing they were going through, and the thought of drinking alone was a bit depressing. I wasn't sure what to expect at The Locker Room. Despite efforts, we had been unable to speak with anyone there in advance of our trip. Pulling up to the run-down strip mall, the expectation fell even lower. And then I saw it and there was no question I was in the right place. The windows had been painted gold, with a huge Steelers logo notifying everyone that there is a little piece of Pittsburgh in the Queen City.

As I approached the bar to quench my thirst (Sam Adams Lager is a great beer that does not get the respect it deserves. Rating – "3"), I was not surprised to learn that many fans drive by and do not enter the bar – people think it is a "gentlemen's club." But the only pole dance here is around the Lombardi trophy. This place could pass for a bar in Homestead. Most of the memorabilia was from the '70s. An album on the wall was Fleetwood Sounds – Super Steelers '76, a sports album with play-by-play and interviews from the season. Curious about the album, I asked the bartender if I could interview her and take some pictures. She shot me down. Lucky for me, she called the owner and handed the phone over. That's how I met Bobby and learned about the origins of The Locker Room.

Bobby was raised in Homestead and opened The Locker Room over 20 years ago as a place to watch Steelers games with his buddies. Unlike a lot of bars in Charlotte that have catered to Steelers fans, his has a genuine connection to Pittsburgh. I could tell.

Mancini's bread is shipped in specially for his Game Day sandwiches, served with his "secret recipe" red wine vinegar slaw. Many of his patrons are transplanted Pittsburghers, as well. Bobby said that a lot of Steelers fans relocated to Charlotte when US Airways moved a significant portion of its operations to Charlotte. One of the customers, a record collector, is the source of the albums on the wall that initially drew my attention. Whenever he discovers an old Steelers album, he brings it to Bobby.

The Locker Room is a cool place. It thrives without a website in the era of social media and online advertising. Bobby doesn't do any promotions or advertising. Don't let the strip mall dissuade you from coming into The Locker Room. This is a true Steelers hangout.

mustard. Perhaps not a typical chain after all! And for the opening game this year, former Steelers kicker Jeff Reed made an appearance. He apparently found the Fan Club so engaging that he stayed well beyond his contractual obligations and spent the entire day hanging in Uptown.

Beer Note: I asked about quality local beers and was steered toward Olde Mecklenburgh Brewery. Once I saw the Mecktoberfest, the choice was simple. Quite simply, this world-class Marzen beer is a "4" and, if you ever see one on draft, make sure you grab a pint. Marzen-style beer was originally brewed in the Bavaria region of Germany. Like many other things German, there are very strict rules for this style of beer.

◆ ◆
FITZGERALD'S

201 East 5th Street
Charlotte, NC 28202
(704) 900-8088
www.fitzgeraldscharlotte.com

The next stop took me downtown, to the shadows of the Panther stadium. From the street, Fitzgerald's looked like your typical chain "Irish pub." Ron, the Charlotte Steelers Fan Club president, greeted me and immediately hit me with Charlotte Steelers Club swag, prominently featuring the slogan "Steel Town in Uptown – Bridging the Queen City with the Steel City." In a city that can be described by its transient population, I found deep-rooted Steelers and Pittsburgh traditions at Fitzgerald's. For instance, the Game Day menu revealed Pittsburgh-type items – fried pierogies, capicola and cheese "sammiches" and pretzel bites served with a Yuengling Lager beer

A Bavarian brewing ordinance decreed in 1553 that Marzen-style beer be brewed only between September 29th and April 23rd of each year. The beer was often kept in the cellar until late in the summer and then served at Okto-berfest. Consequently, most Marzen beers are marketed as Oktoberfest beers. Similar to the British IPA, in order to last so long, the alcohol was increased but the hopping was not strengthened as with the British counterparts. The style is characterized by a medium to full body, a malty flavor and a clean, dry finish.

One of the more interesting stories I learned at Fitzgerald's revolved around three friends who have been gathering at the same table together for the past 13 years. When the Steelers score, the three friends stand up, count down, and initiate the familiar chant "Here we go, Steelers, here we go!" Then the DJ plays the newer hometown favorite "Black & Yellow" by local Pittsburgh rapper Wiz Khalifa. Over the years, the guys have aged and their lives have changed. Significant others have come and gone but one thing remains constant – nobody else is allowed at their table! Each insists that their commitment to the Steelers will outlast all others.

◆ ◆ ◆
DELANEY'S MUSIC PUB AND EATERY

117 W. Main St.
Spartanburg, SC 29306
(864) 583-3100
www.delaneyspub.com

The next Steelers stop was purely unintentional. I hit Delany's Music Pub and Eatery with a longtime friend I knew from the days when it wasn't advisable for me to rate beers at 10 a.m. Knowing that I am a craft beer nut, Mike planned to meet me at a small craft beer pub in Spartanburg, SC – RJ Rockers. As I approached and saw an old fermenting vessel on the roof, I started to get excited to taste another fine local beer. Then the crushing disappointment: they were closed on Mondays. I've heard of fine high-end theaters being closed on Mondays, but a brewpub should be open seven days a week.

We decided to walk across the street to the local Irish pub, Delaney's Music Pub and Eatery. As luck would have it, I walked into a Steelers hangout. Really. I would say, "What are the odds?" but having visited quite a few cities by now, I'd have to say that the odds are quite good. Especially if the pub is Irish in nature! The first thing I noticed after walking in the door was the Lambert signed jersey on the wall, the Terrible Towels flying and the Iron City Beer cans. My brothers-in-law would approve. This was old school Steelers territory. As with many of these hangouts, the owner is a huge Steelers fan. Every Game Day he religiously follows the Black & Gold with 50-75 of his closest friends.

I was in the mood for some comfort food, so I ordered the Guinness Stout Stew. It was served in a bread bowl surrounded by mashed potatoes. The obvious pairing for this meal would be a Guinness, but I figured I was already having a Guinness in the stew...I should try another! I choked back the hard feelings about R.J. Rockers and ordered the Patriot Pale Ale. I rate it a "3." It would have been a "4" if I had been able to drink it in the brewpub, fresh from the tap...but did I mention that they are closed on Mondays?

Along with being a Steelers hangout, Delaney's is known for its music. It has been voted the best bar in Spartanburg. (Take that, R.J. Rockers!). Mike and I kicked back and enjoyed the Steelers memorabilia and some great music. A little bit of serendipity to stumble across a Steelers hangout when I was just looking to meet up with an old friend.

Big Al's Pub & Grubberia was my first and only Steelers stop in Carolina. My heart was in two places at once – Big Al's and Jupiter, Florida, where my father was in his final stages with hospice. I must say, though, Big Al's allowed me to forget about Florida for a moment and remember why we started this Journey in the first place: it was to spend time with some of the greatest sports fans and celebrate one of the greatest franchises in all of sports.

When you walk into Paul's establishment, you can't help but notice this is 100% built for the Steelers fans and only for Steelers fans to gather, enjoy and cheer on the Black & Gold on Game Day. I was blown away by his collection of sports memorabilia covering every square inch of wall and ceiling. Real genuine pieces that they just don't make anymore. Everything from game-worn helmets to game-worn jerseys to the ever-popular seats from Three Rivers Stadium. This was really a museum for Steelers Nation. They treated us like kings. We noticed that they had flyers strategically placed in the bar announcing that the Always a Home Game team would be coming through. They had great stories and they were sincere and genuine in the time they spent with us. I must also tell you the food was fantastic. Thank you to everyone at Big Al's for letting me leave my problems at the door and enjoy a nice afternoon before flying out to Florida to say goodbye to my dad.

St. Louis
Home of the Rams

Shawn's Two Cents

This trip started on a distinctly more somber note. So far, we've traveled together to visit the bars. We each have our own roles that we fall into on the road. Josh is the celebrity, he is engaging with the fans, and he pulls out all the great stories from them. I am the one who handles all of the logistics. I capture the stories, I make sure that we have bars to visit, places to stay, and that we fulfill our commitments. I keep our noses to the grindstone so that there will be material at the end of this Journey for a book. And of course, I have the fabulous job of assessing the beer! But I am visiting St. Louis alone. Josh's father has been gravely ill for a long time, becoming much more so since we started our Journey. I have been impressed by how he has handled the pressure of visiting with fans when concerns about his father (and mother) weighed heavily on him. Just before we were to leave for St. Louis, Josh's father passed away.

After spending weeks on the road with Josh, it was eerily quiet making the 10-hour drive from Pittsburgh to St. Louis alone. This wouldn't be a Big Board filming, so the rest of the crew stayed home. Despite the silence, there was a distinct feel of following in the footsteps of Clark Griswold as I drove past the World's Largest Golf Tee, and then the World's Largest Wind Chime. Where was Christie Brinkley in the red Ferrari? All I could think of as I pulled in to East St. Louis was the scene where he rockets off the highway into a less than desirable neighborhood. I made sure I did not stray off the highway.

✦ ✦
HELEN FITZGERALD'S IRISH GRILL & PUB

3650 S. Lindbergh Blvd.
St. Louis, MO 63127
(636) 299-0645
www.helenfitzgeralds.com

Our research clearly showed that there was only one place to watch the game in St. Louis – Helen Fitzgerald's. So there I was, at the bar and asking about local beer. I was immediately told that Anheuser-Busch was the local beer. Note to self: better rephrase my question next time. I can't believe that Bud Light Lime (Josh's favorite beer) was actually the local "craft" beer and Josh missed it. I finally settled on a Pumpkin Ale from O'Fallon Brewery. O'Fallon's is a brewery located in a St. Louis suburb. I rate the Pumpkin ale a "3," but someone who likes a gourd in their beer might give it a higher rating. I guess you could consider it like drinking a V8? You'd be getting your fruits and veggies in while drinking beer. Maybe this is a "4" after all? It was a very good seasonal variety, lightly spiced and well balanced.

Then I thought about Josh and everything he was going through. I needed to have a beer for him, being the good, considerate friend that I am. As I ordered the beer, I was reminded of the following story:

One Friday afternoon, a Steelers fan walks in to a Black & Gold bar and orders three Iron City drafts. He quietly drinks his pints and leaves the bar. This continues for months. Eventually the bartender asks the man why he orders three beers at the same time. The man proceeds to tell him that he has two brothers and how they left Pittsburgh to explore the world. They were very close and agreed that they would drink an Iron for each other every week, for as long as they live. The Steelers fan said that he had been following this tradition for nearly 20 years. One day in early spring, the man entered the bar and ordered only two drafts. The bartender felt deeply saddened and, when he delivered the beer, gave his condolences and said the beers were on the house. The Steelers fan looked at him quizzically. The bartender explained, "I see that you ordered only two beers so I assumed that one of your brothers had died. I am so sorry." The Steelers fan laughed heartily and said, "Hell no, my brothers are all fine, I just gave up beer for Lent!"

I smiled to myself and thoroughly enjoyed Josh's Urban Chestnut Zwickel. It was also from O'Fallon's. I'd rate it a "3." This is a rather old, rare and unique German beer style. Its low alcohol content and malty finish is a taste worthy of Mr. Miller's palate.

I then met Paul, the president of the St. Louis Steelers Fan Club. The Club slogan says it all, "A little bit of the 'Burgh in the Lou!" This is an amazingly organized and well-run club. Not only do they have very traditional Game Day menus and drink specials

Steelers fan ever since. Interestingly, because he is a mechanic, he is unable to wear a wedding ring. On their 12th anniversary, however, Jared and Kirsten found a way to commemorate their love for each other and for the Steelers. They got matching Steelers tattoos on their ring fingers. As we said earlier in this book, "fan" is short for "fanatical."

at Helen Fitzgerald's, they also organize a weekly 50/50 raffle. Each season the club supports a different charity. The current charity is the Fisher House of St. Louis, which is "Dedicated to our greatest national treasure...our military service men and women and their loved ones." What an excellent example of Steelers fans strengthening the bonds in their community.

As I spoke to the great Steelers fans in St. Louis, I met Kirsten and Jared. Jared became a Steelers fan because of his mother. One might say that this is a good lesson for a mother to teach, but her reason might be considered a bit unorthodox. According to Jared, his mother admired the way Terry Bradshaw looked in his football pants! Regardless of the questionable beginnings, Jared has been a diehard

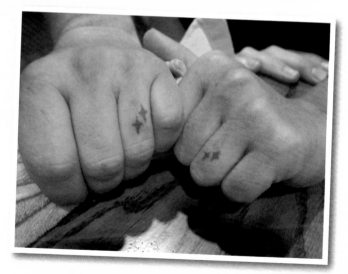

fans that show up week in and week out to cheer on their Steelers. Shawn told me that this was one of the finest visits he had and was welcomed with open arms. Not surprising; it seems to be one of the most common themes between Steelers fans across the country. It doesn't matter if you're in New Jersey or San Francisco or, yes, even in St. Louis or Indianapolis, Steelers fans always welcome you with a handshake and then send you off with a hug.

I guess I should discuss why I wasn't there with Shawn. It was a sad day for my family and me. I lost my biggest fan. This fan was my

My apologies go out to Helen Fitzgerald's in St. Louis and the Main Event and the Nickel Plate in Indianapolis. I was so sorry for not being able to join Shawn on this part of the Journey. I would've loved nothing more than to meet all the wonderful dad and he taught me everything I know. It's that simple. He was a great husband, great grandpa, a great father-in-law and amazing dad. He wasn't one of those dads that made me do things I didn't want to do. He did, however, make sure whatever I did decide to do I was going to do with everything I had. He would always say, "don't waste your time and don't waste my time." He would always remind me and ask me if I got better today. No matter what sport I played, he never missed an event, a game or a tournament. He would tell me all the things I did bad and made sure he told me everything I did well five times.

My finest football memory took place in 1996. We were playing Philadelphia in a preseason game. It was a night game, and my mom and dad drove down with their buddies. I ran out of the tunnel and ran across the field to the visiting side. There he was with all his buddies, looking like the happiest guy in the world. We both looked at each other and knew what it took to get there. I know for a fact that we both had tears in our eyes after that one. Tears of joy. I loved him as much as a son could love his dad. I hope my son looks at me the way that I looked at him. Richard Kent Miller was a great husband, brother and dad. He will be missed very much.

I would have enjoyed being at Helen Fitzgerald's Irish Grill & Pub. I would have ordered a Bud Light Lime and joined Shawn at the bar with the good people of Helen's. I will say I do have a story from St. Louis. It was the first time I've been fined. It wasn't a cool story, like getting into a fight with the other team or getting thrown out by the refs. No, I got fined by my own team. I was punting

against Sean Landeta. He punted for St. Louis at the time. But let's go back a bit. He used to play for the New York Giants about the same time I was in high school punting for East Brunswick High School. A few years passed and I found myself in Scottsdale, Arizona, in junior college. The Giants used our practice facilities for three days. Being a Jersey boy, I knew about this team all too well. It was such a cool feeling hanging out, getting to know these guys. Sean and I would go off to the side and he'd help me with my kicking and punting. He told me then, if you practice this and stick with it you could get a shot in the NFL. That's all I had to hear. Okay, let's fast forward seven years and here I was, punting against Sean Landeta. Very, very cool. After the game he said, "Hey Josh, what do you say we trade jerseys?" Okay with me, I thought. So we did. I walked off that field in St. Louis with Sean Landeta's game-worn jersey. I couldn't wait to get this thing up on my wall. As I walked into my locker room our equipment guys asked me, "Where is your jersey Josh?" Well, I learned a lesson here. You're not allowed to exchange jerseys after a game. That cost me a nice chunk of dough. Well worth it. Sean Landeta is one of the greatest guys I've ever met playing the game. He still remains a good friend of mine today.

Steelers Tattoos

Indianapolis
Home of the Colts

Shawn's Two Cents

I continued my solo journey across America's heartland as I pulled into Indianapolis, not knowing what to expect. Growing up in Southern California in the mid-'80s, my only knowledge of the area was from TV sports coverage that showed the moving vans leaving Baltimore and moving the Colts to Indianapolis. It was big time sports news. Now, images of Larry Bird floated through my mind. Oh yeah, this is basketball country. Were there really going to be Steelers fans here?

I was nervous, but I knew I had two places lined up to check out – the Main Event and the Nickel Plate Bar & Grill. Once I got to the Main Event, I felt like Alfred E. Neuman, "What, me worry?" Dave has been a Steelers fan from his childhood days and we traded stories and talked about beer over delicious Indiana tenderloin. Then it was off to the Nickel Plate Bar & Grill. The Black & Gold were out in full force. The Nickel Plate is home to the Indianapolis Steelers Fan Club. So while the ghosts of Larry Bird and Peyton Manning might haunt Indianapolis, rest assured that there are more than enough Steelers fans there to know that when the Steelers play at Lucas Oil Stadium, it is Always a Steelers Home Game!

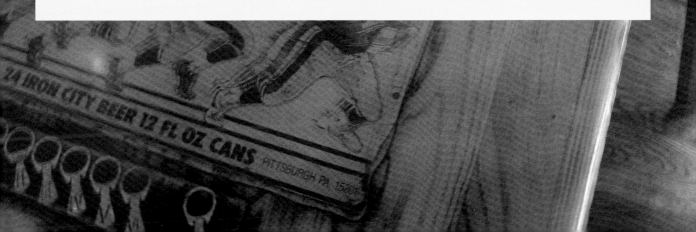

Entering the Main Event in South Indianapolis, I noticed the welcoming environment. There was a mix of people and everyone seemed to know each other. I expected someone to yell "Norm!" Of course, my name isn't Norm; I haven't gained THAT much weight yet on the beer and bar food diet and, admittedly, Norm had WAY more hair than I do.

Eventually I spoke to Dave, the owner and commented on the friendly atmosphere. He said that was exactly what he tried to cultivate at the Main Event. Indianapolis is a blue-collar town, like the Pittsburgh of old. Dave likes the idea of a neighborhood bar and wants everyone, especially Steelers fans, to feel welcome.

I also found out that Dave, like me, is a home brewer. Enough about the city and the Steelers, let's talk beer! Dave is a big fan of stouts – specifically his own chocolate stout. Sadly, he did not have any available for tasting. When I explained that I was a hophead, he suggested that we try the Dragonfly IPA from Upland Brewing in Bloomington, Indiana. The Dragonfly is a very well balanced American IPA. A very drinkable IPA. I give it a "4" – order it if you see it!

Knowing that a pure liquid diet is a sign of trouble, I figured I would try some food. The local specialty is "Indiana Tenderloin." The pork tenderloin slices are flattened and tenderized, then hand-breaded and fried. The "patty" is fried, served on a bun with all the fixings. Locals never order the tenderloin with cheese. In an effort to fit in, I opted to pass on the cheese. The Indiana Tenderloin was delicious.

The recipe for the tenderloin was one of the two reasons Dave purchased the Main Event. He wanted to take over an existing establishment; his criteria were rather simple: (1) find one with a good quality tenderloin recipe; and (2) figure out which bar draws the most Steelers fans on Game Days. Dave's love of the Steelers can be traced back to his youth, when his parents took him to Pittsburgh. In a single weekend, he saw the Panthers, Penguins and Steelers all play and win. He has been all-Pittsburgh since that day.

The back room at the Main Event is dedicated to the Steelers on Game Day. He said the room is always packed with Steelers fans, regardless of the team's record. Interestingly, since the NFL started broadcasting games Thursday through Monday nights, the only team that can still bring out the crowds is the Steelers. Even in Indianapolis, it is always a home game!

★ ★
NICKEL PLATE BAR & GRILL

8654 E. 116th Street
Fishers, IN 46038
(317) 841-2888
www.nickleplatebarandgrill.com

The next and last stop in the "Miller Lite" road trip was the Nickel Plate Bar & Grill. My expectations were high, given that the Indianapolis Steelers Fan Club meets here on a weekly basis, and I was not disappointed. I was greeted before I got out of the car by Steelers fans waving Terrible Towels and chanting "Here We Go, Steelers!" as they prepared for Monday night's encounter.

This group formed back in 1996 when five Steelers fans asked the owner if the Nickel Plate would open on a Sunday afternoon for them to watch the game.

The bar opened for them and the club has grown. For the opening game in 2013, there were over 250 fans sporting the Black & Gold. The fan club has over 350 active members. Every year they hold a pre-season party where fans come out to enjoy each other's company and celebrate the upcoming season.

I soon found Kurt, one of the owners, and a huge Steelers fan. I asked why someone in the land of Larry Bird and all things basketball would be a fan of the Black & Gold. His answer surprised me: Joe Gilliam. I had to admit that I had never heard of the player. Now I know there are some of you out there yelling "Rookie" at me. Okay, this is a JOURNEY. I am learning and Josh wasn't along to school me about Joe. I am discovering things about the rich Steelers traditions on this trip, and I was about to get another lesson. As it was explained to me, in 1972 Joe was drafted in the 11th round out of Tennessee State University, two years after the infamous coin toss in Chicago that allowed the Steelers to draft Terry Bradshaw. Coming out of training camp two years later, Gilliam out-played Bradshaw and was named the starter for the soon-to-be historic '74 season. Six games into the season, however, Coach Chuck Noll suspected illegal drug activity and removed Joe from the starting position. Bradshaw took over and four Super Bowl rings followed. It was crazy to see the passion with which Kurt told the story – it all happened so many years ago.

It was time to test the Nickel Plate's food. I ordered Indiana Tenderloin (again!). When I declined the cheese I received a knowing smile from the server. I was in with the cool kids. I asked Kurt about the local craft beer. He recommended a cream ale. I had some bad (good? Not sure) flashbacks to Genesee Cream Ale from my college days. Kurt told me that the local cream ale is only served in a can. That got my full attention. As a self-appointed beer sommelier, I am a connoisseur of fine canned beer. And no, that is not an oxymoron. Light is the #1 enemy of all beer and bottling beer is the best way to wreck a good beer. I popped the top of a Sun King Sunlight Cream Ale...a beautiful sound. Sunlight Cream Ale is brewed locally in Indianapolis. I'd give it a "3." It was pretty good.

After watching the first half of the game I bid farewell to the fan club and Kurt and headed out the door. Between the Steelers playing poorly, having a six-hour drive ahead of me and without Josh by my side with his wisecracks, I was in a bit of a down mood as I hit the road for the long drive home.

Chicago
Home of the Bears

The trip to Chicago was the inaugural run for the Always a Home Game RV. We were fortunate enough to have the fine folks at Clem's Trailer in Elwood City loan us a 32-foot motorhome for the Journey. We had the RV wrapped with our logo and hit the road with George and Abbey Way, a young, enthusiastic aspiring journalist. Ready for the new adventure! The "new adventure" included sleeping at a turnpike rest stop. Note to self: the next time someone explains how to operate the furnace on the RV, pay attention! It was bitter cold in the RV. The two fearless leaders had no frickin' clue how to operate the system, so poor Abbey was sleeping in two hoodies, sweat pants and multiple blankets. She was still freezing cold.

As we approached Chicago, we drove the RV by the major sports venues in town – Soldier Field, the United Center and Wrigley Field (no offense to White Sox fans, but there is nothing classic or memorable about Caminsky – or whatever the new corporate name is). Basically, we wanted to taunt Chicago with a little bit of the 'Burgh. Maybe the rest of the 'Burgh would have picked something a bit cooler than two middle-age guys in a Black & Gold RV to do their taunting, but we forged ahead. Our concerns about driving a Steelers vehicle in enemy territory were well founded. As we made our way toward Wrigley, Chicago fans were blocking our way and yelling at us. We were hoping they would start throwing some deep dish. We also realized that it is difficult to merge an RV into traffic when everyone around you would prefer to slash your tires. We captured all of this for the video on the Big Board.

♦ ♦ ♦
DARK HORSE TAP & GRILL
3443 N. Sheffield Ave
Chicago, IL 60657
(773) 248-4400
www.darkhorsechicago.com

The first stop was the Dark Horse Tap & Grill, and we were lucky – there was a parking spot right in front of the bar. We thought it would be perfect to get a photo of the RV out in front. A guy approached us and represented himself to be the owner, welcoming us to the Dark Horse. We asked him to join us for the picture.

Walking in, we immediately felt at home. The Dark Horse is a true Steelers joint. We struck up a conversation with fans sitting at the bar. They were incredibly interested in our Journey and asked about the crazy fans we have encountered. Coming off the trip to St. Louis, I told them about the tattooed wedding rings. Much to our surprise, Kim at the bar told us she was Kirsten's sister! She said we would have the complete trifecta if we met the family patriarch in South Florida.

Kim and Kirsten's father is anxiously awaiting the Always a Home Game crew to roll into the Sunshine State. (We have cleverly timed that trip for the December cold in Pittsburgh!). Because the family name is Stewart, their dad will be the one (maybe only one?) sporting the Kordell jersey.

Beer Note: Knowing the rich craft brew history in the Chicago area, I was eager to sample some of the local brews. I found Andy, the bartender and general manager, and asked for a recommendation. He suggested the Revolution Anti-Hero IPA, a local brew from Revolution Brewing. Score "4."

If you are a hophead, this is a must-have.

We asked about ownership and how the Dark Horse attracted Steelers fans. Andy apologized that the owner was not around to talk with us. He was at the game. At the game? Who the hell was that out front who took the picture with us? Andy looked where we were pointing and said that guy was the owner of the Packers bar next door. Photo-bombed by a Packers fan. Guess even a Packers fan wants to be in a book about the greatest NFL team on the face of the earth.

Andy started telling us about the Steelers rituals at the Dark Horse. They handed out black-and-gold beads and Terrible Towels to all in attendance at the opening game of the season. They also have a "signature shot": ½ Jaegermeister and ½ Goldschlager. Very tasty. And they feature Iron City and IC Light on Game Days.

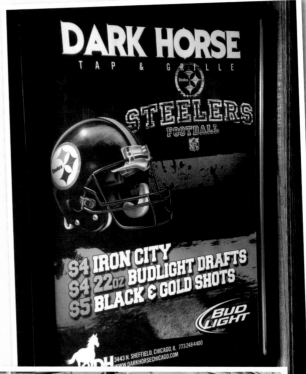

We bade goodbye to Andy and the Dark Horse crew and headed to our next stop. The Dark Horse "signature shot" gave me all the confidence I needed to get out of the tight parking spot, with Josh helping from the curb. All was going well until I backed up into the tree. It was in front of an Asian restaurant. The tree branch grabbed hold of the RV's awning in an effort to keep us from fleeing the scene of the crime. Applying copious amounts of gas and lunging forward, I ripped the limb violently from the tree. As I headed down the street, Josh was running after the RV, with the owner of the restaurant yelling and chasing after him.

over 2,000 and more than 800 active members. Crowds of over 300 gather on Game Days. The club has been meeting long before it became "formalized" way back in 1989. Steeler Steve and Commissioner Clyde greeted us upon our arrival and escorted us to a table in the German-style beer hall.

Prost! itself is great. The club relocated there recently because it was more welcoming of families. Prost! is fully committed to the Steelers fans. One hour before kickoff each week, a Steelers menu

We made it to our second stop, Prost!, the new home for the Chicago Steelers Club. The club is very organized and efficiently run, with a distribution list of

replaces the regular menu. The highlight: a giant pretzel. Just to kick things up a notch, we decide to issue a throwdown – Josh versus a member of the local club in a giant pretzel-eating contest. The club offered up an 18-year-old boy. As any parent of a growing boy can attest, they are ALWAYS hungry. Josh never stood a chance. Rather than bore the readers with the details of Josh's humiliation, let's focus on the classic line he offered as he took the walk of shame back to our table. Even in defeat, his comic genius was evident as he offered, "I just ate two yards of yeast..."

Beer Note: Since we were at a beer hall during Oktoberfest, I felt obliged to sample some of the finely crafted German beers. As one would expect in such a fine establishment, Prost! featured 1-litre mugs of Hacker-Pschorr Oktoberfest straight from Germany. Now, as I've made clear, I'm a huge proponent of American craft brewing. But I believe that this is the world's best Oktoberfest beer, and feel that the beer gods would be angered if I did not enjoy one every September. Easily a "5." I only regret that I did not bring my lederhosen for this trip.

After enjoying the best of Prost! it was time for the Big Board filming. Word began to spread through the bar and fans scrambled to get onto the screen for the live feed back to Heinz Field. One woman in particular was insistent that we get a picture of her "Keisel voodoo doll scowl." Before our eyes, this attractive woman transformed into a "Fear the Beard" lookalike. Worried that she might hit like Keisel too, we used her impression as the introduction to our video.

♦ ♦ ♦
DURKIN'S

810 Diversey Parkway
Chicago, IL 60614
(773) 525-2515
www.bar1events.com/durkins

The last stop in Chicago was unforgettable. Walking through the door at Durkin's makes you feel as though you are in the 'Burgh. The entire bar is an homage to the Pittsburgh Steelers. Greg, known locally as "Coach," greeted us and introduced us to the staff, then ushered us to a large framed picture on the wall. It commemorates a special time in Durkin's history. On February 1, 2009, the Pittsburgh City Council declared it to be Durkin's Day in Pittsburgh to honor the dedication to the city exhibited by a bar in Chicago. The bar celebrates the day each year. This commitment is reflected in the staff. Durkin's runs ads asking for Pittsburgh expatriates to work as servers. They feel strongly that hiring "locals" most easily maintains ties to Pittsburgh. Based on the excellent service, we think they have it right. We were not surprised to find that the drink special was $3 Iron City bottles.

Coach's love for the Steelers was put to the test during the last Super Bowl. Unfortunately, his wife is a Packers fan. When it was time to watch the game, she expectantly arrived before kickoff to take a seat at the bar. Out of respect for the Steelers, Coach banned his wife on Super Bowl Sunday. She was forced to watch the game someplace else. Ouch!

Coach's patrons show him that same kind of commitment. We learned that Durkin's was initially a "two room" bar. Of course, the number of Steelers fans showing up on Sundays soon exceeded the occupancy limits of those rooms. There was an empty space behind the bar, part of an old car dealership, and the landlord offered it to Coach, who was willing to take it on, but not able to complete the renovation. Pittsburgh pride came through. The Steelers fans came in on nights and weekends to complete the work. The sense of pride is evident on the faces of the fans as we enjoyed the game in the back room. If you plan on visiting this special Steelers room, do not expect to find a table. Every table is reserved for longtime fans at Durkin's!

This was our inaugural trip in the RV – a memorable one indeed. Ten-plus hours at 65 mph and a $120 gas tank. Allow me to introduce the starting lineup for this road trip. Captain and driver for most of the time was Shawn Allen, my partner who cracks his knuckles more than any human being I've ever been around. Georgie Boy, our camera guy. It would take him two and a half hours to eat a Snickers. Also with us was young, pretty Abbey Way, currently employed by CBS and trying to make her own path as a reporter. And then there's me. This leg of our Journey had a little of everything in it – plenty of highs and lows. The lows seem to happen in bunches: standing in the rest stop parking lot brushing your teeth with bottled water... eating a granola

bar in the same parking lot, pretending it's steak, and knowing that in 3½ hours we would be on the road again.

But there we were on our way to Chicago, which I have to say was a great mini-trip. First up was the Dark Horse, definitely a Steelers place. It passed the Steelers test.

Prost! was a cool German bar. Everything in this place seemed to be big – the beer, the food and the personalities. First, there was the crazy Keisel girl. She seemed extremely normal...until we started talking about the Steelers. She had a Brett Keisel voodoo doll. And there was the pretzel-eating contest that Shawn and Abbey entered me in. I guess the picture says it all.

Durkins: We had pulled off a great Big Board show at Prost! and I was ready to go home. Did I

mention it was an 8:00 game? That meant we had to drive home through the night from Chicago to Pittsburgh. I asked Shawn if we really needed to go to Durkin's. He explained to me why it would be best if we stuck to the plan. I'm glad we did. This place was hopping. It must have had 500 Steelers fans. Loud, crazy Steelers fans. The older people were on the inside of the group and it got younger and younger toward the walls. As we were about to leave, the Steelers scored a touchdown. Coach grabbed Abbey and started to polka around the room with confetti shooting all over the place from the ceiling. As usual, Shawn was right – we didn't want to miss this.

Nothing is scarier than driving a 32-foot RV at four o'clock in the morning and the other three people with you are sound asleep. We did shifts.

Two hours in the top bunk, two hours in the passenger seat, then two hours behind the wheel. Not sure how we made this one happen but we did.

Phoenix
Home of the Cardinals

Shawn's Two Cents

After our visit to the Windy City, we were headed out West to Phoenix, Arizona. No RV this time, no cross-country drive. We were laying out the cash. With our good friend Domenic Mantella along with us, Josh and I flew out to Phoenix (okay, coach, not first class). Two days and one night in sunny, dry Arizona. We were like three guys going through a mid-life crisis. We rented a red Camaro.

Driving through Phoenix, we noticed something that every city should adopt. Along the side of the two-lane highway were the most interesting plants and cacti. As any idiots would, we began to ask each other what type of plants were growing on the side of the road. Then we were saved the embarrassment of saying, "Dunno, looks like a cactus," by these signs that identified the plants. Can't say as we've seen these signs anywhere but Arizona.

We only had two places lined up in Phoenix, Harold's and Pittsburgh Willy's. Harold's we had heard of. I'm pretty sure most Steelers fans in Steelers Nation have heard of Harold's. It exceeded all expectations. Pittsburgh Willy's was a surprise. Pittsburgh natives Randy and Cindy have dreamed up some crazy concoctions to put on hot dogs. I'm not sure how or why they work, but they do. The dogs are delicious and the Steelers memorabilia is pretty fantastic too.

♦ ♦ ♦
HAROLD'S CAVE CREEK CORRAL

6895 E. Cave Creek Road
Cave Creek, AZ 85331
(404) 488-1906
www.haroldscorral.com

For most of our trips, we have no idea what to expect when we arrive, and that is a huge part of what makes the Journey so cool. That was not the case for our trip to Arizona. Harold's Cave Creek Corral is world renowned for its Steelers fans and how they celebrate the game each Sunday. It seemed as though every Steelers fan that has ever left the Golden Triangle has either visited Harold's or heard about it. We had to go.

The first thing that hits you at Harold's, besides the horses tied up outside the entrance, is the size of the place. Anyone that says "everything is bigger in Texas" has not been to Cave Creek, Arizona. Harold's is the largest Steelers hangout we have ever seen. Danny, the owner, had reserved a table for us in the middle of the action. It's a good thing, too, because seating is so scarce; over 400 people have paid a PSL (personal seat license – though we shouldn't have to define that for all you season ticket holders at Heinz Field) to reserve a table for the season. Harold's routinely attracts crowds in excess of 800 fans on any given Sunday.

After taking in the spectacle that is Harold's (there is not enough space in this chapter to describe all the memorabilia on the walls), we took a look at the custom Game Day menu. It started with a great-looking buffet and included all the classic Pittsburgh dishes, along with their own blend of Southwest-themed items. Because our bodies were still on East Coast time, we felt it appropriate to begin drinking at 10:00 a.m., along with 800 of our new best friends! Josh was quickly encircled by a group of Steelers fans. Everyone wants to do a shot with a former Steelers great. You will have to travel to Harold's to learn the names of the shots. Good taste prevents us from repeating the names.

Beer Note: I ordered a Kilt Lifter Scottish Ale from Four Peaks Brewing in Tempe. My expectations were low for this style of beer in such a warm weather climate. I thought a good Scottish Ale could only be brewed in a cold, gray and rainy climate. Wrong! The Kilt Lifter is a tremendous, bold-tasting ale that goes perfectly with a hamburger. Rating – "3."

As we worked our way through the crowd, with polka music and Steelers fight songs spinning in the DJ booth, we came across one of the PSL holders at a table in front of the big screen. He told us a story of how he was watching a game and a big guy stood there blocking his view. Eventually, the fan got up and tried to shove the guy out of the way, but he didn't budge – just turned around. It was Andy Russell, staring down at him. After apologizing, Andy joined him for the rest of the game. That was one of the great things about Harold's, he told us – you never know who might show up (like Josh Miller and Shawn Allen!).

I noticed a guy in a Chiodo's Tavern shirt. He ambled over to strike up a conversation, saying he wears the shirt to see who is a real Pittsburgher. He confirmed

our authenticity. The conversation took a turn towards Trivial Pursuit. The fan asked if I knew that Josh had once been a "Fighting Artichoke." Little known fact, people: before becoming an All-American while attending the University of Arizona, Josh was indeed a member of the Scottsdale Community College Fighting Artichokes. Steelers fans certainly know football and appreciate the finer (more mundane?) aspects of those who don the Black & Gold.

Just about then, the Fighting Artichoke mounted a horse in the Harold's parking lot. Josh was taken with the idea that the fans at Harold's ride their horses to the bar to watch the game. He admitted to dreaming of being a cowboy as a kid and the crowd at Harold's wanted to bring a piece of that dream to life. He came back inside with a bit of a swagger in his step.

The energy was high at Harold's...until the mood changed in an instant. At 12:10 p.m. local time, with 5:11 remaining in the 4th quarter of the game in London against Minnesota, Steelers Nation stood still. The DJ turned off all the sound on the TVs and calmly announced that L.C. Greenwood had passed. There was a moment of silence; everyone stood in silent prayer for the Greenwood family, for the Steelers family. It is one of those moments etched in our collective minds.

To make an already sad day even more sobering, the Steelers lost the game. We were disappointed that the Steelers did not win, and that we missed a Harold's tradition here: when the Steelers are victorious, Danny will slide down one of the tables covered in shaving cream and crash through a tower of toilet paper (go to YouTube and search "Steelers Shaving Cream Slide" and see for yourself).

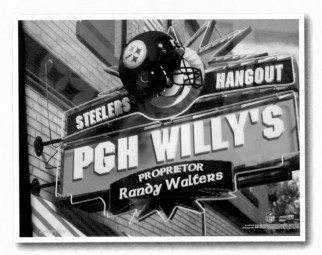

As we headed to Chandler, our next destination, we did a Google search because we had no idea where we were. Forty-plus miles later, we pulled into the parking lot and knew we were in the right place. We saw an old pickup truck with "Pittsburgh Willy's" painted on the side.

This stop on our Journey was slightly different from many we have experienced – Pittsburgh Willy's is not a bar serving alcohol. Rather, it is a hot dog shop serving "the best wieners in Arizona!" But unless you knew the place, you would think that you were walking into a sports memorabilia shop in downtown Pittsburgh. The walls are covered with unique items and classic pieces, like the 1996 Pittsburgh Steelers team photo. In the lower left hand corner is a young looking punter...Josh Miller! We all got a good laugh. On a Journey full of coincidences, we were about to experience another one.

At the counter we met Randy and Cindy, both Pittsburghers; they attended Monongahela and Charleroi high schools. Cindy has a unique connection to the Steelers, or should we say "the Pirates." Her uncle was none other than Joe Santoni. Diehard Steelers fans know where this is going; the rest of you, hold on for the ride. In the 1930s Joe was a tremendous Pittsburgh sports fan. Like many Pittsburghers of his generation, he worked in the mills. One day, he saw that the *Pittsburgh Post Gazette* and Art Rooney, Sr. were holding a contest to rename the professional football team in town. Feeling a strong passion for the team and the industry that supported the town, Joe submitted the name – Pittsburgh Steelers. As the winner, Joe was given season tickets for the next year. He remained a season ticket holder until shortly before his death in 2003.

One thing that has become clear on our Journey is that everyone wants Josh to tell a story. Steelers fans love to hear about his historic clashes with Bill Cower, or how he launched a 75-yard punt during a critical juncture of the game with the Jaguars in 1999. They always ask about the Pittsburgh Steelers fan base and how it compares to other teams he has played for. Josh was fortunate

enough to play for another NFL team with a passionate fan base, the New England Patriots. What's Josh's comparison between the two groups of fans? Say you have a flat tire and are stranded on a highway. A fellow Patriots fan will stop, make sure everyone is okay and call for someone to help fix the tire. A fellow Steelers fan will stop, fix the tire, then proceed to tell you what the coach should be calling during the game. But as we sit down to talk to Randy about Pittsburgh Willy's, we realize that Josh's story might not be just a folk tale. It seems that shortly after Randy moved to Chandler he was stranded on the side of the road with a flat tire. (We are not making this up!). He had a Steelers bumper sticker on his car. A fellow Steelers fan stopped to help. The tire could not be repaired and the guy took the damaged tire into town to have it repaired. He then brought it back to the stranded vehicle to make sure that Randy had a way back to Chandler. We can only guess that it happened during the off-season, so there was no talk about the actual play calling.

Another amazing story from Andy: he started his business based upon a slogan from an Ameriprise commercial starring Dennis Hopper. He had always wanted to own a hot dog business and Dennis Hopper was just the man to make him do it. As Randy quoted the commercial, "Flower Power was then, Dreams are now." He started with a single hot dog cart and built his business by serving great food and caring about each customer. In 2008 he was ready to move into his current fixed location, then tragedy struck. Randy had a heart attack just as the final preparations for opening were taking place. He needed to open the doors to keep up with payments. His loyal customers,

Steelers fans, stepped in and finished the work. The only way to really understand the deep connection between Randy and his customers is to visit the shop. This should be on every Steelers fan's bucket list.

We were getting dangerously close to singing kumbaya and I do not do emotion, but we were saved by HOT DOGS! The menu at Pittsburgh Willy's is laced with references to Pittsburgh traditions. We ordered one of almost everything, starting with the The Pittsburgher – made with chipped ham and barbeque sauce. It is easy to see why Pittsburgh Willy's is consistently voted the best dogs in the Valley of the Sun. The only thing missing was pierogies. Then Randy told us that they serve handmade pierogies every Wednesday. And the coup de grace... For those of you not already in the know, July 23rd is National Hot Dog Day. Randy wanted to make something special for the occasion; enter the Twilly, a Big Willy hot dog with a Twinkie for a bun, topped with peanut butter sauce and bacon. What else can we say about Pittsburgh Willy's – one of a kind!

Harold's Corral has grown to legendary proportions. Once word got out that we were doing a book on Steelers bars, every Steelers fan I came into contact with told us about Harold's, the Graceland of all Steelers hangouts. I went to junior college in Scottsdale, Arizona, then on to the University of Arizona in Tucson. I couldn't wait to go back to this state I loved. But in the seven years I was in Arizona, I never saw anything like Harold's Corral – a must-see for anyone who calls themselves a Steelers fan. You know right away you're leaving everything that's normal behind and entering something very special.

As Shawn and I learned, it's not uncommon to get 800 Steelers fans showing up during the regular season. Like any other bar, the first thing we do is look around and see what the sports memorabilia looks like. Major thumbs-up in that department. We saw things on the wall that we knew we would not see anywhere else in the country. We also noted

that no other team was represented – anywhere. It was really incredible to see 300 people show up two hours before kickoff, all wearing Black & Gold and telling us, "Wow, the crowd is thin today." Would have fooled me. My man Danny, who owns the bar, is exactly what I thought he would or should be, or should I say what I was hoping he'd be – a guy who is ga-ga over the Steelers and a guy who makes sure every one of his customers feels like they're at home.

There were a couple of memorable moments for me personally at Harold's. Believe it or not, as a kid growing up in the '70s in New Jersey, I was a gigantic Steelers fan. Big fan of Mean Joe Greene. Loved the commercial with "Hey kid, catch." Our day at Harold's had started out with so much upbeat energy, but with five minutes and 11 seconds remaining in the 4th quarter, with the Steelers playing Minnesota in London, the score became irrelevant. Suddenly, 300 to 400 Steelers fans that had been partying two hours before kickoff were silent and in disbelief as we heard the announcement that L.C. Greenwood had passed away. There was a moment of silence for one of the greatest Steelers of all time, and a silent prayer in honor of the Greenwood family and the Steelers Nation family. I hate to end on such a sad note. That is why I'll mention the fact that I got on a horse for the first time in 42 years at Harold's. Fulfilling a childhood dream of becoming a cowboy.

Jacksonville
Home of the Jaguars

Shawn's Two Cents

Man, is Florida flat. Living in beautiful Western Pennsylvania, we take rolling hills and foliage for granted. As we drive around the country we are continually surprised by the varying terrain and constantly reminded by how beautiful and diverse the topography is across Steelers Nation.

The trip to Jacksonville is unique for the Always a Home Game team. We were traveling on a bye week, so our initial expectation was low. We knew that lots of people from Pittsburgh escape the snow and ice and retire to the land of perpetual sunshine and oranges (aren't the statistics always that Allegheny County and someplace in Florida have the oldest average age of residents in the country?). But we didn't think that anyone would show up to meet us without a game.

✦ ✦
PLANTATION BAR AND GRILL

3754 Roscommon Drive
Ormond Beach, FL 32174
(386) 615-8948
www.plantationbarandgrill.com

Then we got a call from Joy. Joy is the enthusiastic founder and leader of the Black and Gold of Flagler County. She took it upon herself to organize a tailgate party at the Plantation Bar and Grill. Rather than divide the different fan bases in Jacksonville, Joy brought her group together with the First Coast Steelers Fan Club for the momentous occasion. At this point in our Journey, we are not surprised that Steelers fans work together to support their team. There are no ugly rivalries among Steelers fans.

The Black and Gold of Flagler County started in 2013. It has a strong focus on charitable endeavors

and we were amazed by what they've already accomplished. The club supports "Rush the Bus," to gather school supplies for kids, "Operation Once in a Lifetime" to help soldiers in every branch of the service – and they were heavily involved with the NFL program "Play 60." In fact, when they found out that Larry Foote was coming to participate in Play 60 on his birthday, the club baked him a cake. As the story was told, he was so humble and appreciative, that the club members were as touched as he was. The fan members we spoke to boasted proudly about the tradition of Steelers players embracing fan support – no egotistical superstars, just caring people that happen to play a game on Sundays.

The Black and Gold Club produces a monthly newsletter filled with updates on the club and interesting Steelers facts. The club T-shirts feature a lineman in a three-point stance. We were introduced to Jack, the model for the player – or that's what we were told.

Everyone was asking him to get into the stance. He kindly complied. Even though he was a few years our senior, we knew we would get pancake blocked if he moved in our direction.

Beer Note: At the bar the bartender made our choice for us. He served us Rooney's Old Irish Style Ale. For those of you not in the know, we are talking about the Rooney family. The Rooneys have a long history with beer. According to the Rooneys' Beer Company website, back at the turn of the 20th century, the Chief's father, Dan, opened a family pub on the corner of Corey and General Robinson Streets, later the home of Three Rivers Stadium. In 1933, the family expanded to brewing at General Braddock Brewing Company in Braddock. They produced four beers: Rooney's Irish Red Ale, Rooney's Lager, Rooney's Pilsner, and Veterans & Civilian Pilsner/Lager blend. Eventually the brewery closed. Then in the late 1990s, Joe Rooney, of the Florida Rooneys, resurrected the brand name and began selling the beer as drafts in

Florida. When they looked to expand into bottles, they came back to Western Pennsylvania and the Penn Brewery on the North Side. Rooney's Beer Company is run by Patrick J. Rooney, Sr. (son of Art Sr., the Chief) and his family. I am slightly embarrassed that this is the first time I have tried this local Pittsburgh beer and I drove over 800 miles to do so. My first impression: this is a great local craft alternative to Smithwick's (a strong compliment). This Irish ale has traditionally heavy malt flavorings with a slight spice aftertaste. Overall, a very drinkable beer and a perfect pairing for the phenomenal tailgate food we were about to experience.

The Plantation Bar and Grill had roped off a huge portion of the parking lot for the tailgate. There were pop-up tents and chairs, and a large screen TV playing Steelers highlights all day. We followed our noses to the grill and opted for the pulled pork sandwich and fries. And it wasn't just another Steelers fan manning the BBQ, it was an actual chef. The guy behind us in line remarked to him, "Maybe you should put on some gloves while serving the food." In one of those classic lines, the chef responded, "I am old school, I don't need no stinkin' gloves." Given his commanding presence, nobody was going to question him. After enjoying one of the best BBQ sandwiches ever, we weren't about to question him either.

(Note: Not long after our visit, the owners of the Plantation Bar and Grill emailed us to let us know that the Plantation Bar has closed and is opening up as The Loop Sports Bar and Restaurant. At this time we don't have any additional information, but we wanted to include the photos and details of our visit to the Plantation as it existed when we were there.)

One particular shadow box drew our attention. As it was explained to us, a longtime customer had attended every Super Bowl game that the Steelers have played. He had saved every ticket stub and pin from each game. The fan had recently passed away and the collection in the shadow box was given to Giuseppe's, where the fan had enjoyed watching the games every weekend. Time and again on this Journey we see the connection between fans and their Steelers hangouts.

Giuseppe's is a family business, operating since 1982. They believe that the way to be successful is to embrace tradition and put out the highest quality product available. They hand-make all the pizzas and cook them directly on stone rather than on metal screens.

Giuseppe's is also known for the food challenges. One person has 30 minutes to eat:

✦ The Pittsburgh Extreme (including chips and a pickle spear)
✦ 10 buffalo wings (5 must be extra HOT)
✦ One slice of cheesecake with cherries
✦ One 32 oz. beverage of your choice

✦ ✦ ✦
GIUSEPPE'S STEEL CITY PIZZA

3658 Nova Road
Port Orange, FL 32129
(386) 761-4717
www.giuseppessteelcitypizza.com

We left the Plantation tailgate in high spirits and headed south looking for Giuseppe's Steel City Pizza. It seemed like we drove forever, which reminded us of just how big this city is. The drive was worth the effort. Giuseppe's is a Steelers hangout like no other. The memorabilia on the walls were so diverse and interesting that we stood gawking like the out-of-state tourists that we were. One of the more unique things about Giuseppe's is the graffiti on the wall. The owner's son did it and it gave a real Pittsburgh steel mill feel to the place.

OR

Two people have 60 minutes to eat:

✦ Giuseppe's 28 inch 60 slice party pizza with cheese and 5 toppings of choice

✦ A 32 oz. beverage of choice for each person

As of our visit, there were only two people who had successfully completed the individual challenge (check out Giuseppe's website to see a video). Considering that we had gorged at the tailgate party, we graciously passed on the challenge. That doesn't mean that we didn't order. I ordered one of the "Super Bowls," the Buffalo Chicken Bowl – a freshly baked bread bowl filled with chopped chicken breast and hot buffalo wing sauce, then topped with mozzarella and cheddar cheese and baked. Delicious!

✦ ✦
LATITUDE 30

10390 Philips Hwy.
Jacksonville, FL 32256
(904) 365-5555
www.latthirty.com

Latitude 30 was our final stop in Jacksonville. It's home to the First Coast Steelers club. Wanda, the club president, told us they've been around for more than 20 years and currently have more than 200 active members and 400 "not so active" members. Their home is an amazing 50,000 square foot facility. On Game Days, Latitude 30 allocates the First Coast Steelers Club the entire movie theater. They get their own private wait staff and a customized menu featuring, of course, Iron City.

We met with this club earlier at the tailgate, so we went to this bar just to get a sense of how big it really was. When we pulled into the parking lot, we were

met with a familiar face who recognized the RV – with good reason. The guy who wrapped the RV, Gary, has a son, Bryan, who lives in Jacksonville. When we saw Bryan we recognized him from the picture in the Sign-A-Rama South display room. The picture shows two guys in Iraq standing in front of a huge Steelers logo. The picture was taken at the Kirkuk Air Force Base in Iraq. Captain Bryan McAfoose (Franklin Regional) and Captain Doug Whitehead (Penn Trafford) were both members of the 823rd Security Force Squadron out of Moody Air Force Base in Georgia. They came across the painted logo at a base in Iraq. It turns out that the logo had been painted by troops from the Pittsburgh Air National Guard. The Steelers connection in the armed forces is a very powerful thing. It unites people in the most difficult of situations.

Didn't know what to expect on this one, other than a 14-hour drive ahead. Roll call on this trip was Shawn, Domenic Mantella and Josh Miller. Dom and I have had many discussions into the wee hours of the morning about preparing, cooking and, yes, eating all kinds of food. Dom comes from a wonderful Italian family. His family members own their own restaurants, his mother is a bakery chef and his family makes their own wine, picks their own olives and are connoisseurs when it comes to cheese. Dom came up huge on this trip. He brought the most amazing Italian sandwiches and home-made desserts. He sold shirts, bracelets and even filmed segments of the Journey. He handled a lot of the driving and babysitting. He was the team MVP on this trip, for sure.

Each one of our visits is supposed to be an hour, but I think we stayed at the Plantation Bar and Grill for three to four hours. We were signing autographs, taking pictures and giving hugs. A common fact about Shawn Allen – he hates hugs. Can't explain why, he just hates hugs from anyone outside his family. So having this knowledge at my fingertips, I went around the country encouraging everyone to make sure they get a few hugs in on Shawn. Not nice but it was fun. I grew up with the notion that if you want to be good at something you need to practice and take a lot of reps. With that theory at the forefront, I just assume Shawn needs a lot of hugs. As we were leaving, I told 25-50 people to give Shawn a big farewell hug. Needless to say, Shawn wasn't very happy with me. I, of course, thought it was very funny and vowed to keep it going. I figured this was going to happen in all 32 NFL markets, like it or not.

place in Florida called Steel City Pizza. Then we walked into the place and our jaws dropped. I've never seen anything like this, even in Pittsburgh. A family pizza joint honoring the Steelers and serving fantastic food was exactly what we needed. I am not doing this place justice through words. This is a must-see if you're ever in Jacksonville. So there we were with full bellies and loading up the RV for the long trek back to Pittsburgh. In case you're curious, everyone in Giuseppe's gave Shawn a hug goodbye.

At the Plantation, Joy was the woman responsible for throwing an amazing tailgate party that took up a huge parking lot in a strip mall. They roped off an enormous section and had three grills going full blast. I had the barbeque pork sandwich and it was amazing. One thing about Steelers fans I can say is that they love to have fun and party in large groups. The crew at the Plantation was very educated Steelers fans with huge football IQs. I am always surprised, shocked and honored when someone comes up to me and tells a story of my playing days.

Giuseppe's Steel City Pizza was an absolute treat. I had zero expectations other than that I wanted a great slice of pizza. As we were getting close, I was thinking about how strange it was to have a pizza

Atlanta
Home of the Falcons

Shawn's Two Cents

Being longtime Pittsburgh residents, we appreciate all our local sports – so we still hold a grudge against Atlanta and the tragic ending to the Pirates' 1992 season. Still, Atlanta is home to Steelers favorite Hines Ward…and it's nice this year to still be talking about the Pirates in September! As we drove past the Steelers' "home field" in Atlanta, the Georgia Dome, we compared the Atlanta skyline – and the skylines of all the other cities we've visited – to Pittsburgh's. Nothing comes close to emerging from the Fort Pitt tunnels and seeing the Pittsburgh skyline, with Heinz Field shining proudly on the North Shore. It's got to be one of the best urban views in the country.

Of course, one of the good things about the Steelers hangouts in Atlanta is that they aren't downtown. We have come to realize why so many RVs are on the road towing extra, smaller cars. A 32-foot RV is a pain in the ass to park! That said, as we pull into our first parking lot, we also realize how much fun it is. The Steelers Fan Club of Atlanta cheered loudly as we pulled in – followed by others on the outside decks "booing" loudly. On the bright side of things, everyone thinks we are #1 – they just express their feelings with different fingers.

◆ ◆
HAMMERHEAD'S SEAFOOD & SPORTS GRILL

**415 Peachtree Industrial Blvd.
Suwanee, GA 30024
(770) 945-3570**
www.facebook.com/HammerheadsSeafoodSports

We meet Jeff, president of SFCOA, at Hammerhead's, the newest gathering spot for the club. We decide to talk in the parking lot because it is so noisy that it would be difficult to conduct any sort of meaningful interview inside. We learn that the SFCOA was formed in 1990 at, of all places, an Atlanta Falcons bar, the Falcon Inn. Really, who else but the Steelers could form their own fan club at an opposing team's bar? Although it was over twenty years ago, the longtime members still recall the time the home opener was not available because lightning struck the satellite dish just before the game was about to begin. We are not talking about one of the 18" DirecTV dishes, but

the enormous 8' models from back in the day. Shortly after, the club moved to Barnacle's where they stayed for nearly twenty years. During that time the membership grew from the low 20s to over 300 current active members. The club has been involved in many charitable endeavors with their hometown hero Hines Ward. Then, the unthinkable happened. Pittsburgh was screwed again by the Atlanta Braves!

Former Atlanta Braves pitcher John Smoltz purchased Barnacles. In what was clearly an anti-Pittsburgh move, he turned the Steelers hangout into a hip hop dance club. I wonder if the dance moves there resemble the lumbering "dance" Sid Bream performed as he painfully scored that run in 1992. Regardless, the SFCOA was left without a home. Fear not. One of the club's founding members opened a new restaurant. The club quickly established a relationship with Hammerhead's and now you can find hundreds of Steelers fans each week cheering on the Black & Gold.

Beer Note: Wandering up to the bar in search of a great local beer, I saw an advertisement for Sweetwater Brewery. I had never noticed their ad slogan before "Don't Float the Mainstream." It inspired me to order a pint. Sweetwater Brewery began in the early 1990s in Atlanta and has a strong lineup. I have enjoyed the 420 Extra Pale Ale but wanted to try something new. I decided to go with the Sweetwater Blue – definitely not the usual direction for a hophead, but I have heard great things about this award-winning beer. I was not disappointed, as the blueberry aroma was refreshing without overpowering. A solid "3."

The Steelers fans in Atlanta are just like the fans we have met all across the country. Warm and friendly, educated about football – and they love to tell stories. And like all Steelers fans, they support their team. The fans at Hammerheads told us that when the Steelers come to town there is an all-out media blitz in an attempt to curb Steelers fever. The last time the Steelers played in Atlanta there were ads placed online and in local papers asking (begging?) Falcon fans NOT to sell their tickets to Steelers fans. More roadblocks: the Falcons instituted special rules for the purchase of Steelers game tickets. All purchasers were required to buy tickets to a second game if they wanted a ticket to the Steelers game. Try as they might, the ploys did not succeed. The Georgia Dome became another home game for the Black & Gold.

✦ ✦ ✦
SMITH'S OLDE BAR
1578 Piedmont Avenue NE
Atlanta, GA 30324
(404) 875-1522
www.smithsoldebar.com

The next stop was Smith's Olde Bar. We were expecting a very traditional Irish pub and were pleasantly surprised by what we found. Smith's is a combination pool hall, music hall and drinking pub. The music memorabilia dominates the first impression...then you notice the Black & Gold intermixed with the music.

Shawnee, the president of Steelciti, introduced herself. Steelciti is the second Steelers fan club in Atlanta, started in 2010. These fans were looking for more than just a place to watch the game on Sundays;

they wanted to be a part of something professional with a purpose. As Shawnee says, it is about what is in your heart and the passion and drive that leads to bleeding Black & Gold. Steelciti gives back to the community on a year-round basis. Its slogan is "A social organization committed to community service." They also have a very interesting initiation for new members. Words cannot adequately describe this almost religious ritual and unveiling, but I highly encourage you to check out their Facebook page.

As Shawnee gave us a personal tour of Smith's, their home away from home, she let us know that she knew her football. She was hitting Josh with great plays during his career, specifically talking about his huge punt against Jacksonville in 1999, saying, "That's right, baby, I remember you." The entire room was packed with Steelers fans. The current mailing list is over 600; this proved to be a problem when they all showed up for the last Super Bowl. Fortunately, the fire marshall was also a Steelers fan.

Beer Note: I went to the bar to continue my "beer float" with SweetWater Brewing Company. I ordered the LowRYEder IPA. As you might guess, this is an American IPA made with rye. The rye is apparent from the time you lift the glass and catch the aroma. Yet like many of my favorites, the citrus characteristic of the hops comes through and I enjoyed another fine beer from SweetWater. Of course, I had a Miller Lite to deliver, so I headed back to the pool hall. Josh and the Steelciti members were laughing and telling war stories. We had only been there a few minutes, but they looked like old friends. Steelers fans are like family anywhere you go.

I was looking forward to this trip for some time. A lot of ex-Steelers live in Atlanta – Hines Ward, Kordell Stewart, Carlos Emmons, Greg Lloyd and many others. Atlanta is a fun, passionate sports town. They love their Hawks, Braves and of course, Falcons. Believe it or not, Atlanta is one of the places where I got yelled at the most; more so than New York or even Oakland in the black hole. I really believe Atlanta flat-out hates punters in general. Atlanta allowed me to grow skin like an iguana. That actually helped me in my career. But I wasn't here to play football this week. I was here to check out two very cool Steelers joints that happen to like punters.

Hammerhead's and Smith's Olde Bar: Hammerhead's was a nice group, a little older and maybe 15-20 deep. I remember that they all sat patiently waiting for an opportunity to explain why they were Steelers fans. In these trips across the NFL markets, we've found that most of the Steelers fans we encounter were at one time living in Pennsylvania. No exceptions here in Atlanta. There were a few college games going on inside and everybody wanted to see our big Always a Home Game RV, so we went outside and took some wonderful pictures and sold a handful of shirts. That was a great start to a very long weekend. Let's not forget we already had 11 hours on the road, with one more bar to visit in Atlanta...and then on the road again.

There's a saying out there that size doesn't matter. People will fight vehemently that size does matter and that bigger is always better. Well, that's not the case with Smith's Olde Bar. This group of Steelers fans might've been five, six or seven deep

and some of the most knowledgeable fans we've come across
on this Journey. The passion
and love that they have for the
Steelers would match any as
well. Tonight this old bar had
an intimate crowd. I loved it. I
remember high-fiving, laughing
and just having a great time as
if I'd known them for years. We
took a bunch of pictures and
told a ton of stories that for me
personally will last a lifetime.
Of course, like most visits they
all seem to end the same way –
with Shawn and his finger
pointing to his watch. It
was time to get back on the
RV because we were off to
Jacksonville or Carolina. I'm
not sure anymore. That is
the common theme, that
Shawn, thank God, kept us
on some kind of schedule.
Because if he didn't, I'd
still be in Kansas City or
perhaps even Washington.

New York

Home of the
Giants

Home of the
Jets

Shawn's Two Cents

If any of our readers have met Josh, they know that he is a very engaging and charismatic person. In general, this works to our advantage. Steelers fans are always excited to meet and hang with him on our Journey. In New York City, his magnetic personality had interesting consequences – the homeless were also very interested in speaking with Josh. I have no idea if they knew who he was or just sensed that he was a good guy who would stop and listen to them.

One guy in particular immediately engaged Josh with his quotation of Scripture before switching to, "Bagpipes should be played indoors." He was very insistent on this last point. Josh would have stayed to continue debating the benefits of playing the bagpipes indoors versus outdoors, but we had a schedule to keep.

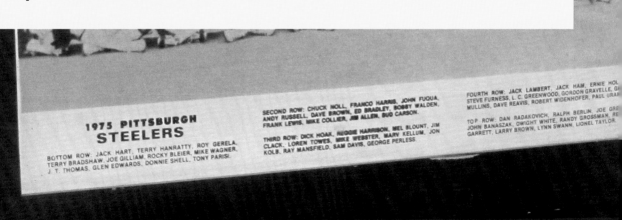

1975 PITTSBURGH STEELERS

BOTTOM ROW: JACK HART, TERRY HANRATTY, ROY GERELA, TERRY BRADSHAW, JOE GILLIAM, ROCKY BLEIER, MIKE WAGNER, J. T. THOMAS, GLEN EDWARDS, DONNIE SHELL, TONY PARISI.

SECOND ROW: CHUCK NOLL, FRANCO HARRIS, JOHN FUQUA, ANDY RUSSELL, DAVE BROWN, ED BRADLEY, BOBBY WALDEN, FRANK LEWIS, MIKE COLLIER, JIM ALLEN, BUD CARSON.

THIRD ROW: DICK HOAK, REGGIE HARRISON, MEL BLOUNT, JIM CLACK, LOREN TOEWS, MIKE WEBSTER, MARV KELLUM, JON KOLB, RAY MANSFIELD, SAM DAVIS, GEORGE PERLESS.

FOURTH ROW: JACK LAMBERT, JACK HAM, ERNIE HOL... STEVE FURNESS, L. C. GREENWOOD, GORDON GRAVELLE, G... MULLINS, DAVE REAVIS, ROBERT WIDENHOFER, PAUL URA...

TOP ROW: DAN RADAKOVICH, RALPH BERLIN, JOE GRE... JOHN BANASZAK, DWIGHT WHITE, RANDY GROSSMAN, RE... GARRETT, LARRY BROWN, LYNN SWANN, LIONEL TAYLOR.

HIBERNIA BAR & GRILL

**401 W. 50th Street
New York, NY 10019
(212) 969-9703
www.hiberniabar.com**

The first stop was Hibernia Bar & Grill. We got there early, just before 11:00 a.m. We were not the only Steelers fans waiting for the bar to open. A group of

fans from out of town were standing out front. They wanted to make sure that they got good seats at the bar for the game.

We met Sean, one of the partners, and he gave us a tour of the Steelers memorabilia on the wall. They had

a cool (weird? disturbing?) print of Marilyn Monroe in a Roethlisberger jersey. That was something we'd never seen before. We asked Sean about the history of Hibernia. He told us that Hibernia became a popular Steelers hangout after the closing of Scruffy Duffy's. We had heard about Scruffy Duffy's and were excited to check it out when we were doing our initial research for the Journey. But, as Sean explained, Scruffy Duffy's became a victim of large-scale real estate development in the city. Many of its former patrons now come to Hell's Kitchen to hang out in a traditional Irish pub and cheer on the Steelers. We were bummed about Scruffy Duffy's, but Hibernia is a great place to catch a game and hang with Steelers fans. One of the traditions that Hibernia-Steelers fans have created: they all drink one Iron City for good luck each week before the game before switching to a more traditional "pub ale" for the rest of the game.

♦ ♦ ♦

THE IRISH EXIT

978 2nd Ave
New York, NY 10022
(212) 755-8383
www.irishexitnyc.com

The next stop was The Irish Exit on 2nd Avenue. We struggled getting there because we ran into a parade on our way from Hibernia. Apparently, parades are a relatively normal thing in this city. Eventually we bailed on the cab and walked the parade route.

The Irish Exit is touted as the #1 Steelers hangout in NYC and it's not hard to see why. The walls are covered in memorabilia and people in Steelers jerseys occupied every seat at the bar. We asked Patrick, the general manager, about the unusual name. He explained that an "Irish exit" is when someone leaves a party without saying goodbye. Ahhh! We've been doing this for years and didn't know it was a legitimate, culturally recognized phenomenon. Maybe we

can use it as a signal for the rest of the Journey – "Josh, time for the Irish exit." As you can imagine, it takes forever to get Josh out of a bar – both because everyone wants to say one last thing to him and because he's just a naturally friendly guy. The Irish exit might keep us to our schedule a bit better!

Patrick also explained that The Irish Exit has more in common with Pittsburgh's North Shore than a love for the Steelers. Apparently, there is some sort of common ownership between The Irish Exit and McFadden's.

Patrick was brought to NYC specifically to open a bar for Pittsburgh Steelers fans. Those fans enjoy the "Iron City Tower," a tall, cylindrical beer-dispensing tower that holds six Iron City beers at once. The Irish Exit also has a Steelers Game Day

menu featuring Chuck Noll Nachos, Polamalu Pierogies, Tomlin Tower Package (the tower as described above, along with a huge selection of appetizers) and the Joe Greene Quesadillas.

We also noticed some Iowa Hawkeye paraphernalia on the wall, so we asked whether there was some kind of connection. Patrick told us that back in 1979, then coach Hayden Fry wanted to build the Iowa football program. He believed that dressing the team

in a winner's image would spur the team to become winners. So he reached out to Joe Greene, who was able to send Fry the home and away uniforms of Steelers quarterback Terry Bradshaw. Fry also gained permission from the Steelers to overhaul Iowa's uniforms in the Steelers' image.

Between college Game Days on Saturdays and Steelers on Sundays, The Irish Exit is packed all weekend. The Irish Exit goes all out on Game Day. The DJ is constantly giving updates on bar specials and engaging with the fans. At every break in play the fans are treated to Steelers fight songs and polka music. It's a great place to be to watch the Black & Gold.

Beer Note: Since it was still early, I decided to have a breakfast beer in a traditional Irish style. I ordered a Guinness. Josh decided it was time to order a Loose Goose. Patrick looked at him and searched his memory for a moment then said, "I give up." He knew nothing about the Loose Goose, but was about to be educated. A few years ago in our neighborhood there was a small movement (spurred by Josh) to rename the Bloody Mary. A few guys started ordering the Loose Goose at a local club after a round of golf. Josh, with his totally dry delivery, orders one and says "Oh…around here they probably still call it a Bloody Mary." The look on a bartender's face is priceless. So many of them just go along with it. We encourage all readers to jump on board our renaming wagon!

predictive analytics-based engine for sports performance. If you are a fantasy sports junkie, this is a site worth investigating. It has contracts with many of the sports news outlets, including ESPN and *Sports Illustrated*. Nik picked up a passion for the Steelers while obtaining his degrees from Carnegie Mellon. The day we went to Reservoir Bar, another company was conducting a research study about fans and the probabilities associated with certain outcomes in NFL games. Presumably, they had chosen Nik to interview both because of his background and because of his love for the Black & Gold! Once the interview crew found out that Josh had played for the Steelers, he was brought into the interview too.

✦ ✦
RESERVOIR BAR
70 University Place
New York, NY 10003
(212) 475-0770

As we reached the third stop on the tour of NYC, we were surprised to see a video crew conducting an interview with a guy in Steelers gear. We went over to chat with him and found that he was Nik Bonaddio, the founder and CEO of NumberFire, which is a

The Steelers crowd was not as large as usual at the Reservoir Bar on our visit. According to the bartender, most of the regulars had gotten tickets and made the road trip to the Meadowlands to see the Steelers pick up their first win of 2013. Generally, at least 20-30 fans are there each week.

A breakfast burrito with a Guinness is a tremendous way to end a day, or start a day for that matter. We thoroughly enjoyed the food and the atmosphere at Beckett's. We spoke with Ronan, the manager. We told him about our book and our commitment to donating a portion of the proceeds to help the older players who did not benefit from the huge contracts of today. He made an immediate connection to the struggles that many of the Gaelic football players have after their careers. Ronan was incredibly supportive of our efforts, saying that it made sense for Steelers fans to take on such an endeavor because they were the most compassionate sports fans in the world. That's just his opinion, of course, but we tend to agree.

◆ ◆
BECKETT'S BAR & GRILL

81 Pearl Street
New York, NY 10004
(212) 269-1001
www.beckettsnyc.com

Our final stop in the Big Apple was at Beckett's Bar & Grill, the perfect place to rest before the long drive back to Pittsburgh. There was a large outdoor seating area on a street outside the back of the pub. Rows of tables were all packed with guests enjoying a Sunday afternoon in the city. Granted, the hostess was wearing a Jets jersey, but she claimed that the Steelers were her second favorite team, and she showed us where the Steelers fans meet each week. Interestingly, Beckett's uses caution tape to segregate the space off. She suggested we try the breakfast burrito. I'm not sure whether we've had more beers, burritos or cups of coffee on this Journey, but we went with the recommendation.

Oh yes, the New York Bars. I had mixed emotions about this weekend's trip to New York City. I grew up in New Jersey and I understand the loyalty to New York teams. That was one of the reasons we decided not to take a mammoth RV wrapped in the Always A Home Game logo. I was expecting the worst and was very pleasantly surprised when it turned out to be okay. It's funny, when we started on this trip and talked about the 32 NFL markets, we had New York as being one of the places we may have trouble. Being from New Jersey, I have seen a lot of weird things happen when it comes to sports teams. The Rangers hate the Islanders and the Jets hate the Giants and of course the Knicks hate the Nets. But a funny thing happens when an outside team comes into town. They all get together and join forces and hate that team together. Not the kind of hate like "you guys stink" – I'm talking about the baseball bat to the headlights, rock through the window, getting jumped and just all-around bad things that happen in back alleys across America.

Sometimes my imagination gets the best of me. I could just see this New York trip as a lead story in news stations across the country: New Yorkers jump Steelers fans

on a Journey to Steelers hangouts. Needless to say, none of this took place and our trip turned out to be one of the better ones on this Journey. (We didn't even get a "Hey, I got your Always A Home Game right here, pal!" We came across a Spanish parade, went past Ground Zero, Manhattan, Queens, Brooklyn and the Bronx. We had a great time. We've been to so many places that were amazing and always kept saying, "Our wives would love it here." Those six words would be said 100 times during this Journey. I don't know if it's funny or sad, but Shawn and I have now been to more places together than my wife of 13 years and I have been.

As far as the bars go, they were great. Steelers fans are truly out and about in New York and New Jersey. I'm sure Shawn has all the numbers, but I'm certain that on this New York trip I must've had about nine Loose Gooses. I believe some of you may still call them Bloody Marys. Reality hit – an eight-hour drive to get home. That's not bad when you leave in the morning but we started this one at seven at night.

78

Philadelphia
Home of the Eagles

Shawn's Two Cents

Philadelphia. The City of Brotherly Love. But does the City of Brotherly Love have any love for the Steelers? Hard to believe. Philly is pretty rabid about its sports teams. We had three bars lined up to see if we could find some Black & Gold fever in Ben Franklin's stomping grounds. We were headed to the Fox and Hound, O'Neal's Pub and Dave and Buster's.

I had been at a soccer tournament in Maryland, so I drove up to Philly and picked Josh up at the train station. We hit the pubs and met up with Spoonie, Angie, Ross and Steelers PA East – and even a Pittsburgh Harlequins rugby team. Along the way we learned that sometimes in a divorce, the most valuable marital property is the allegiance to the Steelers, and that Josh needs to invest in a better electric razor. Oh yeah, we also learned that there is plenty of Black & Gold fever in the city at the other end of the Turnpike.

✦ ✦
FOX AND HOUND SPORTS TAVERN

1501 Spruce Street
Philadelphia, PA 19102
(215) 732-8610
www.foxandhound.com

We headed to the Fox and Hound Sports Tavern in Philadelphia, knowing it was a big-time sports bar. With our crazy travel schedules, we were there on a Saturday. It looked more like college game day than Terrible Towel day. Veronica showed us a table and immediately apologized when we told her who we were and why we were there. She said the place is always packed with Steelers fans on Sundays but Saturdays are college game days. This is a dilemma we face on a consistent basis. By visiting 100 Steelers hangouts in 140 days, we cannot visit every place during a game. That said, there was still a 10-foot-tall inflatable Steelers guy guarding the front entrance.

Beer Note: We decided to have a quick pint and something to eat. Being in Philadelphia, I felt

compelled to order a beer from Yards Brewing Company. Yards Brewing was started in 1994 and has made some great beers along the way. In 2012, their Extra Special Ale won a medal at the Great American Beer Festival which, as a beer sommelier, I felt I had to attend. (My wife is a lawyer and has to take continuing legal education classes. I think going to the GABF is something like that for me!) I ordered the IPA, which turned out to be a good choice. This IPA is more of a British style, rather than West Coast American. The hops have a slight pine aftertaste, and unlike many of its American counterparts, does not punch you in the face with the hops. Definitely a "3."

Everyone has his or her quirks. Some are endearing, others are annoying. Still others are downright hilarious. Josh falls into the last category when it comes to ordering food or drink. It always happens – he will start to talk to the server or a fan. This does not give him proper time to focus on the menu or be more specific with respect to his order...which leads to a moment of sheer panic. There have been times when Steelers fans are hanging on his every word, listening to a story he is telling about Bill Cower and the "Cower Shower" and the time comes to order. Thus, Josh places "the panic order."

Case in point: at the Fox and Hound, Josh first tried to order a Bud Light Lime, but that was unavailable. Veronica offered to put a lime in a Bud Light. Not understanding the response, Josh said that they make them with lime already in the bottle. Veronica said she could put the lime in the bottle. This went back and forth a few times. Who's on first? Eventually, it got straightened out and Josh was ready to order food. He had decided on wings... blue cheese or ranch? There

was panic in his eyes. Josh said blue cheese. Veronica went to place the order. No, wait! RANCH! Here is a guy who can kick a football 75 yards down the field with 10 monstrously-sized guys charging at him, but he can't order wings without cracking under pressure.

✦ ✦
O'NEAL'S PUB

611 S. 3rd Street
Philadelphia, PA 19147
(215) 574-9495
www.onealspub.com

The next stop in Philly was O'Neal's Pub. This is a traditional urban, shotgun style public house – if you can mix metaphors from the American Southwest and Ireland and end up with anything traditional. Spoonie, the owner, and one of the long-time servers, Angie, greeted us warmly. Angie was not originally a Steelers fan but was converted by her ex-husband. We asked briefly about the ex and the response was quick and firm – the Steelers were the best thing about the marriage and the only thing that was worth a damn! They informed us that to really experience the atmosphere at O'Neal's we needed to visit the second floor, aptly named Steelers Alley.

Beer Note: Before we headed off to the Alley, I needed to pay my respects once again to Yards. This time I ordered my favorite session beer, the Yards Brawler – PUGILIST STYLE ALE. Because this beer is only 4.2% ABV, I love to say, "Let's go another round." The Brawler is also crafted in the style of English session ales, with ruby color and features flavors of freshly baked bread and caramel. A solid "3."

Armed with drinks, we headed to Steelers Alley. We were halted in our tracks by a large group singing "Here we go, Steelers!" Although it was not a Game Day, we had run into the Pittsburgh Harlequins rugby team. This Steelers hangout is also popular with the Pittsburgh rugby teams. When we finally made it to the Alley we understood how it got

its name. This is a narrow second-floor bar dedicated to the Steelers. Spoonie told us that it is packed, standing room only, every Sunday for the Steelers. He could not say enough good things about Steelers fans. We all know that Steelers fans are the best in the world but this fact must be especially true when compared to Philadelphia fans.

✦ ✦
DAVE AND BUSTER'S

500 Germantown Pike
Plymouth Meeting, PA 19462
(610) 832-9200
www.daveandbusters.com

The final stop on the City of Brotherly Love tour was Dave and Buster's in Plymouth Meeting. We were scheduled to meet the Steelers PA East, but did not know where we could find them in the enormous sports bar. Never fear. As soon as we walked through the door the hostess welcomed us and told us that the entire back room had been reserved. After hearing that the Steelers PA East had well over 100 fans in attendance each week and a mailing list of over 500, we knew why they'd need the whole back room. As we learned first hand, the management at Dave and Busters loves Steelers PA East. When the bar was recently enlarged, the first thing done was to allocate the new larger space to the Steelers fans. By providing the separate room, weekly drink specials and private wait staff, they are truly committed to maintaining a Steel City presence in Philadelphia.

We sat down to enjoy a cold beverage with Ross, the president of the fan club, and realized once again that Steelers fans are "smarter than your average bear." The discussion quickly turned from how the team could improve to how the league could improve. Most people think of the NFL as a multi-billion dollar freight train that is rolling down the tracks, but Ross and his band of Steelers fans had a list of ways to improve the experience for the fans. Ross also talked about the fan club's commitment to charity. One of their members, Fergie, had succumbed to cancer. So each year the club holds a fundraiser to benefit the cancer society in Fergie's name. The bond between Steelers fans does not end when the final whistle blows on Sundays.

After a long day visiting with fans of the greatest team in the world, we were dead tired. We were checking into the hotel and we noticed a buzzing sound. We got into the elevator and the buzzing sound got louder. We thought there must be something wrong with the HVAC so we just went to the room. The buzzing was still noticeable and we just hoped we wouldn't hear it once we got inside. In one of those frustrating moments we realized the key did not work so we went back to the lobby.

When we returned to the lobby, still with the buzzing, we asked another guest if he heard it. He listened closely and agreed that there was a faint buzzing sound. The three of us walked around the

lobby listening to the HVAC vents, trying to identify the source of the sound. The guy behind the desk didn't hear anything. As we rode the elevator back up to our room for the second time, a Chinese food delivery guy joined us. We asked him about the noise. He said it was the first time he'd heard it although he delivered food to the hotel all the time. It was really loud at this point.

We finally got into our room and the buzzing was still going strong. We were about to call down to the front desk to get someone to fix the problem when Josh set his travel bag down. The buzzing sound was more muffled. He opened his bag up and discovered that his electric shaver had been making the noise for the past 20 minutes! We just cracked up.

Iknew finding Steelers bars in Philadelphia was going to be very tough. Even if they had Steelers bars in Philly, I was sure they were going to be underground – the kind of bars that you need a secret handshake to get in or a password. Or knock three times on the door and say the words "Franco-Bradshaw" and "Cowher" and then the door opens. Well, once again I was wrong and have proven that I watch way too much TV. All we needed to do was go to the Fox and Hound Sports Tavern. We just walked in, found a booth in the back and made ourselves at home. It was a Saturday and every TV in the house was focused on college football. Very nice people worked there and they swore up and down that Sunday was Steelers day at the Fox and Hound. They answered enough questions correctly to validate that they were Steelers fans, so we took pictures and headed out.

I remember O'Neal's very well. You notice two things right away when you walk through the door. One is the amazing front of the bar. It was very cool how it opens up to the street. Second is Spoonie. He is a very big man. This guy comes to work every day and loves what he does. Everyone should be this happy when they come to work. Spoonie is a very cool guy who clearly is a big Steelers fan. He had the upstairs dedicated so the Steelers fan base can watch the game. If you didn't like something going on at the bar, you just go ahead and tell Spoonie about your problem. He would probably tell you "Tough shit" and enjoy yourself. You would, however, feel better about getting it off your chest. He's built a very nice business by making this a neighborhood bar that caters to a loyal fan base. I am a big fan of Spoonie and if I'm ever in Philly again, I would definitely stop over at O'Neals Pub. It's a safe bet that you would need a phone number for a car service if you weren't within stumbling distance of home.

At Dave and Busters, we met a great group of people. There's a very loyal fan base. We learned that 100 fans will show up every weekend to cheer on their Black & Gold – regardless of the record. This group's email blast goes out to 500 members weekly. It's a very passionate and organized fan base.

Steelers Tattoos

Baltimore
Home of the Ravens

Shawn's Two Cents

Baltimore. Home of the Ravens. Home of Ray Lewis. Really – what sincere Steelers fan wants to travel to Baltimore, unless it is for the purpose of vacation or checking out the Inner Harbor? But word was that there were some Steelers hangouts worthy of visiting in Baltimore. We figured we had nothing to lose, except more liver cells. So we fired up the Always a Home Game RV and hit the road.

1996 PITTSBURGH STEELERS

♦ ♦
OUTTA THE WAY CAFÉ

17503 Redland Road
Rockville, MD 20855
(301) 963-6895
www.outta.com

The first stop in Baltimore is the Outta the Way Café. From the moment we walked in the front door we knew this was a great place to relax and hang out. The motto says it all: "Good food, good 'tude." Adopting that theme, we ordered the fish tacos. Serendipitously, the draft beer selection featured Heavy Seas Brewing.

Beer Note: I believe in lifelong learning. Because I am so committed to continuing education, I've attended Pittsburgh's Craft Beer School since its inception in 2006. Each month, the Pittsburgh Cultural Trust presents Beer School. My classmates and I enjoy a sampling of four different beers and presentations from beer experts and craft brewers. A few years back, one of the founders of Heavy Seas was the featured speaker. I recall this being one of the best sessions,

not only for the quality of the beers, but because of the engaging personality of the founder. He insisted that rather than clapping, each person should respond with a pirate "Aargh." By the end of the night, there were almost 300 people talking like pirates. I thoroughly enjoyed a Loose Cannon [rating – "4"].

Josh and I noticed a quote on the bottom of the menu:

House Rules: *"All other NFL games are not Steelers conflicts …when the Black and Gold plays, nothing else exists. ~ Chip and Brian"*

This is a very clear indication that even in this "Outta the Way Café" every week is a home game for the Pittsburgh Steelers. The guys explained that regardless of the record, or whether the game is nationally televised, the bar is packed to capacity every game.

Over our most excellent fish tacos, we began talking to the guy next to us at the bar. As it turned out, he was a professional hockey official and had connections to Sidney Crosby. He remarked that Pittsburgh is a great sports town. Initially, he was only a fan of the Penguins, but as he met Penguins fans – who were of course also Steelers fans – he started to root for the Steelers and now is a regular at the Outta the Way Café on Sunday afternoons!

can collection to custom art from Fred Carrow. While hanging around just gawking at all the cool stuff, we were approached by Buxy himself.

Buxy told us his story of attending IUP and then moving to Ocean City to tend bar after graduating. In 1999, he decided that it would be prudent to open his own Steelers-themed place. Now he is a mainstay in the community and a destination for every Steelers fan at the Shore. When we asked about his favorite piece of memorabilia he got a very serious look on his face and there was a long silence. Finally, he said that it was his Terrible Towel signed by Jack Lambert. A worthy choice!

Buxy also described how the market in Pittsburgh has appreciated his efforts to bring a little bit of

✦ ✦ ✦
BUXY'S SALTY DOG SALOON

28th Street Bayside
Ocean City, MD 21842
(410) 289-0973
www.buxys.com

We stretched the limits of the "Baltimore market" in selecting Buxy's Salty Dog Saloon, but it proved to be one of the best decisions we've made on this Journey. We were rewarded as we pulled up. They had announced our arrival on the marquee out front. The collection of Steelers memorabilia at Buxy's is tremendous, ranging from signed items to a fantastic beer

IPA is continuously hopped for 60 minutes (thus the name) and is only 6% ABV, which makes it very aromatic and quite drinkable. The 60-minute IPA is a definite "4."

Being an early morning stop, and having to film for the Big Board, Josh ordered a Loose Goose. Josh was informed that he was about to have the best Loose Goose of his life (nice how quickly Buxy's Salty Dog picked up on the nomenclature). This house specialty is made from George's ~~Bloody Mary~~ Loose Goose mix, which is based in Georgia. We thought it

Pittsburgh to the Shore. *Pittsburgh Magazine* has run stories on Buxy's, and the Steelers' Pre-Game show with Tunch and Wolf has also filmed there. The current offensive coordinator, Todd Hailey, is an off-season resident of Ocean City and is a regular at Buxy's, along with the local fan club, the Pittsburgh Steelers Fan Club of Ocean City.

Beer Note: At the bar, the beer list was as impressive as the memorabilia. I settled for 60-minute IPA from Dogfish Head. The 60-minute IPA is, in the words of Dogfish Head founder Sam Calgione, the de facto session beer for hopheads. This dry, yet balanced,

was odd that one would head to Ocean City, Maryland, to get a drink from Georgia, but then again we were in Maryland to cheer on a team from Pittsburgh. Josh reported that it was one of the top three all-time best Loose Gooses.

The menu at Buxy's had so many great looking items that it was difficult to make a decision. Then they told us about the Game Day specials. As soon as I heard they were seafood pierogies there was no need to go any further.
The perfect combination of the Shore and Pittsburgh. Hands down, one of the best pierogie dishes I've ever tasted.

TODD CONNER'S RESTAURANT & BAR

700 S. Broadway – Fells Point
Baltimore, MD 21231
(410) 537-5005
www.toddconners.com

The final stop in Baltimore was at Todd Conner's in Fells Point, in an historic neighborhood. Like many historic neighborhoods, parking is at a premium. We started to get nervous about parking a 32-foot RV in an urban environment. About three blocks from Todd Conner's we spotted two open parking spaces. Josh proceeded to execute one of the most incredible parallel parking jobs in the history of parallel parking. I firmly believe that even PennDOT driving instructors would have given him a standing ovation.

We made our way to Todd Conner's. Our timing could not have been better. The Steelers flag was flying proudly outside the bar and we entered just as the Steelers pulled off the dramatic win against the Ravens. The place went crazy! Good thing the game was over, too, or we never would have been able to

meet the owners. It was so crowded. After several rounds of "Here We Go" the place began to empty out enough for us to get seats. When we met Nikki we knew we were in for a great visit.

Beer Note: I asked Nikki about the beer and she asked if I had ever tried The Brewer's Art. I had heard of the local Baltimore brewery because they can their beer, but had never tried one. She insisted that I try her two favorites, The Brewer's Art Ozzy Ale and Resurrection. The Ozzy ("3") is a very rich and dry Belgian ale. It did not have the sweet aftertaste that you get with some of the traditional Belgian ales (Chimay and Duval). The Resurrection is a brown ale and might have been one of the best brown ales I have tasted in a long time. When you see this beer it is a must-have – "4." This is one of the few times I have been very pleased with a beer when it isn't an IPA.

We then settled in to enjoy some of the food. Nikki took tremendous pride in telling us about the menu, including the fact that they roast all of their meat fresh, in-house. She also mentioned how they experimented with local flavors in traditional dishes. This prompted me to try the Old Bay seasoned buffalo wings. They were awesome! As she puts it, Todd Conner's is "A Steelers slice of Heaven in Baltimore!"

There is no doubt that this is a great place for Steelers fans to congregate on Game Days, but Baltimore is a huge rivalry town. We asked about the flag outside. Nikki said they keep the Steelers stuff on the walls all the time, but for "safety" reasons, the flag is only displayed outside on Game Days. Then we asked about the unique name of the bar. Nikki's husband filled us in. They had been eager to have their first child, but like many couples, it was taking longer than expected. They were about to partake in fertility treatments, but those were going to be very expensive. At the same time, the opportunity to invest in the bar arose. Faced with a very difficult life decision, they reached a compromise. They invested in the bar and named it after the already agreed-upon name for their first child – Todd Conner. It looked to us like their "first baby" was doing quite well.

The bar was a huge success. Of course, the Steelers gods rewarded them for their devotion. Shortly after opening Todd Conner's, Nikki became pregnant with their first child. They now have two daughters, never would have used the name Todd Conner anyway, and have a cool Steelers hangout as part of the family, as well.

As we were leaving, it seemed like we were saying goodbye after a family meal. There were hugs all around, to which Georgie Boy said, "That is the first time I've ever been hugged by a stranger." Georgie could not have been more wrong. We may have walked in as strangers, but we left as friends. We have one more thing to say to Nikki…"Aaargh!"

I was definitely looking forward to the Baltimore trip. I had heard great things about the Salty Dog and couldn't wait to meet Doug, the owner. Very cool guy, loves his Steelers but most importantly, loves the community he lives in and the loyalty of his patrons. You can tell that it is a family that just happens to gather at a bar.

The first couple things you notice when you enter the parking lot of Buxy's Salty Dog is an army truck with Steelers camo all over. I don't need to tell you how cool that looks. When you walk into the place you can't help but notice sports memorabilia that you've never seen before. I asked myself, where did he get these items? And the Salty Dog made one of the best Loose Gooses I've had on this Journey.

If you ever find yourself in Ocean City, please go out there and spend a couple hours. Ask for Doug, tell him you're a Steelers fan and enjoy a wonderful afternoon. This is definitely a place to vacation with the family and have dinner. And it's a block away from the beach. This was one of the most enjoyable stops along the way.

I was ready to go home after the Salty Dog. I didn't think we needed to drive all the way back to Baltimore from Ocean City for one more bar. I am so glad we did. Todd Conner's was packed wall-to-wall with Steelers fans. The most noticeable difference about this bar compared to all the others we have been in was the age of the crowd. It was a younger, hipper crowd. They all took after the owners of the bar, Nikki and her husband. This was a very cute couple that absolutely loved the Steelers. I enjoyed listening to Nikki tell her story of the food, the Steelers fans, the beer, the community and most importantly, their own magical story of the immaculate conception. It was getting late and we didn't want to leave. I could've stayed there all night and listened to the younger generation of Steelers fans tell their stories and why the team is so important to them. Whenever I'm in Baltimore I will make sure that I drop by and say hey to Nikki and the hip little group that hangs out at Todd Conner's.

Seattle
Home of the Seahawks

The trip to Seattle began as one might expect. We started the final approach into SeaTac airport and after about 15 minutes we looked out of the window. Nothing but fog. Then smack! We hit the runway. It was raining and visibility was no more than 10 feet. Welcome to Seattle.

After our visit to Baltimore and the East Coast, we were making a cross-country trek to Seattle. I'd been to the area before, both to hike the Cascades and Olympics and to kayak around the San Juan Islands. I'd even been to a Mariners game to catch Ichiro Suzuki. But I'd never gone looking for Steelers Nation. That was about to change.

We had three places lined up to check out – Cheers Bar & Grill, Fremont Dock Restaurant and Fado Irish Pub. During our sojourn we learned that some Seahawks fans did not take the loss in Super Bowl XL graciously, that Seattle has "interesting" public art and that a lot of CMU grads live in the Seattle area. We know the crowd at Seahawks games is loud, but with Northwest Steelers Nation and the Seattle Steelers Fan Club, there will be plenty of Terrible Towels waving when the Black & Gold take the turf at Century Link Field.

Most of the time we are writing about the Steelers memorabilia or the beer selection, but Cheers requires a slightly different focus. On the shelf behind the bar there were three or four bottles of every type of liquor you could dream up. So, between being the headquarters of Northwest Steelers Nation, the prime location by the double-sided fireplace, and the ability to create any kind of drink a customer orders, this is a great place to catch a Steelers game.

✦ ✦
CHEERS BAR & GRILL

2611 Pacific Avenue
Tacoma, WA 98402
(253) 627-4430
www.cheersdowntown.com

We picked up a car at the airport and shot over to Tacoma to visit Cheers, the home of the Northwest Steelers Nation. Unfortunately, the leader of the club, Will, was unable to meet us, but the owner of the bar was quick to point out how many Steelers fans show up for each game. Cheers reserves a section near a huge double-sided fireplace for the fans.

Beer Note: We settled in at the bar, eagerly anticipating the selection of West Coast IPAs. Of course I use the term "we" very loosely here. One of us was eagerly anticipating Bud Light Lime. Ninkasi Brewing out of Eugene, Oregon, was the featured brewer so I selected the Total Domination IPA. Maybe my expectation was too high, but this was just an average IPA – a "3."

✦ ✦
FREMONT DOCK RESTAURANT

1102 N. 34th Street
Seattle, WA 98103
(206) 829-8372
www.fremontdock.com

The Fremont area is known for its counterculture and unique residents. Since the early 1970s some Fremont residents have been referring to their neighborhood as "The Center of the Universe."

The Fremont Dock is a great neighborhood bar. The atmosphere was very comfortable and inviting, but the Steelers memorabilia was in short supply. We asked the bartender and he said that the place used to be covered in Steelers stuff, but after the ill-fated (if you are a Seahawks fan) Super Bowl, the owner took down a lot of it. It seems that too many of his regular customers did not want to see the Steelers stuff every day and be reminded of the Seahawks' loss. That said, there are still a large number of fans that gather at the Fremont Dock on Game Day.

Beer Note: I asked about a local beer. The bartender smiled and mentioned a brewer that happened to be 50 yards away from us. The Fremont Brewery is located right next to the Dock. We sampled the Interurban India Pale Ale. I highly recommend this IPA; there was a slight spice aroma and distinct citrus hop aroma. Since the ABV is below 7%, this is a very drinkable beer. A "4." This particular beer was named for a popular outdoor sculpture in Fremont – "Waiting for the Interurban." Outdoor sculpture is not something we were particularly interested in, but it turns out we should have asked about other pieces in the neighborhood.

As we left the Dock, there were a lot of one-way streets and the GPS was not as clear as one would like in giving directions. We wound up driving under the Fremont Bridge, looking for a way to get on top of the bridge. Suddenly, we were staring at a mammoth troll palming a VW Beetle. Because we were staring at the statue and not paying attention to the road, we almost caused a huge pile-up. Cars from all directions swerved to avoid the gawking tourists dressed in Steelers gear. We suspect we were not the only ones to have been caught staring at the troll. Word of advice: if you travel to Fremont, ask about the troll.

✦ ✦
FADO IRISH PUB & RESTAURANT

801 1st Avenue
Seattle, WA 98104
(206) 264-2700
www.fadoirishpub.com/seattle

The final stop in Seattle was to meet the Seattle Steelers Fan Club. They hang at Fado's Irish Pub on 1st Avenue in downtown Seattle. Well, with the rain and the fog, we were starting to believe all of the stories about Seattle. After walking around downtown we confirmed another: there IS a coffee shop on every corner.

Beer Note: Because we again found ourselves in an Irish pub (note to self: why are they always "Irish" pubs? Where are the Portuguese pubs or Ecuadorian pubs, the Polish pubs or the Ukranian pubs?), I decided to have a Black and Tan. There is a lot of history and controversy surrounding this drink. In England, the Black and Tan is a mixture of 50% Guinness and 50% Bass Ale, while in Ireland, the preference is for 50% Guinness and 50% Harp Lager. So many of my friends of Irish descent will not only give me a hard time for drinking the English version with Bass, but they also object to the name. Due to the political issues associated with the English troops sent into Ireland (commonly referred to as the Black and Tans), the Irish refer to this drink as a Half and Half. Regardless, in Fado it was a Guinness and Bass and very delicious.

We have heard from many bar owners that Steelers fans are the most serious about the game and the team's performance. As we engaged the Seattle Steelers Fan Club, they started to tell us about the team, the play calling and other very technical aspects of the game. We are convinced that Steelers fans know more about football than any other fan group. One fan even recalled a story about Josh. He did not remember the game, but told a story about a very tense moment when Josh did not back down from another player's aggression. The fan was so impressed that he went out the next day and bought a #4 Miller jersey.

The fan club is made up of a lot of CMU graduates. Amazon is a large employer in the Seattle area and they love to hire CMU graduates. So the Seattle Steelers Fan Club grows with every hire! The club has bounced around a bit but finally found a home in Fado's. There's a free buffet for the opening game of the season and there are between 70-100 fans for

each game. The distribution of Iron City is not prevalent in Seattle, but the club has discovered that it is available on the local Navy base. So they go on the base and buy Iron City to bring to the games each week. We asked if they drank a lot of Iron and, true to lots of the clubs we have visited, they have a tradition where they each have one Iron then move on to another beer. The beer of choice at Fado's is Manny's Pale Ale. Not ever having heard of this, we tried one. It was amazing – a strong "4." Manny's is produced by Georgetown Brewing in Seattle and is only placed in kegs. They do not bottle any beer. This means only local distribution, but very fresh beer. We highly suggest you try one if you are in the area.

It was a long flight out to Seattle, complete with an incident that involved a passenger behind me heaving the contents of his stomach. Not so wonderful unless you like that kind of smell. So it took me a while after we landed to get some enthusiasm going again. I started to rally when I found myself standing in front of the Pike Place Market in Seattle. Amazing how the smell of fish can seem like an improvement over being trapped on the stinking plane with no way out. I can be a tourist as good as anybody. Even went to the original Starbucks. It was a great time.

I will say this for the 12th MAN, they are a loyal bunch. Now they don't expand nearly as far as Steelers Nation, but in their own backyard they are loyal. This brings us to Cheers Bar & Grill. This place looked like a very cool hangout. Definitely one of those dive bars where the same guys have

been coming for the last 15 years, and when you walk in, everybody stops what they're doing and looks at you and then goes about their business. Shawn and I sat down at the bar, had a drink, took some pictures, asked some questions and then were on our way.

We headed to Fado Irish Pub & Restaurant to meet the Seattle Steelers Fan Club. I would be remiss if I didn't bring up the troll that lived underneath the bridge with his big giant hand covering a Volkswagen. You might be asking how many Loose Gooses I had been drinking. That would be a fair question. I didn't have

any. From what I understand, this was art. Very scary, creepy art.

We made it to Fado's in plenty of time to meet a very cool fan club. They not only love their football, they love their hockey and baseball too. I remember looking back and thinking, if I made a pie chart of what we spoke about, it would be 30% baseball, 50% hockey and 20% football. This was a great night for me as I learned that no matter how much you know about a sport you played there's always room to learn more. It was nice to know Seattle had a wonderful Steelers presence.

San Diego
Home of the Chargers

Shawn's Two Cents

From Seattle to San Diego. Both West Coast, but totally different vibes. As Jimmy Buffet says, "Changes in latitudes, changes in attitudes." Fish taco stands replaced all the coffee shops. Who wouldn't want to live here? My brother went to college at San Diego State. Best five years of his life! He hasn't left the city since.

Don't get us wrong, we love Pittsburgh. But year-round sun and the beach and 70 degrees? And you can still find people to watch the Black & Gold with? Sounds like a great place to hang. Our first rate team of interns found us three places where Steelers Nation allegedly gather on Game Day. We were on a mission to find out whether The Library, McGregor's Grill & Ale House and Bub's Dive Bar & Grill were the real deal. Along the way we ate way too much Mexican food. But Todd Brown of Bub's Dive Bar introduced us to a new delicacy – tater tots. Yes, he has managed to elevate the humble tater tot to new heights. You can enjoy your spud with a good beer and hang with your fellow fans.

✦ ✦
THE LIBRARY
7459 Mission Gorge Rd
San Diego, CA 92120
(619) 583-5839

A significant other asks you where you've been all day. Your response: "The Library." And you aren't even stretching the truth. Perfection. It turns out that Steelers fans have figured this is a great place to hang out and connect with other fans and their team. The Library is a classic dive bar dedicated to featuring the Steelers on Game Day. There are a number of pool tables and four large screen TVs. We didn't see any volumes on Shakespeare or Twain but the bartender told us that the loyal fans in Black & Gold religiously "study" every Sunday that the Steelers play.

Wheat and to no one's surprise, he loved it. Chrissy, the bartender, told us that lots of Steelers fans gather at McGregor's on Sundays. She said that they still get more Chargers fans but the Steelers are a close second. So the verdict is out on whether McGregor's is, in fact, the #1 Sports Bar in San Diego when it comes to the Steelers. It is a good place, however, to catch a beer, some grub, and a Steelers game if you are in the area.

◆ ◆
McGREGOR'S GRILL & ALE HOUSE

10475 San Diego Mission Rd
San Diego, CA 92108
(619) 282-9797
www.mcgregorssandiego.com

Our Journey continued in San Diego as we visited the reputed #1 Sports Bar in San Diego, McGregor's Grill & Ale House. Of course, in our opinion for it to be #1, it must be a Steelers hangout. McGregor's is also known for its beer list. They have a great selection of local craft beer. One of the favorites is a nationally acclaimed brewery – Stone. I ordered the IPA, which, truth be told, is one of the less hoppy beers in their impressive lineup. I let Josh try the IPA; the reaction was immediate bitter beer face and "Did they do that on purpose?" Clearly, Josh is not a hophead, but that does not mean that he should drink mass produced American lagers. I ordered him a Hanger 24 Orange

Bub's has grown consistently. It recently doubled its physical space to accommodate all the fans. Todd has created a great Game Day atmosphere. There is a raffle for a Steelers jersey each week and when the Steelers win, everyone in the bar gets a free beer!

It is a given that every TV is tuned to the Steelers game, but they also have a DJ that plays Steelers-themed music and traditional polka during the game breaks. The fans start to line up at 8:00 a.m. to get a good seat for the game. For the most recent Super Bowl the fans were lined up at 6:00 a.m. To pass the time until Bub's opened, a game of football broke out right there on Garnet Avenue. The support for the

♦ ♦ ♦
BUB'S DIVE BAR & GRILL

**1030 Garnet Avenue
San Diego, CA 92109
(858) 270-7269
www.bubsdive.com**

The final bar in San Diego turned out to be the mecca of Steelers fans in Southern California. At first glance, it appeared to be just a great little hangout in Pacific Beach. After further inspection, we realized that every wall was covered with Steelers memorabilia and that there were Terrible Towels hanging from the rafters. If any of our readers visit Bub's Dive Bar, look for the Josh Miller signed towel. For us, Bub's gets to be called the #1 Sports Bar in San Diego!

The owner of Bub's, Todd Brown, is from Pittsburgh and specifically recruits Pittsburgh natives to work in the bar. The connection is so strong that employees are even issued Steelers-themed dog tags to wear while on shift. Initially opened over 15 years ago,

team goes beyond Game Day celebrations and Bub's helps to manage charity events to support Troy Polamalu's foundation.

Beer Note: Beyond the Steelers, Bub's is known for its great beer selection and tots menu. Tater tots are featured prominently on the menu and the varieties are incredible. They have everything from Artichoke Tots to Buffalo Wing Tots. Then there is the beer list. The first order was for the Ballast Point Sculpin IPA (rated 100/100 by Beer Advocate, a beer that had been on my wish list for quite a while. This is a perfect example of a West Coast IPA and the first "5" of the Journey. I followed this up with another of my favorite beers, the Bear Republic Racer 5, a great IPA that is no longer shipped to Pennsylvania. Hands down, this is the best Steelers hangout for a hophead so far on this Journey.

If I were ever going to be sick of Mexican food, it would definitely be on this West Coast trip. Shawn and I had breakfast burritos, chips and salsa and fish tacos every day. San Diego was no exception. It was kind of funny; we would stuff ourselves on Mexican food then swear we would never do it again. Four hours would go by and we would agree we were in the mood for Mexican food. That continued for four days straight. As I'm writing this, I'm in the mood for Mexican food again. Fish tacos to be exact.

So there we were in San Diego, with the weather in the 70's, constantly filled with Mexican food, driving along visiting Steelers bars. I can see why people live here all year round. But even after seeing all that San Diego has to offer, I can honestly say that it's not for me. It's a great place to visit and hang out for a week with your family and friends but I'm pale, and with the sun out here I'd catch on fire.

We came out here to visit three bars. First up, The Library. I can only imagine how many kids told their parents that they were going to the library Friday and Saturday nights, hoping they were getting one over on their parents and that they'd never find out.

McGregor's Grill & Ale House was a pretty cool place to hang out and watch a football game. The cute girl behind the bar promised us it was a Steelers bar and that they gather every weekend. I have to give her the benefit of the doubt because she was cute. The coolest thing I will take away from this bar was I had my first big boy beer – a Hangar 24 Orange Wheat. It wasn't a Bud Light with a lime or a Miller High Life; it was a beer that was actually on Shawn's hit list. I could tell Shawn was proud of me, like a dad watching his son hit his first home run in a baseball game. I guess it's true, you always remember your first.

On to Bub's Dive Bar & Grill. I'm not saying we saved the best for last, I'm just saying that's how it turned out to be. This place is an absolute must, whether you like the Steelers or not. Garnet Avenue alone is worth the trip. Bub's Grill is 100% Steelers Nation crazy. It just happens to be around a corner from the beach. No windows, just open air with nothing between the bar and the street. This place was an absolute treat. Not only is there a strong Pittsburgh connection, with Todd Brown being from Pittsburgh, but the people working there are also from Pittsburgh. If you work there and you're from Pittsburgh, you get special Pittsburgh dog tags. They take care of each other and have a family atmosphere that you can't miss. They're involved in many charities, including a few Steelers charities. And if you look closely at the walls and ceiling, you will find Steelers sports memorabilia that you've never seen before. Truly one of the best stops on the Journey. We had the time of our lives there.

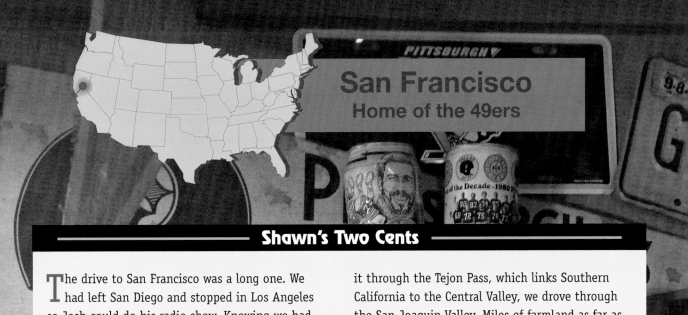

San Francisco
Home of the 49ers

Shawn's Two Cents

The drive to San Francisco was a long one. We had left San Diego and stopped in Los Angeles so Josh could do his radio show. Knowing we had a lot to check out in the Bay Area, we headed out after his show straight into L.A. traffic. We opted to take Highway 5 and the more direct route to San Francisco rather than the more scenic Pacific Coast Highway. It would save us time. The PCH does offer breathtaking views of the ocean, along with razor sharp switchbacks, granite cliffs, forgotten beach towns and roaring surf. But we discovered that I-5 offered its own unique views. Once we made

it through the Tejon Pass, which links Southern California to the Central Valley, we drove through the San Joaquin Valley. Miles of farmland as far as we could see. I couldn't help but think of Bruce Springsteen's album "The Ghost of Tom Joad."

We finally made it to San Francisco and geared up to check out four Steelers hangouts – Shanghai Kelly's, Giordano Bros. Mission, Giordano Bros. North Beach and Pittsburgh's Pub. I sampled good beer, I know Josh enjoyed a few Loose Gooses, and we had some really good beef jerky! It was a memorable trip.

Beer Note: The beer selection at the bar was incredible. I selected the Lagunitas IPA. I have what I believe to be a personal connection with Lagunitas. When I was at the Great American Beer Festival in Denver a few years ago, my friends and I were hanging out at a local bar and a stranger asked what beer I was drinking. At the time, I was thoroughly enjoying the Lagunitas IPA. The stranger introduced himself and told me that the Lagunitas was "his beer." We spent the next 30 minutes discussing their entire beer lineup and the quality that goes into each batch. As the Steelers know, customer loyalty is the key to success. Those 30 minutes made me a fan of Lagunitas for life. It was like meeting Jack Lambert in a bar and having him talk about his favorite games with me. For the record, the Lagunitas IPA is a "4."

Josh and I went in search of Mark, the owner. We asked how Shanghai Kelly's became a Steelers hangout. He told us how one of his regular customers, Brendan Coyne (Central Catholic and Penn State), was a huge Steelers fan. Brendan had some ties to the Rooney family, as well. His grandfather on his mother' side was Art Rooney Sr.'s brother. Well, Brendan had trouble finding a way to watch the Steelers games in Frisco way back in 1994 and asked Mark to open his bar at 9:30 a.m. and put the game on. Reluctantly, Mark agreed. He expected it to be a "one and done" scenario. He gave his keys to one of the bartenders and asked him to accommodate Brendan. Much to his surprise, the bar was packed and the guys came back week after week. Before long, more than 80 Steelers fans eagerly rushed into Shanghai Kelly's every Game Day. It is now a regular gathering spot for local and traveling fans.

✦ ✦
SHANGHAI KELLY'S
2064 Polk Street
San Francisco, CA 94109
(415) 771-3300
www.facebook.com/ShanghaiKellys

The first stop in the City by the Bay was Shanghai Kelly's. Our publisher, Paul, who used to live here, had given us a heads-up about Shanghai Kelly's. It sits on the corner of Polk Street and Broadway and isn't very big. As we walked in sporting the Black & Gold, we were accosted by a kid in a Michigan State sweatshirt. He was meeting a bunch of his college buddies in town so they could watch the Steelers play. One of his friends was a reporter for WTAE in Pittsburgh and he heard Always a Home Game was going to be in town.

As we were about to leave, we encountered another Steelers fan group headed in the door. These guys had traveled all the way from Hawaii for the game. They told us that they try to make the trip every time the Steelers play on the West Coast. They also invited us to the Islands to check out their local hangout. Journey Two – the Sequel! We need sponsors for this trip!

We discovered that Giordano Bros. wasn't just dedicated to the Steelers, it was homage to all things Pittsburgh. It was painted Black & Gold and covered with Steelers memorabilia. There were signs from Kennywood – we spotted one from the Thunderbolt and one from the Jack Rabbit. (Sadly, there were no Potato Patch fries.) There were also two seats from Three Rivers Stadium. There is a weekly raffle drawing and two lucky fans get to sit in the stadium seats and watch the game on their own TV. How cool!

Beer Note: When I asked about local craft beer, Adam suggested the San Francisco Brewing Alcatraz Amber. One of Adam's friends recently revived the old brewery and was just beginning production. The beer was a very solid crisp Amber – I'll give it a "3." It is cool to see entrepreneurs resurrecting some of the older beer labels and creating great new beers. Josh

♦ ♦ ♦
GIORDANO BROS. – MISSION
3108 16th Street
San Francisco, CA 94103
(415) 437-BROS
www.giordanobros.com

We headed to the Mission District in search of Giordano Bros. We found the bar but struggled to find parking, which is a nightmare in San Francisco. We finally found an open spot with a parking meter, but had no quarters. Luckily, we were in a high tech city. We downloaded an app for the iPhone that allowed us to make payment. It would also send us a notice when the meter was about to expire and we could add more time without going back to the car. What a great app!

opted for a Loose Goose. As persuasive as Josh can be, he couldn't convince Giordano's to go with the new name; they had already renamed it! They call it "The Bleeder." He went with it and was glad that he did. Adam prepared one of the best drinks of the trip. Because many of the Steelers games on the West Coast are very early in the morning, having a quality Loose Goose is key to the success of the bar (and Josh's attitude). Giordano Bros. has this area covered.

On all the signage and menus, Giordano Brothers is referenced as "Giordano Bros." – like "Primanti Bros." of Pittsburgh fame. We learned the connection went deeper than the abbreviation. Adam told us that the Mission location was actually the second to open in San Fran. The original spot was our next stop – the North Beach location. Adam joined the partnership when the second store was opened. The founders, Jeff and Allison, approached the Primanti folks in Pittsburgh when they were opening North Beach location and asked if they could replicate some of the menu items. Gaining consent, they sent their baker to Pittsburgh to learn how to make the bread.

In addition to the sandwiches, pierogies are a staple on the Giordano Bros. menu. We asked about the favorite menu item (apparently, unlike Primanti Bros.

it isn't Iron City). We were surprised by the answer ... beef jerky. Curious, we had to try some. The jerky is shipped in from Texas. It was incredible – the perfect combination of spices but not too spicy. It almost melts in your mouth. We highly recommend placing an order.

We spent a lot of time talking about the Steelers and Pittsburgh in general with the staff. One guy, Charlie, seemed to be one of the most ardent advocates for the city. Assuming he was from the 'Burgh, we asked where he had grown up. Much to our surprise, this wasn't a guy from Polish Hill or the South Side Slopes. He was born and raised in San Francisco. He explained that Pittsburgh is a city of "we," unlike so many other places where it is a "me" culture. We couldn't agree more, Charlie!

location? Probably too caught up in the excitement over the parking app. The tagline reminds us of the number of places we've discovered on this Journey where Steelers fans gather to watch their team. While they all might be a good place to grab a drink with friends, some places really do show an extraordinary passion for Pittsburgh and the Steelers. Giordano Bros. embodies Pittsburgh and the Steelers every day, not just on Game Days.

The North Beach location has a different vibe. It is much more about food and the dining experience. It feels a bit like the Strip District. All the sandwiches are served on

◆ ◆ ◆
GIORDANO BROS. – NORTH BEACH

**303 Columbus Avenue
San Francisco, CA 94133
(415) 397-BROS
www.giordanobros.com**

After the awesome experience at the Mission location, we headed off to North Beach. Upon arrival, we noticed the tagline "A Pittsburgh Tradition in San Francisco." How did we miss this at the Mission

THE ANSWERS TO YOUR Q'S:
1. YES, THE FRIES ¼ SLAW ARE ON THE SANDWICH.
2. COPPA IS SOMETHING LIKE PROSCIUTTO.
3. HOT CAPPIOCOLA IS SPICY ITALIAN HAM.
4. WE DON'T SERVE LIQUOR.
5. YES, THE OWNERS ARE FROM PITTSBURGH.
6. YES, WE ARE LIKE PRIMANTI BROS.
7. WE ACCEPT VISA ¼ MASTERCARD ONLY.
8. THE SANDWICH HAS BEEN MADE THE SAME WAY FOR OVER 70 YEARS, SO WE RECOMMEND YOU DON'T TRY TO CHANGE IT.

paper and the line was out the door. We spoke to Jeff (West Mifflin) and he told us how he met his now wife Allison (Export) at a Steelers tailgate party. (By the way, this isn't the first romance/marriage we've heard of that the Steelers helped to bring together!)

Beer Note: When I asked about the beer, the offering was the Green Flash Brewing West Coast IPA. This multiple-award-winning IPA has a crisp grapefruit aroma and is incredibly smooth. One would expect a bitter aftertaste, given the 95 IBUs, but the guys at Green Flash have perfected the West Coast IPA and brewed an easy drinking beer. Another "4", as expected. San Francisco is a great city for craft beer.

We found another group of Steelers fans that traveled to San Francisco for the game. They informed us that this was the sixth consecutive year for the "guys trip," and that the Steelers are 0-5 so far. With that luck, we suggest that perhaps they stay home next year?

◆ ◆ ◆
PITTSBURGH'S PUB

4207 Judah Street
San Francisco, CA 94122
(415) 664-3926
www.facebook.com/pages/Pittsburghs-Pub

For the final stop in San Francisco we headed to the beach. Pittsburgh's Pub is located a few blocks off the beach just south of Golden Gate Park. It is a very traditional neighborhood/dive bar – without a doubt one of the friendliest bars on our Journey. It's the kind of place where Bob, the bartender, knows exactly what all the regulars want and pours all their drinks without their having to ask. He is a very laid back guy for an ex-bouncer.

Beer Note: As with most bars of this ilk, the common drink is a shot and a beer. I decided against the shot and opted for an Anchor Steam. A trip to San Francisco would not be complete without enjoying one of the original craft beers in America. I had toured the brewery with my wife years earlier and it brings

back fond memories. There are varied stories about the brewery's unique name. My recollection from the tour is that the steam came from the fact that the brewery originally had no way to chill the boiling wort, so the beer was fermented in open containers on the roof of the brewery. As the cold air came in off the Bay, huge steam clouds would form over the brewery, thus the name. The story might not be true but I like the image of huge "beer clouds" hanging above the brewery, so that's the one I'm repeating. Regardless, Anchor Steam is a "4."

We noticed an old Terry Bradshaw album behind the bar. Bob told us that the owner, Dan, was from Latrobe and that he never missed a game. A Terry Bradshaw jersey – that's Steelers memorabilia, for sure. A Terry Bradshaw album? That is true dedication! The Pittsburgh's Pub has been dedicated to Steelers fans since its inception and it gets huge crowds on Game Day. In many cases it pushes its occupancy limits. Given the warm and inviting atmosphere, we can see why it is packed on Game Days.

San Francisco was one of my favorite trips on this Journey. I was able to see my family that lives out in redwood country. You forget how beautiful Mother Nature is and how feeble our existence really is in the big scheme of things. We stayed at Fisherman's Wharf, which was an absolute treat for me. I would wake up at five in the morning and run along the water and hear all the seals yell and scream along the edges. Nothing feels better than going on a nice long run and knowing you can eat whatever you want for the rest of the day. There isn't a better place to cheat on your diet than Fisherman's Wharf. But we were on a mission, one that would allow us to visit three amazing Steelers hangouts.

First on the list was Shanghai Kelly's. We found out about this bar compliments of our publisher at St. Lynn's Press, Paul. When you walk in, it feels like you are in a subway car. Long and narrow, with very little room to stretch, breath or sit. As we hung out and had a beer we were able to meet some people, chitchat about anything football – and suddenly our subway car grew and it felt very comfortable. This bar was filled with regulars who were kind enough to listen to our stories and send us off with just enough stuff for the book. Shanghai Kelly's is a legit Steelers place. You know the famous quote, "Size doesn't matter." I believe that to be true in this case. Although small,

Shanghai packs a punch. Definitely a place I would visit again.

Giordano Bros. I can honestly say I had one of my top three Loose Gooses in this joint, although they call it a Bleeder. It's so great when we go into a place and the first thing that jumps out at you

is cool sports memorabilia. Not over the top, in your face memorabilia, but subtle quality pieces that belong in a museum type of memorabilia. It was accompanied by loyal, hard-core owners with plenty of Pittsburgh roots. I'm not sure how long we stayed at Giordano's, I do know that the time spent was enjoyed. If memory serves and I think it does, I had award-winning beef jerky that was out of this world. Shawn, on the other hand, was in heaven because of the beer selection. He went on and on about how you can't find this beer on the East Coast. I kind of tuned him out and just extended my hand and said, "Yes, I know I'm driving." Whenever your travels take you to San Francisco, please look up Giordano Bros. because the food is out of this world. Truth is, the chefs came to Pittsburgh to learn how to cook Pittsburgh-style eats.

Next up was Pittsburgh's Pub. This place was an absolute dive. It was three blocks from the beach and you could smell the salt water. It was incredible. We had such a good time there. I remember I got into a heavy conversation with two Irish guys with thick accents. We were buying each other drinks and laughing out loud and just hanging out as if we were buddies for life. I don't know how it happened, but even after we left I had an Irish accent for at least five hours.

Shawn's Two Cents

Oakland was the last leg of this four city West Coast tour. We had seen Seattle in all its high-tech glory, basked in the laid back atmosphere of San Diego, rolled through the hills of glorious San Francisco and all that was left was Oakland. Home of the Raiders. The Steelers' arch nemesis through most of the '70s. Can you imagine two more different owners than Dan Rooney and Al Davis? This rivalry gave birth to one of the most storied plays in NFL history: the Immaculate Reception.

The 408 Steel City Mafia had invited us to tailgate at the game, but we just didn't have it in us to fight the crowd and traffic at the stadium. We decided instead to check out their home turf, The Blue Chip Sports Bar in San Jose, as well as Cheater's Sports Bar in Sacramento and Francesca's in Mountain View. Admittedly, none of these were in "Oakland," per se. But our research told us that Steelers fans gathered there. Besides, Sacramento and Oakland are less than 90 miles apart. It could take longer to drive from the Pittsburgh Airport to Monroeville through the Squirrel Hill Tunnels during rush hour traffic and nobody is going to argue that bars in Robinson Township and Murrysville aren't both in Steelers Nation. However spread out they may be, Steelers Nation is in the greater Oakland area. Bruce and his memorabilia, the 408 Steel City Mafia and the South Bay Steelers Fan Club are making any game in Oakland feel like a home game for the Steelers.

Bruce told us that he had owned the bar for 17 years. He has been committed to showing Steelers games since day one. Cheater's Sports Bar has been featured in the Sacramento Bee as the place to watch Steelers games in the Capitol City. Along with showing the game, Bruce rewards the fans with free food each week. On our visit there was free chili for all fans in attendance.

Coincidentally, the day we were there another former NFL punter was in the house. Chris White, drafted by the Indianapolis Colts in 1985, was hanging at Cheater's. Even guys who played for other teams know that the places to watch NFL games are the ones where the Steelers fans go!

✦✦
CHEATER'S SPORTS BAR

3221 Folsom Blvd.
Sacramento, CA 95816
(916) 736-0563
www.facebook.com/pages/
Cheaters-Sports-Bar/109572895746297

Our Journey through the East Bay brought us to Cheater's Sports Bar in Sacramento. The large, inflatable Steelers player was just the first glimpse of the memorabilia housed inside this bar. What was different about the memorabilia at Cheater's was that most, if not all, of it was signed. We spent quite a while checking out the cool pieces and had figured out that Bruce owned the bar long before we met him. One of the most interesting pieces on the wall is a picture of Bruce standing on the field at Three Rivers Stadium.

STAIRWAY TO 7

✦ ✦ ✦
THE BLUE CHIP SPORTS BAR
& FAMILY RESTAURANT

325 S. 1st Street
San Jose, CA 95113
(408) 971-2898
www.bluechipsj.com

The Blue Chip Sports Bar is a little different. This Steelers hangout is in the basement of a building that seems like an old shopping mall. Everything around the bar was closed (it was Sunday) and it felt a bit like Raiders fans were luring us into some sort of trap. Our overactive imaginations were laid to rest when we walked through the Blue Chip's front door. The hostess took one look at our Black & Gold attire and said, "Head around to the back room." She said it so routinely that we knew plenty of people had come this way before us.

The Blue Chip is the home of the 408 Steel City Mafia. Many of the members were actually at the game, so attendance was understandably light for our visit. The 408 boasts over 120 members and usually exceeds over 60 members for each game. The entire room is painted in honor of the Steelers. We had fun admiring the graffiti murals on the walls and the interesting pieces hanging around the room. The 408 has their own dedicated wait staff that comes around at the end of each quarter and passes out free shots to the fans.

After our stop at The Blue Chip, and reeling from the free shots, we were hungry. We noticed a purple building with a huge iguana on the sign. It was a sign from the heavens. A burrito joint! The Iguana features the "Burritozilla." This is a 5-pound burrito that is as big as a linebacker's arm. Delicious and big enough to induce a food coma. We were ready to get on the plane and sleep for the entire flight back to Pittsburgh, but there was one bar left to visit.

◆ ◆
FRANCESCA'S SPORTS BAR
2135 Old Middlefield Way
Mountain View, CA 94043
(650) 965-1162
www.francescasbar.com

The final stop was Francesca's Sports Bar, the home of the South Bay Steelers Fan Club. The fan club formed about 10 years ago and has over 125 registered members. As with The 408, many of the members were at the game. Really, we can't expect the fans to miss seeing the Steelers in person just to hang with the Always A Home Game crew. We aren't bitter, honest.

Andy, the current leader of the club, was born and raised a Steelers fan. He hails from Uniontown and Indiana, PA. After attending Carnegie Mellon, he headed to the West Coast, but stayed close to his Western Pennsylvania roots. This is a common theme we've discovered of Steelers fans across the country. The South Bay Steelers Fan Club is a bit different

in its makeup, though. The fan base is younger and we learned that 80% of its members were NOT from Pittsburgh. Interesting. They may have had a long-lost relative that once lived in Pittsburgh – but many really enjoy other people from Pittsburgh that are ardent Steelers fans and they've become fans of the Steelers winning tradition.

The South Bay Steelers Fan Club has been gathering at Francesca's for three seasons. Mike, the owner, is very supportive. He ships Iron City and Yuengling in for each game (he pays more for shipping than the cost of the actual beer!), and he always runs a special for the fans. As appealing as an Iron or Yuengling would be, I opt for one of my all time favorite beers – Bear Republic Racer 5. The name says it all – "5." For a short time, Bear Republic was imported and available in Pennsylvania, but no longer is. I don't know what went wrong, but I hope it gets cleared up soon. In the meantime, I'm taking this last opportunity for another great West Coast IPA.

Oakland was our final stop on our West Coast swing. We were tired, cranky and exhausted. I believe this represented our fifth day away from our family and Shawn and I were getting on each other's nerves. I hope we gave Oakland a fair and legitimate look of what life was like being a Steelers fan there. I do remember this was the worst football game the Steelers played all year. Terrelle Pryor, a Pittsburgh guy, was starting quarterback for the Oakland Raiders. He went 10/19 for 89 yards and 0 touchdowns and 2 interceptions. His offense had one first down the entire second half.

I can't begin to tell you how bad that is. Sadly, Oakland won the game. Just an awful and embarrassing loss for the Pittsburgh Steelers. So there we were, cranky and on the last day of our Journey, having to witness that wonderful performance. So please keep that in mind as you read about our Oakland bars. In all fairness to Oakland, we may not have been all there.

So whether it's Cheater's Sports Bar and its amazing chili and very cool sports memorabilia, or The Blue Chip Sports Bar that for some reason was also the second Steelers hangout that was underground

and had a record of three patrons sound asleep at the tables, or the last but not least, Francesca's Sports Bar, that had a 70-year-old woman dressed in a Steelers Santa cheerleading outfit, I will speak highly of all three establishments and can honestly say that they were memorable.

Boston
Home of the Patriots

Boston fans may be almost as fanatical as Steelers fans. They love their Patriots, their Celtics, their Red Sox and their Bruins. It wasn't surprising then that our advanced research told us Steelers fans generally gathered in only two bars in Boston. I guess there is safety in numbers. So we put Lir and Roggie's into the GPS – my phone GPS, that is. We had decided to take the RV to Boston. On a purely objective level, it was a good decision. We left late Saturday night and drove for a number of hours. It was just Josh, Domenic and me, so when we got tired, we pulled off and slept right there. The RV had everything we needed. We drove the rest of the way Sunday in comfort.

What we hadn't thought through was navigating the RV with Boston drivers. Thank God the "Big Dig" was over. I can't imagine that nightmare. We also thought it would be fun to parade our pride in the Black & Gold around Boston. The RV wrap looked "wicked good." I'm pretty sure the citizens of Boston might have disagreed, though, but with that accent, who knows? Lir offered up a great atmosphere, despite a horrific beer blunder on my part. And Roggie's was filled with loyal fans who cared more about watching the kickoff than seeing the end of some other overtime game. It felt like home! Then we hit the road, making it back to the 'Burgh some time early Monday morning.

BLACK AND GOLD FOREVER

LIR

903 Boylston Street
Boston, MA 02116
(617) 778-0089
www.lironboylston.com

As we pulled into Boston, I called my brother-in-law to confirm the stops on our Journey. As you may recall from the introduction, my indoctrination into Steelers Nation began in the basement of my now-wife's family home. Her youngest brother, Mike, was the most vocal of the siblings in his support of the Steelers and now lives in enemy territory – Boston. He is married to Nancy, a person who is fantastic in every possible way except for her fanaticism concerning the Patriots. She and Mike are fighting for the loyalty of their children. Four kids who could be Patsies or Steelers fans! Mike was going to bring my nephew Jake along to the bars. The news on the other end of the phone was not good...he had gotten a call from a friend with tick-

ets to the game. Not only were we going to miss out on spending the afternoon with one of the Steelers' greatest fans, but now we had to navigate the traffic without a local.

We forged onward. Lir is a traditional pub located on Boylston Street, just off Copley Plaza in downtown Boston. This sounds really cool on paper, but is murder when trying to park an RV. Fortunately, Dom came to the rescue. Because the game was being played at Foxboro, Abbey and George weren't along on the trip and we had extra room. Dom came for the 22-hour ride. Surely he thought he'd be hanging out in the bars and having fun. Nonetheless, he manned up and double-parked the RV in front of Lir. (In case you haven't been to Boston, nobody seems to think twice about double-parking in this city.) We got out and Dom eventually just drove around the block over and over and over...

Given the Steelers and the Pats rivalry, we were expecting a rowdy group. But the bartender greeted us in a Pats jersey, and we thought we were in the wrong place. When we introduced the book, and ourselves, her demeanor changed and she offered to get us a beer.

Beer Note: I made a tragic "cool wine label" mistake. I'm not a wine drinker, but many of my friends are and I admittedly pick out wine based entirely on the way the label looks. I'm sure that my friends have opened some of the bottles I've bought them and thought them complete swill. Well, at Lir I chose a beer based upon the tap handle. The Big Wave Blonde by Kona Brewing had a really cool wave and surfer on the tap handle, so I ordered one. I should have known that ordering a Hawaiian beer in Boston was not good when I'm trying to stick with local craft beer. The Big Wave Blonde started off with a very hoppy aroma but disappointment soon followed as the bland liquid crossed my lips. The rating is a "2" and I will learn from this mistake.

Beer (if you call it a beer) in hand, we made our way through the bar in search of Matt. Matt loves Steelers fans. He showed us the second floor, reserved every game day for the group Yinz in Boston. Yinz has been meeting here for a number of years and had over 100 fans for the opening game of the season. Lir offers food and drink specials for their Steelers fans and lets them hang banners on game days. Matt

said that the fan group recently split into two factions. The downtown group meets at Lir and the suburban group watches the game at Roggie's. Josh and I smiled. Our interns rock! Our next stop was Roggie's.

♦ ♦
ROGGIE'S BREW & GRILL

356 Chestnut Hill Ave
Brighton, MA 02135
(617) 566-1880
www.roggies.com

Fortunately, Roggie's was in the suburbs and located right next to a bank – closed on Sundays with a wide-open parking lot! Dom escaped the RV. Walking in, we noticed the walls were covered with chalkboard paint. Cool chalkboard drawings surrounded the bar and many were of labels from the beers Roggie's served. This was my kind of art.

Beer Note: Still reeling from my poor selection on the last beer, I asked about a local IPA and was directed to the Red Hook Long Hammer IPA. I was confused. I had always thought that Red Hook was a brewery in the Pacific Northwest. I learned that they also operate a brewery in Portsmouth, New Hampshire. I was hooked. It is easy to see why this beer is one

of the best selling IPAs on the market. It has a great hop aroma with a sweet, malty finish. This is not a hophead's first choice, but a good starting point for someone looking to try an IPA for the first time. A solid "3."

We met John, one of the owners, and he told us that Steelers fans had been meeting there for the last 10 years. Roggie's has a special room dedicated to the Steelers. We made our way down to the basement and saw dozens of Steelers fans waiting for the game to begin. As we entered, we noticed that the early NFL game was in overtime. One of the teams had the ball, 1st and goal, in overtime. Most NFL fans would consider this a very crucial point in the game but nobody at Roggie's cared. The Black and Gold were taking the field and all the TVs were changed to make sure the fans saw the kickoff in the only game that ever really matters on Sunday. The instantaneous switch of channels made us recall the famous "Heidi Game" – though there is no connection between the Steelers and a little girl in the Swiss Alps. For those not old enough to remember, the Heidi Game, or "Heidi Bowl," was a game played on November 17, 1968. The game is remembered for its exciting finish, when Oakland scored two touchdowns in the final minute to overcome a 32-29 New York lead. The problem was that NBC controversially broke away from the game with the Jets still winning to air "Heidi" at 7p.m. in the Eastern Time Zone. Fans around the country missed the final two touchdowns.

Beer Note: We started talking to one of the Steelers fans at the bar, Richard, who offered insight into the beer selection at Roggie's. Richard referred to himself as a "beer snob," but I would describe him as more of

a highly educated scholar of local brewing customs. Richard suggested we try Clown Shoes Galactica. Clown Shoes is a local brewery that I knew made a great Black IPA, but I was unfamiliar with Galactica. The Galactica is an Imperial IPA or Double IPA with 8.0% AVB (almost twice the alcohol content of a typical American lager). With many higher alcohol beers there is a very strong aftertaste due to the high alcohol content. This beer was different. The over-the-top hop aroma, but malty finish, masked the alcohol and made this a dangerously good beer. Definitely a beer that should be on your list. Give it a "4."

The basement at Roggie's is a great place to watch a game. It is almost like you have a huge man cave and 50 of our closest friends can come over and watch the Steelers. They welcome all traveling fans to join them for Game Day.

It was a very good time for our trip to Boston. I kind of had this trip circled on the calendar. I had some very good times here personally, professionally and with the family. We lived in Franklin, MA, for four years. Our third child, Ava James Miller, was born in Rhode Island, I won a Super Bowl ring with the New England Patriots and we made some lifelong friends. Oh, I also had the greatest meal ever at a place called Zebras. So yes, I was looking forward to this trip for a long time. People always ask me what it was like playing for Coach Belichick. The follow-up question was always, what was the deal with Spygate? People give me way too much credit for being a punter and thinking I would have any information regarding that. I always tell them I knew nothing, heard nothing and saw nothing. I look at life like a book. If you're fortunate enough to have a bunch

of chapters, good for you. I will always look back at my New England days as a wonderful chapter of my life.

I do remember Roggie's very well. I remember thinking it was kind of funny how they treated the Steelers fans. They allowed the Steelers fans to take over the downstairs of the bar. It was almost as if they didn't want anyone to see that they were hiding Steelers fans. But every week 100 fans would be squirreled away in the basement for the game. If you went upstairs during the game, you wouldn't see any signs of a Steelers game. It was all going on downstairs. They welcomed you with open arms, treated you as if you were family, but made sure you stayed in the basement. I knew this was one of Shawn's favorites right away. There must have been about 50 different kinds of beer taps behind the bar. Shawn looked at me after his fourth step into the bar and said, "You're driving." That was it. Still, a wonderful time was had by all. The funniest part of the entire afternoon was that not one person down in the basement wanted to watch the conclusion of the overtime game that was being played while we were sitting around waiting for the Steelers game. Right at 4 o'clock they turned the channel because we can't miss the kickoff. Steelers fans are amazing. Nothing else matters to a Steelers fan but their Steelers. Kind of nauseating if you aren't a fan. Kind of cool if you are a fan or an ex-Steeler. That's how I feel the rest of the world looks at Steelers Nation.

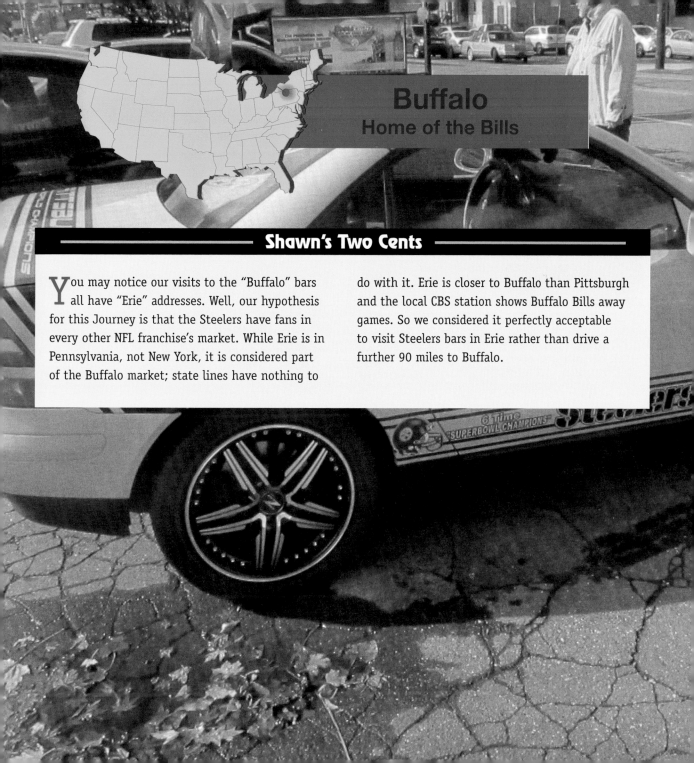

Buffalo
Home of the Bills

Shawn's Two Cents

You may notice our visits to the "Buffalo" bars all have "Erie" addresses. Well, our hypothesis for this Journey is that the Steelers have fans in every other NFL franchise's market. While Erie is in Pennsylvania, not New York, it is considered part of the Buffalo market; state lines have nothing to do with it. Erie is closer to Buffalo than Pittsburgh and the local CBS station shows Buffalo Bills away games. So we considered it perfectly acceptable to visit Steelers bars in Erie rather than drive a further 90 miles to Buffalo.

★ ★ ★
THE PITTSBURGH INN

3725 W. Lake Road
Erie, PA 16505
(814) 833-0925
www.thepittsburghinn.com

The Pittsburgh Inn was packed. It feels like the kind of place my grandparents took me to growing up – it appeals to all generations and everyone can find something to eat. The difference here is that everything is decorated with Steelers memorabilia, mostly donated from patrons, and there are Steelers fight songs playing over the PA system.

Even more impressive than The Pittsburgh Inn's support of the Steelers was its support of our soldiers. We had wandered into the vestibule and noticed that it was covered with pictures of local men and women who have served our country. We learned that a few years ago, owners Tom and Robin Weunski started sending care packages to soldiers overseas. This practice has grown and now patrons join in and help support their efforts. In the past three years alone they have sent over 2,000 packages. If you visit, make sure that you see the pictures and make a donation. It is humbling to see how Steelers fans continue to think of others beyond the Black and Gold.

The trip to the Buffalo market is one of the shortest of the Journey, so we had many volunteers join for this leg of our crusade to find the best Steelers hangouts in the country. Our friends Don, Mike, Abbey and George joined us. We had a full RV for this trip. The day started with a Loose Goose for those not driving.

The first stop was The Pittsburgh Inn. As we pulled into the parking lot, we noticed the huge sign announcing our arrival. We sensed this was going to be a good day. Experience had taught us that it could be difficult to get large crowds to show up two hours before a game. This was not the case today;

Beer Note: Mike is a fellow home brewer and it was nice to have him along. Josh's eyes tend to glaze over when I talk beer. Mike and I tried the Erie Brewing Co. Railbender. The Railbender is a heavily malted/lightly hopped ale with a slightly higher alcohol content than a brown ale. This provides the perfect warm aftertaste for which the style is known. Unlike some of the Scottish ales that have a distinct smoky characteristic, Erie Brewing has produced a clean caramel taste without the smoky distraction. The Railbender is one of the best – rating "3."

Our attention was drawn out to the parking lot to see a fan's car. John Sample had an unusual Mercedes. We have seen many Steelers vehicles on our Journey. They tend to be trucks or SUVs, but John showed up with the first sports car. He was kind enough to send us some of the decals he created so we could add them to the Always a Home Game RV. Thanks, John!

Finally, after checking everything out, it was time to sit down and have something to eat. The secret to The Pittsburgh Inn's success, Robin told us, is that she stays behind the bar and Tom does all the cooking. Tom likes to experiment with different flavor combinations. We tried apple spice wings – they were awesome! He combined his favorite pork chop and chicken wing recipes for an interesting twist on traditional favorites. It was the perfect combination of sweet and spice. It is a must-have if you visit.

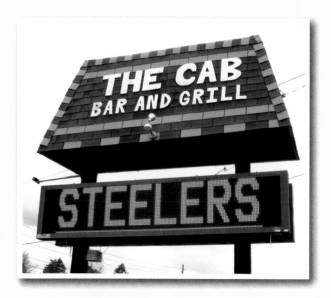

✦ ✦ ✦
THE CAB BAR & GRILL
5442 West Ridge Road
Erie, PA 16506
(814) 838-0507
www.the-cab.com

Next stop was The Cab. It had a catchy tag line – "If you're gonna drink, use the cab." Clever. Walking in, we noticed that the entire place was Black & Gold. Welcome home, Steelers fans! The owner, Bob, moved to the area from Pittsburgh and has remained a lifelong Steelers fan. The Cab has played host to Steelers fans for the past 20 years and has no plans to stop. The bar has separate smoking and non-smoking sections, each of which was decorated with Steelers memorabilia and packed with fans on the day we visited. One of the highlights is the annual game where Bob hosts a pig roast. We missed it this year but Bob promised to hold one when Always a Home Game returns. We will have to put that on the calendar for next year.

The Cab's chili has been voted the best in town. Rumor has it that the gumbo is also phenomenal. Georgie Boy agreed and Bob was kind enough to give us a gallon to take home. Bob embodied yet another common Steelers fan trait – generosity.

Beer Note: I tried to get a good local beer to go with the spicy chili, but when I asked for an IPA, I was told, "we do not carry that brand." I opted for a Sam Adams Boston Lager (rating – "3"). Not a bad beer, I just had my sights set on a very hoppy ale to pair with that delicious chili.

We sat around The Cab enjoying ourselves thoroughly and somehow the conversation drifted into quoting old movies (that seems to happen quite often with guys of a certain age). Don threw out a classic John Candy line. Abbey looked at him blankly. Don was astonished and asked, "Haven't you heard of John Candy?" The response was a hilarious, if somewhat painful, "Don, you are twice my

age." The room fell silent as yet another old guy went down for the count. Then we all burst into laughter at his humiliation.

got into an altercation on the field with an opposing player and he thought it was so cool that the Steelers were so tough that even their punter was a scrapper. So he went right out and bought a #4 jersey and wore it for the remainder of the year. He later admitted that he also loved Josh's crazy hair. With that, he and Josh toasted with Lombardo's specialty shot, Fire in the Hole, a fireball whiskey and hot sauce. Passing on the shot, I asked for the beer list and was directed to the cooler. You've got to love a real neighborhood bar like this. Of the selection available, Yuengling Lager was the best option. Nuff said...

✦ ✦ ✦
LOMBARDO'S TAVERN

**915 W. 21st Street
Erie, PA 16501
(814) 455-7821
www.facebook.com/LombardosTavern**

The final stop was at Lombardo's Tavern. This is a Steelers hangout and neighborhood dive bar and a great way to end the day. One of the patrons at The Cab told us about Lombardo's. Keep in mind that it is a smoking bar if you plan to visit. As we pulled in, we recognized the Steelers Mercedes parked along the street. Superfan John was inside and offered to buy us a drink.

We walked in and noticed a very elaborate custom piece of memorabilia at the back of the bar. We began speaking to the owner about it when he recognized Josh. He told us that he recalled the day that Josh

Buffalo week was a fun one. It was a Big Board game and we were headed to a place that came highly recommended, The Pittsburgh Inn. I know what you're thinking – this place is in Erie, not Buffalo. You'd be correct, but they show Buffalo away games in this market so we decided it counted. I'm glad we decided to go because we found this to be one of our fonder memories along the Journey, thanks to Tom and Robin Weunski. They made us feel like we were home. You can easily tell that The Pittsburgh Inn is one of those places where everybody in town gathers to eat amazing food, gossip and watch their beloved Steelers play. Tom and Robin did an incredible job of getting the fans in two hours before kickoff for the Big Board filming.

I could go on and on about the food, particularly the apple spice wings. I could also ramble on about the sports memorabilia that covered every square inch of the establishment. But the one thing that really stood out for me was the respect that Tom and Robin show for the people who have fought for our country. They have pictures and letters on the wall – brothers, sisters, sons, daughters, moms, dads, and grandpas as well. And then to find out that they have sent over 2,000 packages over the last three years to all these soldiers...don't know about you, but that is cool in any book.

We had an amazing time, and I know we had more fun on this trip than we told our families we had. That's the funny thing about this book – we had to make it seem as if this was work and not fun.

The Cab Bar & Grill: I remember this place well. Usually it takes something pretty special to stand out from the other 99 establishments. This was the place where Shawn almost drove the 32-foot RV into the bar. When the RV was parked and we both got out, we noticed that the RV was two inches away from the low-hanging roof. To this day he says that he did it on purpose, but there's no way in hell he would be able to pull that off on purpose. We got very lucky.

My memories of the Cab Bar & Grill are good ones. Bob the owner was nice enough to give us five gallons of gumbo. I'm sorry, legendary gumbo. I also acquired a fishing buddy who since that visit has sent me pictures of salmon swimming upstream. Each and every picture has come with an invite. So I definitely will come back up that way and fish with the new friend I met at the Cab Bar & Grill. Yes, he is a Steelers fan.

Lombardo's Tavern: Let's just say people come here to cheer on their Steelers and drink, and not necessarily in that order. Hard-nosed, tough people

pass through here. I'm glad we did it during the day. Yet again we came across a place and felt like we were in someone's kitchen having fun, laughing and sharing stories.

Shawn and Josh collected t-shirts from many of the stops on their Journey. Here is an example of one of the six quilts Joyce Allen (Shawn's mom) made to be auctioned off – see www.alwaysahomegame.com for more details regarding the auction.

Detroit
Home of the Lions

Shawn's Two Cents

The next Big Board trip was Detroit and we were worried. We'd found out that the local Steelers fan club were all chartering a bus and making the pilgrimage to Pittsburgh to watch the game at Heinz Field. We had visions of showing up at the Detroit bars and having nothing to show. So we thought about the road trip TO Detroit and realized that we would be passing a perfect Steelers hangout on the way. Why not?

♦ ♦ ♦
BILLY'S BLACK & GOLD
514 Sharpsville Avenue
Sharon, PA 16146
(724) 981-2030
www.billysblackandgold.com

Billy's is equidistant from Cleveland and Pittsburgh, but Billy's is Black & Gold all the time. Just walking into the place is like walking into a museum dedicated to the Steelers, the Penguins and the Pirates. Of course the Steelers take top billing. Opened in 1988, Billy's has been dedicated to Steelers fans since day one, and that commitment was returned ten-fold in 1996. On August 1, 1996, a fire gutted the structure. The Steelers fans rallied and the community pitched in to rebuild Billy's in time for the 1997 season. Understandably, owners Bill and Carol speak fondly of the community of Steelers fans in Sharon, PA.

As with many husband and wife teams, the roles are clearly defined. As Carol puts it, the secret to their long relationship is that Bill does not cook and she does not tend bar. Carol's real expertise is as an artist. She hand painted the murals that highlight the Black & Gold décor. The coup de grace is the Pittsburgh Skyline (featured in our Big Board presentation). She also paints Ukrainian pysanky eggs, with a Pittsburgh motif, of course.

Billy's displays a number of interesting shadow boxes. Carol told us that former Steelers play Steve Courson (1978-83) had built all of them. We noted an original team photograph of the first Pittsburgh Steelers (then known as the Pittsburgh Pirates), a set of Myron Cope's headphones and scores of other interesting items including an original Franco's Italian Army seat cushion. All the tables and chairs were repurposed from the Allegheny Club at Three Rivers Stadium. Some of the actual stadium seats are on display as well.

The game had not yet started, and Bill was testing the flashing lights and buzzer that he sounds when the Steelers score. Poor Georgie Boy, who was setting up the camera, looked as though he was about to have a heart attack.

On Game Day there is a strict dress code. No opposing jerseys or colors are allowed. Bill said it was necessary back in the "mill days" when the Steelers and Browns rivalry was at its peak. Although no longer necessary,

the tradition is carried on with pride. Billy's food is fantastic – all handmade and prepared fresh onsite. They were preparing "fire dogs" for the game. That's a hot dog wrapped in bacon then deep-fried, sprinkled with cayenne pepper and placed in a bun topped with marinara sauce and mozzarella cheese. The regular menu is full of references to Steelers players past and present (with a few Pirates and Penguins thrown in for fun). Everything from the Jack Ham & Cheese sandwich to Webster's Wings and Polamalu's Pierogies.

The bar in the center of the restaurant is set up in a triangle shape – just like Billy's logo and Pittsburgh's Golden Triangle. The center cooler has a great feature where bottled beer and kegs can be stored and served, instead of in the basement, like most bars. It's like having a can dispenser in your refrigerator and the beers just roll out one after the other. The beer selection was only average, with Sam Adams Boston Lager being the closest thing to a true craft beer. That said, the place is so cool that any beer would taste good here.

We heard one of the best stories from a Steelers fan during this trip. Bob, the former mayor of Sharon, PA, told the story of a Cleveland morning radio talk show host who wanted to intensify the Browns–Steelers rivalry. His plan was to burn a Terrible Towel outside Billy's Black & Gold early one morning before the AFC Wild Card Playoff game for the 2002-03 season. He would then go on the air live from Quaker Steak and Lube (the original location in Sharon) and tell the world he had broken the hold that the Steelers had on the Browns. To foil the plan, a group of Steelers fans spent the night at Billy's, armed with Super Soaker squirt guns. When the DJ arrived, they soaked him with the water guns. Then, to complete the prank, Bob had one of the Sharon police cruisers pull up and place the DJ in cuffs and haul him away in the back of the cruiser for loitering. Of course, he wasn't arrested but rather taken to the site of his "live" show. So rather than ending the curse, he became a part of it. The Steelers won the game 36-33 later that day at Heinz Field.

We could have spent all day with the people at Billy's. But we needed to head to Detroit in search of more Steelers fans.

◆ ◆
TE ROMA
24436 Van Dyke Ave
Center Line, MI 48015
(586) 757-7575
www.facebook.com/pages/Te-Roma

The first stop in Detroit was Te Roma. We had a difficult time locating the bar because we were in the middle of a massive rainstorm, coming down so hard we thought all of the roads were going to flood. Following several expertly executed U-turns, we arrived to a warm greeting from the owners. The Steelers memorabilia was understated but there was no doubt that Steelers fans have watched many games here. It all started more than 25 years ago with a satellite dish and one Steelers fan. The numbers grew over the years and now the fans line up every Sunday to watch the Black & Gold.

Beer Note: I inquired about local craft beer. Bells Brewery in Kalamazoo, MI, is one of the best craft breweries in America. Te Roma featured a full line and I chose the Two Hearted Ale, one of the top rated IPAs in the country and one of my personal favorites. I rate this beer a "4" when it is served in a bottle, but one night I found it "on cask." This is when the beer is carbonated in the keg and drawn into the glass by a manual pump rather than forced by CO2. This produces a less carbonated beer and makes the beer much smoother and more flavorful. Anytime you see a beer "on cask," it will likely be the best tasting beer in the bar.

Like so many of the bars catering to Steelers fans, Te Roma goes that extra mile and serves Iron City on Game Day. During the build-up to Super Bowl XL in Detroit, Te Roma was the headquarters for many local Pittsburgh radio shows and live broadcasts back to Pittsburgh. During the game, fans consumed 20 cases of Iron City. We also confirmed the rumor that Larry Foote's mother had a standing reservation at Te Roma for many years. As we looked over the menu, the owner mentioned that they served the best ribs in Detroit, enough to get us to try them. The ribs are excellent.

Warren, Michigan

◆ ◆
VIVIO'S FOOD AND SPIRITS

3601 E. 12 Mile Rd
Warren, MI 48092
(586) 576-0495
www.vivioswarren.com

The rain had slowed to monsoon-like conditions as we headed to Vivio's Food and spirits, our final stop. We pulled into a dark parking lot and took vastly different approaches to getting inside the bar in as dry a state as possible. Josh took his time, proceeding cautiously and avoiding the puddles. I, on the other hand, launched myself out of the car full force and landed straight in a large puddle. With soaking wet shoes and socks (at least my socks were wet) we grabbed a high top table in Vivio's. An intoxicated Lions fan began verbally assaulting us. It was difficult to understand his exact point, but I think he spent the next 15 minutes trying to convince us that the Steelers were the best-run organization in the league and that the Lions were the worst. We weren't going to argue his point.

Once he stumbled away, we started to take in some of Vivio's ambience. There was Steelers paraphernalia all over. The design favors the defense and Polamalu and Lambert are featured heavily. There was a "Charles Barkley Turrible Towel" hanging on the wall. We never found out the story behind how it got there.

Vivio's has been a Steelers hangout since the owner relocated from Arizona in 2008. Each week, the Steelers fans gather there to cheer on the Black & Gold and enjoy the "knife and fork" sandwiches. Vivio's also has an extensive craft beer list. Given that it was a cold and wet night and my socks were still wet, I thought that a Scottish Ale was appropriate. Founders Brewing Co. in Grand Rapids, MI, is known for its great beer and the Dirty Bastard Scottish Ale is one of their best. The best description comes from the Founders' website – "It is so good it is almost wrong." Rating – "4."

I remember Detroit as being one of our most underrated and unexpected, coolest, pound for pound, trips of the Journey. Let's start with Billy's Black & Gold. Now I know this place is in Sharon, PA. It's not exactly Detroit. But if you look at them from space, or Google Earth, they are very close together. Billy's is probably one of the all around, top to bottom, coolest bars on the Journey. I'm talking legendary sports memorabilia – items you had no idea ever existed and you wonder how they hell they got them. The next great thing about Billy's was the food, amazing and unique. The two owners treat the bar as if it is their home and everyone inside is family. I'm talking Steelers, Pirates and Penguins. If you're ever close to Billy's Black & Gold, stop by and give a big hug to Bill and Carol.

Te Roma was up next. This place was definitely in Detroit. It had a different kind of vibe than Billy's. It was a sports bar and you could tell it was a place for Steelers fans to come and watch a game. One thing stands out about Te Roma's – I had the best ribs on the Journey there. Unbelievable sauce and I think just by looking at the meat funny it would fall off the bone. I'm a big fan of the rib and I'm so glad I decided to have it.

Vivio's Food and Spirits was our last stop in Detroit. Could be one of the more memorable stops, as well. First, it was pouring down rain. Shawn got out of the car hurrying to jump across what he thought was a small puddle and somehow found himself in water up to his waist. I've never laughed so hard in my entire life. Right after that, there was a drunken Detroit fan's definitely unfunny rant. But the best memory was a mental note. We have been in Florida, Arizona, the Carolinas, Atlanta, Denver and everywhere else. It was in Detroit that we came across the cutest waitress on the entire Journey.

Dallas
Home of the Cowboys

Shawn's Two Cents

Over the long Thanksgiving weekend we were tackling Texas – both Dallas and Houston – and then on to New Orleans It was going to be rough away from the family but we were ready to see how Steelers fans in Texas country spend Game Day. There are times when we talk about taking this Journey when someone will say, "Every team in the NFL could do a book like yours." Generally, we politely disagree and point out that in Pittsburgh there is not a bar dedicated to [insert whatever NFL franchise you choose]. One of the names that comes up the most often during these discussions is Dallas. With the Cowboys being "America's Team," we feared that support for the Black & Gold might be hard to find. Wrong!

AUSTIN AVENUE GRILL AND SPORTS BAR

1801 N. Plano Road
Richardson, TX 75081
(972) 907-8003
www.austinavenue.com

First stop, Austin Avenue. As soon as we got out of the rental car wearing our Steelers gear, someone in the parking lot came up to us and asked about the Thanksgiving Day game. He was from Plum Borough and was a lifelong Steelers fan. He confirmed that Austin Avenue is packed with fans every Sunday. As the conversation continued, he asked if we had been to "Frisco" yet. Assuming he meant San Francisco we told him "yes," thinking he was going to ask whether we had tried the beef jerky that Giordano Bros. ships in from Texas and sells at their San Francisco pubs. We told him that we loved Texas beef jerky. He had no idea what we were talking about. He was talking about Frisco, Texas, not San Francisco.

Beer Note: We met Margo and asked about the local beer. Other than the large commercially brewed beer (Lone Star), the suggestion was a Shiner Bock. To me, the Shiner Bock is very similar to Yuengling Lager, a relatively inexpensive beer that everyone will like. The sweet malt dominates the lightly hopped beer and it will not overpower your palate. The rating is a "3."

Margo also told us about the Southern Steel Fan Club of North Texas. They get between 150-200 people each week for the game. The entire bar needs to be rearranged to accommodate all the extra banquet

tables. It's hard to imagine Austin Avenue doing this because the bar is quite large, with a separate smoking section. The Steelers sign and memorabilia are spread throughout the bar. Margo said that the fan club hangs additional banners each week, but that they are taken down on non-Game Days.

The Southern Steel Fan Club of North Texas (currently over 600 members) has met at a number of bars, all of which are now closed. Many of the original members were affiliated with the Black & Gold Brigade but started to think about organizing their own club in 2000. They began meeting at Austin Avenue in

Plano, with weekly attendance reaching 200. Unfortunately, the original Austin Avenue location was ravaged by fire and for the past three seasons the club has been meeting at Austin Avenue II. They may return to the original location if the building process is complete, but wherever they meet they will be cheering on the Black & Gold.

After the first visit we're no longer nervous about finding Steelers fans in Dallas. Now we just hope there is enough time to meet them all. P.S., we think it's time somebody revisits the idea of who is "America's Team."

✦ ✦ ✦
MALARKY'S TAVERN
4460 Trinity Mills Rd.
Dallas, TX 75287
(972) 931-7300
www.malarkystavern.com

As we pulled up to our second stop, we could see that Malarky's was another Steelers hangout. Dozens of Steelers flags were flying proudly atop the building and a Steel City Mafia sticker was on the window next to the front door. The memorabilia was understated but cool. There was a lounge area with a number of leather couches placed in front of dark wooden bookshelves that were filled with books and Steelers memorabilia. Josh's first comment was that it looked like the Art Rooney Sr. library/office that had been recreated at Heinz Field.

We perused the menu and had to go with the Irish tacos. For the uninitiated, an Irish taco is a warm flour tortilla filled with thinly sliced rib eye,

homemade mashed potatoes topped with gravy, and shredded cheddar cheese. It's like Shepherd's Pie Tex-Mex style. It was comfort food and it was delicious.

Beer Note: As expected from an Irish pub, the beer selection was terrific. The local brew of choice was actually from a brewery in Houston – Saint Arnold Brewing Company (Texas's oldest craft brewery). I tried the Amber Ale (rating – "3"), Saint Arnold's flagship beer. This is a multiple-award-winning beer that is usually judged in the bitter category. Bitter beers are similar to pale ales but generally have fewer hops and are slightly darker in color. Most people refer to this style of beer as an "amber" or "red ale" in the United States, while it is more commonly referred to as a "bitter" in Europe. This beer was one of Saint Arnold's first and the recipe has remained unchanged since 1994. Malarky's also serves different beer flights – 5-oz. serving of four different beers – a great way to sample beers and still be able to function the next day.

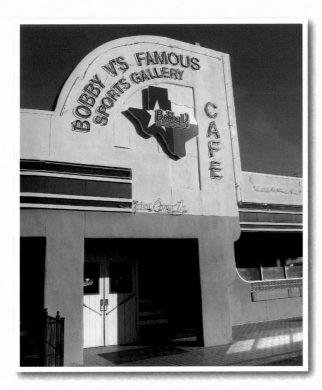

pockets of Steelers items here and there, including an old helmet.

One of the rooms is reserved for the Steelers fans that gather each week. Although they are not formally organized, they meet on a regular basis to enjoy food and drink specials. The craft beer selection was not impressive but we were treated to a Shiner Bock (it may be a requirement to serve Shiner if you operate a tavern in the State of Texas). This "we" means that Josh ventured away from his little comfort zone to try something new. After the great experience with Hangar 24 in San Diego, Josh's beer palate is expanding ever so slightly.

◆
BOBBY V'S SPORTS GALLERY CAFÉ
4301 South Bowen Rd
Arlington, TX 76016
(817) 467-9922
www.bobbyvsports.com

Bobby V's Sports Gallery Café seemed like an odd name, but it all made sense when we walked in. There are pictures, magazine covers, newspapers and other memorabilia on almost every surface of the place. It is truly a gallery of sports. As expected when named after a longtime manager of the Texas Rangers, baseball memorabilia dominates the décor. But there are

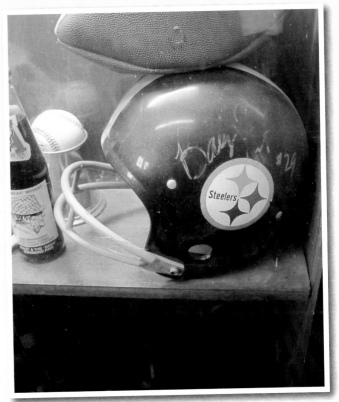

✦ ✦
WOODY'S TAVERN
4744 Bryant Irvin Rd. # 946
Fort Worth, TX 76132
(817) 732-4936
www.woodystaverntexas.com

Woody's Tavern was next up. It was a little difficult to find this place because it's located on the backside of a shopping plaza. Once we made our way around the back, however, we noticed that almost every car in the parking lot had a Pittsburgh Steelers window decal, bumper sticker or license plate frame. Feels just like home.

Woody's is a very large Texas-style bar with high ceilings and TVs all over the place. This is also a smoking bar, which means that it is a strictly 21-and-over crowd. We met up with Becky, the founder of the Fort Worth Steelers Fan Club, and learned that she and the other roughly 200 club members take over Woody's each Game Day. She personally brings pierogies and others pitch in, too, for a little bit of Pittsburgh in Dallas. Becky also has an interesting tattoo on her backside. It's just low enough that she had to warn her mother before a local TV station displayed her tattoo for the world to see.

The Fort Worth Fan Club was founded in 2003 and boasts over 300 members. This year it reached a milestone. It celebrated its first Fan Club Baby. Carrying on the Black & Gold through the next generation!

Beer Note: On the beer list, I noticed Rahr & Sons Brewing Co., a Fort Worth craft brewery. Feeling adventurous, I tried the Ugly Pug, which is a black lager. Many people assume a dark beer is heavy and high in calories (Guinness is actually a "light" beer by calorie standards). Yet the Ugly Pug has a surprisingly light body. Rating of "3."

◆◆ EAGLE'S NEST SPORTS GRILL

**8455 Boat Club Road
Fort Worth, TX 76179
(817) 236-8881
www.eaglesnestsportsgrill.com**

With the proliferation of smoking bars that do not allow families to watch the game, a number of additional Steelers hangouts have emerged. While at Woody's, we had met Lorraine. She started another fan club called Steelers Nation Fan Club of Fort Worth. They meet at the family-friendly Eagle's Nest Sports Grill. This is a new club for 2013 and it's growing every week.

I would love to find out how many NFL play-ers come out of Texas. I'm thinking the actual numbers are very big. Any time you get into a car and it takes you 24 hours to drive across the state you know you're in a big place.

First stop on our Dallas tour was Austin Avenue Grill and Sports Bar. Because of the time change, I was able to sneak a Loose Goose in before the noon hour. The Loose Goose has to be in hand before noon. For some reason, it was meant for the morning hours and I had about 35 minutes to get within that acceptable window of time. You talk about

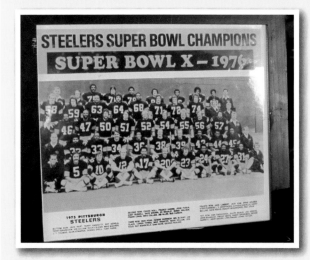

surrounding yourself with numbers – how about 600? That represents the Southern Steel Fan Club. Very nice indeed. Austin's is definitely a place to watch the Steelers play.

Malarky's Tavern: This place made Shawn's top five of the Journey, I'm sure of it. It wasn't an in-your-face Steelers place; it was more discreet. When a Steelers fan/owner opens up an establish-ment outside of Western Pennsylvania he must know that he's treading a very fine line between good business and following his heart. At Malarky's the owner got his point across that he is a Steelers fan, but at the same time allows others to pay the bills for him. Shawn was in heaven standing at the bar talking beer with the boys and I was very con-tent being way in the back with a Loose Goose. If you're keeping score, that's my second of the day.

We made a quick stop at Bobby V's Sports Gallery Café. In my opinion, it's probably not the best place to watch a Steelers game, even though it had thousands of sports memorabilia on every square inch of the wall, ceiling and even countertops. But we are on a mission to visit Steelers establishments and I'm sorry to say that I didn't find too much that made me feel at home.

Woody's Tavern, however, was a different story. We must've seen 12-15 different Steelers decora-tions for cars in the parking lot. Woody's is home to the Fort Worth Steelers Fan Club. They can talk to you about Steelers from the '70s all the way up to free agency of today. On Game Days, ownership allows them one half of the bar. I can promise you the next time I'm in Fort Worth, Texas I will visit this group and try to spend the day with them.

Houston
Home of the Texans

Off to Houston. We'd been to Dallas. I'd lived in Austin and been to San Antonio too many times to count because my parents retired there. But I'd only ever been to Houston for business. It was time to see this town from a different perspective. We were going to check it out with fans of the Black & Gold.

Our crackerjack interns told us that there were three places where the Steelers faithful gathered on Game Day: Papa's Ice House, Frank 'N' Steins Bar & Grill and the End Zone Sports Bar & Grill. What's more, Hwy SixBurgh Steelers Nation promised to show us how the Black & Gold throw it down Houston-style. Boy did they! We learned that the old adage is true – things are bigger in Texas. Mickey, Lucy and Patricia put on a show. Not to be outdone, West Houston Steelers Nation hosts a family friendly version at the End Zone. We really needed a day off after Houston, but we couldn't stay because we had more cities waiting for us.

As we travel the country, Steelers fans are getting engaged in our concept for the Journey, sending lots of suggestions about places that Always a Home Game should visit. A number of fans told us about a place in Houston called Steel City Pizza. Sadly, it's now closed. But we found out where those displaced fans now hang – Papa's Ice House. We made plans to meet a Steelers fan club here for a big tailgate party.

Papa's looks like a barn with roll-up doors and tons of outdoor seating. The unusual thing was that the place was empty. We could not find a Steelers fan in sight. Thinking that everyone else must just be late, we went in and met Rich, the owner. He assured us that this is a huge Steelers hangout. They average 125 fans on Game Days and erect a large projection screen just for the Black & Gold. Rich has been serving the folks from Houston for over 23 years, and he really appreciates the loyalty of the Steelers fans.

Because we were in Texas, we "sauntered" up to the bar. Josh ordered a Loose Goose. He pronounced it "tremendous" and in the top third of all beverages on the Journey. I noticed that there was a beer from Karbach Brewing, a local Houston craft brewer. I tried the Hopadillo. It was awesome (and had a great name). It was another strong, well balanced IPA (a "4") that was very drinkable. The best thing is that it comes in a can! At this point we were feeling pretty good about ourselves. Then disaster struck...

We got a call from one of our interns back in Pittsburgh. The fan club in Houston, The Hwy SixBurgh Steelers Nation, wanted to know where we were. What? We were at Papa's, where were they? Looks like we went to the wrong bar first. In the words of Homer Simpson, "D'oh!" We needed to be on the other side of Houston – which was at least 45 minutes away. We made a mad dash to the rental car and headed south.

◆ ◆
FRANK 'N' STEINS BAR & GRILL

**9907 Hwy 6
Sugar Land, TX 77498
(281) 744-4547
www.facebook.com/pages/Frank-NSteins-
Bar-Grill/143150025731179**

We flew around the beltway (at least they call it a beltway in the Northeast) to try to reach Frank 'N' Steins before the party was over. But no need to hurry: we soon found out the party goes on all night long!

As we pulled in, there were hundreds of people in the parking lot. Remember, this is on a Saturday night and the Steelers played on Thursday night. It was an insane tailgate party. The first thing we noticed were the huge, although probably small for Texas, smokers in the parking lot. Here we found Mickey ("The Godfather"), who is originally from New Kensington, manning the smokers. He generally arrives four hours before kickoff to ensure things will be ready

at the appropriate time. There was enough meat to feed an army – or better yet, Steelers Nation. Next to the smokers are all of the trophies they have won at regional BBQ competitions. One such award was at Reliant Stadium, home of the Houston Texans. They were awarded the "Best Tailgate." Go, Steelers Nation! Mickey let us know that this group not only gets together for Steelers games, but continues to gather year round, performing many charitable activities, mostly to benefit soldiers. They are such a close "family" that they all got together to celebrate Thanksgiving this year.

Frank 'N' Steins also had a tent with a custom Steelers chopper and custom Mustang on display. Replicas of the six Lombardi trophies were also on display under the tent. A mere $5 gets a ticket for the buffet and a raffle (the prize table was amazing!). While we were checking things out under the tent, club members Patricia and Lucy grabbed us by the arms and rushed us inside the bar. They wanted to make sure that we had good seats and got something to eat. Because the Steelers weren't playing a live game, the Hwy SixBurgh Steelers Nation had set up a highlights DVD of the Super Bowl championship seasons.

Buying someone a drink is an interesting concept with this club. In most places, when someone offers to buy you a drink, it is exactly that drink. When a member of the Hwy SixBurgh Steelers Nation buys you a drink, a bucket of beer arrives every fifteen minutes until you tell them to stop! I asked about a local IPA and was told, and I quote, "What the f*&#k is an IPA?" The bartender was helpful and suddenly another pint of Karbach Hopadillo was sitting in front of me. It was even better the second time. Needless to say,

spent a number of years there at Sansone's until it closed and they moved to Frank 'N' Steins. The best way to contact the club is through the Facebook page. Lucy and her daughter Stephanie keep it updated.

We asked Lucy how she became a Steelers fan and her answer suggested another international road trip for Always a Home Game. Lucy is originally from Monterrey, Mexico. Apparently, there is a huge Steelers fan base there. According to Lucy, in the '80s, a lot of people moved to Monterrey to work in the steel industry. Of course all these workers wanted to keep in touch with their beloved Steelers and getting together on Game Day was the best way to do this. A number of Steelers hangouts opened and are still packed every Sunday. Sounds like we need to make sure our passports are up to date!

It is difficult to describe all of the things that were going on during this event. The club has a lot of energy and creativity that is on display each week. One item of note was the "shotski," a waterski that has six shot glasses (one for each Super Bowl) glued to it. After every touchdown six club members do a simultaneous shot. After showing us how it worked, Lucy said one of the more memorable lines from our Journey: "We hate field goals!" With that, we were off to the next stop.

Josh had more Miller Lite than he knew what to do with. I think there were three buckets in front of him by the time I reached my seat.

Patricia and Lucy were the perfect hostesses, aka the "Steeler Lady Divas." They had prepared a color booklet explaining the history of the club and then gotten every member in attendance to sign the cover, so we will always have something to remember that day. It was something we would never forget anyway! The Hwy SixBurgh Steelers Nation started almost 25 years ago in another team's sports bar. This time it was a Buffalo Bills bar. They

The End Zone Sports Bar and Grill was a far more relaxed atmosphere and we quickly settled into a conversation with Justin. He told the story of Sansone's closing and how a small portion of that original fan group had since started watching games at The End Zone. This group was looking for a more family oriented Game Day experience. So they formed a new fan club called the West Houston Steelers Nation.

The West Houston Steelers Nation has a weekly raffle for the 75-100 fans that gather to watch the games each week. They also try to get ex-players to attend watch parties. This past season Mike Merriweather (1982-87) spent an entire afternoon with the fans. Everyone in attendance was impressed with how friendly he was and that he stayed for the entire game. Add this to the list of themes emerging on our Journey – Steelers players love to interact with the fans. The fan club also challenged a local Dallas Cowboys fan club to a flag football game. Although the outcome was not ideal (there are claims that the other team used ringers), the fan club takes every chance to be together and celebrate the Steelers.

Justin told us that a few times a year the End Zone closes the parking lot for a huge tailgate party. When they are not having a special occasion, there are always food and drink deals for the fans. Justin also told us that he is a published author. Pretty cool! We asked him for some advice in writing this book but then discovered that his genre is along the lines of "Fifty Shades of Grey." Not sure how to incorporate that into this book without seriously embarrassing our kids!

Before we started this Journey, Shawn and I decided we should put together some rules in regard to grading and judging the establishments. We flat out decided we were not going to name a #1 Steelers hangout in the country. We decided we would talk about the positives for each place and the good times that we had there. I think we did a good job of keeping true to that theory and game plan. All that being said, I have to say that I had the best time hanging out with Mickey and the Steelers diva ladies, Patricia and Lucy, at Frank 'N' Steins. On a non-Game Day, you wouldn't know that this is a Steelers hangout. But on Game Day? This might be the most fun I had, and we weren't even there on a real Game Day. Let's go down the checklist, shall we? A large crowd of Steelers fans? Yes. Representatives from at least four generations? Yes. Amazing food – pulled pork and six other meats to choose from? Yes. More than three grills fired up and smoke touching the sky? Yes, and they had over 20 different desserts and a bar that seemed to have no end. When someone says, "Can I buy you a beer," what they are telling you is that you will need a cab in about five hours. One beer equals a bucket; a bucket equals five beers. You do the math. It doesn't make sense but this is how they do it and everyone seems to be fine with it. I would have to say the coolest and most memorable thing that I took away from this group and experience was the love they had for each other. It reminded me of one of those crazy family reunions where 150 people show up with name tags and claim to be part of the same family tree. The weird thing about this trip was that there wasn't even a game the weekend we visited. They set up a video and replayed the Steelers' last Super Bowl and watched it as if it were live. I tell you this group knows how to have fun and goes that extra mile to make sure you are getting the full experience of what it's like to hang with them. It's funny because I was thinking, man, they really put on a nice party for Shawn and me, and then I realized that we crashed their party. This was going to happen whether we showed up or not. Many thanks go out to the crazy group at Frank 'N' Steins Bar & Grill. They kind of reminded me of what I was hoping to find on this Journey – a large group of people getting together for celebration and leaving all of life's problems at the door. Celebrating a common cause and truly enjoying each other and of course the Black & Gold. And if you're keeping score, I had all 120 people give Shawn multiple hugs!

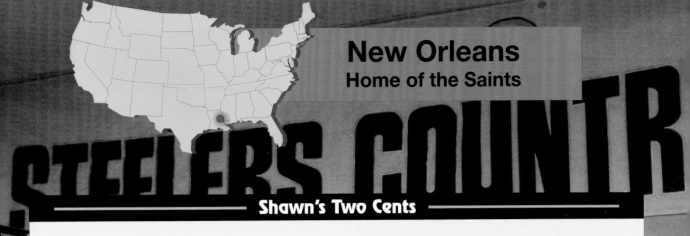

New Orleans
Home of the Saints

STEELERS COUNTR

Shawn's Two Cents

When I think of New Orleans, I admit that the Saints and football aren't the first thing that springs to mind. I think of Mardi Gras, the French Quarter, beignets, jazz, Emeril Lagasse (Bam!)... I once had a palm reader in Jackson Square do a reading. He said that I was going to "live forever." Hey, I could be the oldest Steelers fan someday. Anyway, we weren't here for Cajun cooking or Bourbon Street. We were looking for the fans of the Black & Gold at the Fox and Hound, Cooter Brown's, and Buffalo Wild Wings. Of course, Steelers Nation knows how to kick back and enjoy, so we headed out to greet Tim, the Cajun Steelers Fan Club and the other faithful of New Orleans, knowing we were going to enjoy ourselves. *"Laissez les bons temps rouler!"*

♦ ♦
FOX AND HOUND

1200 S. Clearwater Parkway
New Orleans, LA 70123
(504) 731-6000
www.foxandhound.com

The first stop that day was at the Fox and Hound on Clearwater Parkway. This was the first openly "multi-NFL" team bar. Many of the large chains have similar floor plans for their restaurants. There are usually two party rooms flanking a main bar and dining area. This was the case in New Orleans. One of the rooms was 100% dedicated to the Saints (to be expected), but the other room was used for LSU on Saturdays and the Pittsburgh Steelers on Sundays. The Fox and Hound has a tailgate special package for the fans and is actively trying to increase the number of fans that attend each week.

Beer Note: I went to the bar to ask specifically for Abita, rather than take a chance on another brewery. Abita was founded in 1986 and is a pioneer in the craft beer market. The brewing company is about 30 miles outside of New Orleans. Because Abita is not readily available in Pittsburgh, I was anxious to try some. I asked the bartender about the best selling Abita product and he suggested the Amber. The Abita Amber is a Munich-style lager. My brother-in-law Dave, who is probably as beer-obsessed as am I (and far more Steelers-obsessed) insists that any craft brewer that has a Lager as its flagship beer deserves much respect. I tend to agree. The Abita Amber is a very crisp, well-balanced session beer, and I can see why it is consistently voted the best beer in New Orleans by various publications. The rating is a "3" and I would serve this beer at any social event.

It was a long drive from Houston to New Orleans and we made it in late. The next morning, we headed out to try to find a diner for breakfast. Being that we are both guys and that our wives weren't along to insist otherwise, we refused to stop and ask for directions. Instead, we took the "drive around and just look" approach. We weren't looking for a national chain but a local diner. We were in for a shock. There are parts of New Orleans that are pretty rough. The aftermath of Hurricane Katrina is still very present. We finally found a perfect place for breakfast, but I'm sure we could never retrace our footsteps.

talking Steelers. Cooter Brown's is a short trolley ride from Bourbon Street. This convenience makes Cooter Brown's the ideal spot for traveling Steelers fans to watch the game. Every week there is someone from out of town who stops in to cheer on the Black & Gold along with the regular crowd that always shows up. The best crowds are always the Saturday night before a Sunday game at the Superdome when the Steelers play the Saints. It is standing room only. Everyone enjoys a party in NOLA.

✦ ✦
COOTER BROWN'S TAVERN & OYSTER BAR

**509 S. Carrollton Avenue
New Orleans, LA 70118
(504) 866-9104
www.cooterbrowns.com**

The next stop in New Orleans was Cooter Brown's Tavern & Oyster Bar. This is a beer lover's paradise. They have over 400 different beers in bottles (of course cans would be better) and 40 taps, including 13 taps dedicated to local craft brews. Many of the tap handles are custom made and really cool. I opted for the NOLA Hopitoulas IPA. This is a strong West Coast IPA bordering on Imperial IPA. It has a very strong citrus and pine aroma with a slightly bitter aftertaste. This beer would give Josh "bitter beer face." I should have ordered him one! I give it a "3."

After getting over the excitement of the beer list (sorry, Josh!), we got down to the real business of

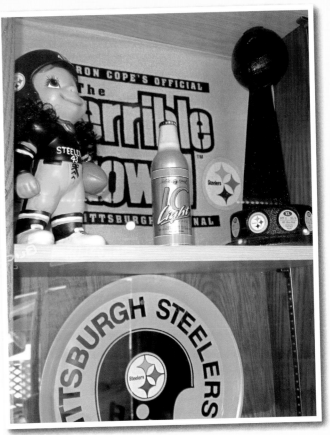

◆ ◆
BUFFALO WILD WINGS
3434 Veterans Memorial Blvd.
Metarie, LA 70002
(504) 252-4606
www.buffalowildwings.com

Our final stop in New Orleans was at the largest Buffalo Wild Wings location in the country. It is also the home to the New Orleans branch of the Steel City Mafia family tree. Boss Tim and his family greeted us. Tim has been affiliated with the Steel City Mafia for quite a while. He remembers finding them on MySpace. Wow, it has been quite a while! Tim recalls his early days growing up in a large Ohio family where all of his brothers liked the Browns. As Tim puts it, he likes a winner and has followed the Steelers as long as he can remember.

This BWW location is huge with a large outdoor deck on the second floor. This deck is where the Cajun Steelers Fan Club (as they are more commonly known) gathers each week to watch the game. Tim was excited to show us the way to the deck. We soon discovered that there was good reason. The aptly titled "stairway to seven" is completely decorated with Black & Gold. There are signed jerseys and other memorabilia that the management gladly put up to support their faithful Steelers fans. Creative and pretty cool – a nice combination.

Beer Note: I took this opportunity to sample another from the Abita lineup. This time I ordered the Turbodog. This is a very dark brown ale with a strong Willamette hop profile (rating – "3" on its own). When doing research for this trip I noticed the Abita website suggests that you pair this beer with spicy Louisiana or Caribbean foods. With this in mind, we ordered the Mango Habañero wings. It was a perfect combination. I highly recommend this pairing (the Turbodog is a "4" with the wings)!

The conversation then turned to the fan club. We quickly realized that we were not in the presence of an ordinary fan. Tim said they have over 1,000 names on the distribution list for the Steel City Mafia in New Orleans, and that this does not account for all the fans

that travel to New Orleans and join them for a game or two every year. Then Tim pulled out the helmet. This was a helmet that came in a kit back when I was a kid – probably from the old Sears catalog. Tim has had it signed by every Steelers player he has ever met. It was full of signatures. Josh was honored to add his name to the collection. Then Tim asked if we wanted to see pictures from his wedding. Recalling the Terrible Towel wave at Ed's wedding in Kansas City we were eager to see Tim's interpretation of a Steelers wedding. Tim went over the top.

Tim dressed in traditional black – not a tux but a home Lambert jersey. His wife was dressed in white – not a gown but an away Polamalu jersey. Both were in what I can only describe as pajama bottoms. The entire hall was decorated in Black & Gold, including the wedding cake.) It was a match made in Steelers heaven.

After we got over the shock of the wedding album, Tim asked Josh a very interesting question. He wanted to know why so many Steelers come back to live in Pittsburgh. The answer was simple and straightforward. "The grass isn't always greener..." Josh said that many free agents are lured away by the talk of winning a championship or by the glamor associated with a big contract, but at the end of the day the most important thing is to be a part of an organization that is committed to winning every year and to having a fan base that will support the team through the good times and bad times. There is not another team in the league that treats its players as well as the Steelers organization and there are no other fans as good as Steelers fans. That is why they come back.

That was very well said by Shawn. Or was that Me? Or was that Shawn quoting me? Either way, that is the truth. Look around and try to find another ex-kicker that has his own radio show in a drive time slot. I will save you the trouble; you won't find it because it doesn't exist. That's what makes Pittsburgh so special. Pittsburgh fans are so loyal, almost to a fault. Doesn't matter if you're a superstar or third-string fullback. The average Steelers fan can smell bullshit a mile away. Stiller fans not only root for the player on the field but they root for the player off the field. That is the difference between Steelers fans and everyone else. If you work hard and give everything you have and managed to keep your nose clean your entire career, you have a fan for life. No

matter what position you played. That is why my wife and I decided to raise our family in Pittsburgh.

Tampa Bay
Home of the Buccaneers

Shawn's Two Cents

The Sunshine State "take two." We'd already visited Steelers Nation in Florida when we went to Jacksonville. Florida is a big state and it's home to three NFL teams – the Jaguars, the Buccaneers and the Dolphins. This time we were headed to Tampa and Miami over a three-day weekend. Our research showed us that there were six bars we needed to check out in Tampa. Black & Gold gather faithfully there on Game Days to watch their team. We met up with Len and the crew from the "Three Rivers Club at the Villages" at Beef "O" Brady's. Tampa is home to more than one Steelers fan club. The Bay Area Black and Gold Club joined us for drinks at O'Briens Irish Pub & Grill. We put some unnecessary miles on the rental car trying to find the Tampa Tap Room. Let's be clear, it really wasn't difficult to find, we just struggled to work our way around the construction. It was worth the effort. Then we headed to Cooter's, which offered us a chance to hang out on the water and expand my palate. Finally, we made it to Rudy's. People had been talking about it all day. It didn't disappoint. We were supposed to finish our Tampa adventure at the Great White Grill. Well, we eventually made it there, but not before it closed. We had the best of intentions and usually I can keep us on track. But Tampa offered too many fun places to hang, too many great fans and too many unique stories to keep to our schedule.

◆ ◆
BEEF "O" BRADY'S

840 South Main Street
Wildwood, FL 34785
(352) 689-0048
www.beefobradys.com

As we flew out to Florida, we were expecting a 50-degree increase in temperature. It was a perfect time to escape the cold and snow of Pittsburgh.

We planned to film for the Big Board in Tampa. There are so many Steelers hangouts in Florida that it was difficult to decide where we should film. Then we were introduced to Len. He is vice-president of the Three Rivers Club at the Villages, a 500-person fan club, and only one of three such Pittsburgh clubs in the Villages. He rallied the Steelers fans and we were ready to meet them at Beef "O" Brady's.

The best way to describe this crowd is a fraternity party for seniors. They were a riot. We had so much fun. They were telling Abbey about all of the amenities at the Villages – over 80 pools, multiple country

clubs, shopping. She was ready to move in. We arrived early and I asked for the beer list. It is safe to say that the flavor profile for the beer list is geared to the customer base – nothing hoppy to be found. The best option was a Sam Adams Boston Lager (rating "3"), so nothing new to add.

When George fired up the camera, the place was rocking. The Three Rivers Club created a lot of excitement and we filmed a great segment for the fans back at Heinz Field. Many of the participants had family at the game back in Pittsburgh so the text messages were flying out telling everyone to look for them. (Hey, these guys may be retired, but they were technologically savvy!)

As we talked to the fans, we heard two remarkable stories. The first was a story about the Immaculate Reception. The lady we spoke to was at Three Rivers Stadium with her husband sulking in defeat as the last 30 seconds of the game were winding down. Then, as we know, one of the most amazing plays in the NFL history unfolded before their eyes. In his excitement, her husband jumped out of his seat and almost knocked her over the railing of the upper tier to her certain death in the crowd below. Fortunately, she was able to grab the rail and tragedy was averted.

The second story came from a gentleman who claimed that Jack Lambert saved his life. He was working on a stadium renovation in 1981. While walking down one of the internal corridors looking at his notes on a clipboard, the Steelers team came rushing out of the locker room and down the hall, heading for a practice session on the field – Jack Lambert leading the way. In a moment of sheer terror, the man froze. Without missing a step, Jack (I feel as though I should be referring to him as "Mr. Lambert") picked him up under his armpits and carried him to an alcove where he calmly deposited the petrified Steelers fan and continued to run to the field.

After the filming, Josh spent a lot of time signing towels for everyone in attendance (and many for their grand-children as well – at least that's the story they told us, maybe the towels are now on eBay). One of the ladies came up to Georgie Boy and asked to have her picture taken with him – to which he replied, "I'm not famous, I just have a beard."

We were having such a good time that we overshot the expected departure time. We did not think this was a big deal, until the Kansas Jayhawks fans showed up for a game and a very lively discussion ensued. We decided it was time to hit the road.

◆ ◆ ◆
O'BRIEN'S IRISH PUB & GRILL

1435 N. Dale Mabry Hwy
Tampa, FL 33618
(813) 961-4092
www.obrienspubtampa.com

Next up: O'Brien's Irish Pub & Grill – home to the Bay Area Black and Gold Club. This club has a classic origin – three guys and a 1987 Mean Joe Green Hall of Fame Iron City Beer can (this sounds like the beginning of a commercial). Back in 1992, a few friends were having a cold one at a local pub. One of the guys had brought the Mean Joe Green Iron City beer can as a gift from Pittsburgh. Another regular at the bar joined them and they decided that Briedy's Pub in Northdale would become their local hangout to watch the Steelers. They ran an ad in the local paper and before the end of the first season they had over 100 Steelers fans for each game. They soon outgrew the initial location

and moved to O'Brien's for the 1994 season and have been there ever since. The official club roster is over 300, but additional fans stop by on Game Day. For the Arizona Super Bowl, there were 4,000 in attendance.

The Tampa Tribune and Pittsburgh news media have recognized the Bay Area Black and Gold Club and the mayor of Pittsburgh even dedicated a December game to the club in appreciation of their commitment to the Steelers. The current officer, Marco, told us about all the other things the club does. They make shirts, cozies and lanyards. For the Miami game they are having a Taste of Pittsburgh party where they have Isaly's chipped chopped ham and BBQ sauce shipped in from the 'Burgh, along with a case of Clark Bars – and in a very Pittsburgh tradition they are having a cookie table.

Marco shared with us one of the more unique ways that the Bay Area Black and Gold root for the Steelers. They will bang Heinz Ketchup bottles on the table (this was the practice long before the Steelers moved into Heinz Field) to cheer the team on. The tag line for the club is, "The home of the 60 minute fan" and the dedication to the Steelers we experienced while there makes us believe every word.

Beer Note: Before leaving on this trip, my brother-in-law and fellow

home brewer Dave insisted that I had to find Cigar City Jai Alai IPA – so by definition he was already rating this beer a "5." I was in luck, O'Brien's had it and in a can! I was a little nervous wondering if this beer could actually live up to its reputation as one of the top IPAs in the country. After the first sip, I was hooked – this is as good as advertised. I think the best description for this beer is what the Alstrom Bros. say on their Beer Advocate website (www.beeradvocate.com), "Seriously epic beer, we can only hope a pint of it is waiting for us at the gates of hop heaven." I can add nothing to that other than to confirm the rating – "5."

As we walked away from the bar, we saw the Stewart #10 jersey. We had met Kim (Dark Horse, Chicago) and

Kristen (Helen Fitzgerald, St. Louis) and remembered them telling us of their father who lived in Tampa and wore a Kordell jersey, but we had forgotten which bar he called home. We met him and started high-fiving each other, thinking that we had met the whole Stewart clan at Steelers hangouts across the country. Then we learned that they also have a son/brother in Portland, Oregon. He is also a huge Steelers fan. Jeez, couldn't he have made the road trip to Seattle? Sounds like we've got to hit Portland on our next Journey. We hate to leave a job unfinished. Besides, Portland has a lot of good breweries.

◆ ◆
TAMPA TAP ROOM

13150 N. Dale Marby Hwy
Tampa, FL 33618
(813) 961-2337
www.facebook.com/TampaTapRoom

A short distance from O'Brien's is the Tampa Tap Room. Due to construction, it was difficult to make it into the parking lot. After circling the entire strip mall we finally made it to the Tap Room. It is a cool place with an excellent beer selection. As we were looking at the taps we noticed that there were plastic shot glasses placed upside down on all of the liquor bottles. Clearly we looked like completely confused idiots because the server came over and asked us if everything was okay. Fruit flies. I think we could have sat and guessed for hours about the reasoning for the shot glasses and we would never have come up with fruit flies.

Beer Note: Not deterred by my ignorance of liquor (I am a beer guy after all), I looked at the beer list. There was a surprisingly strong lineup, but not many local options. I ordered a pint of the Goose Island India Pale Ale (yes, I know it is brewed in Chicago and shipped to Florida). With all of the new craft breweries and different styles of beer, I appreciate breweries that simply name their beer after the style of beer. For example, when we were in Detroit and ordered the Founders Dirty Bastard, Josh had no idea that he was going to get a Scottish Strong Ale. So Goose Island was off to a good start with me. This is an English IPA, in contrast to the American IPA (West Coast IPA), so it is not as hoppy as its counterpart and generally has a lower alcohol content. This award winning beer is a great example of the style. It deserves a "3" rating.

We talked to the owner of the Tampa Bay Tap Room and he told us the bar had recently changed ownership and names. It used to be called "Tanks," which was a renowned Steelers hangout in Tampa for over 20 years. Back in the day there were 100-150 fans for each game. Over time, the numbers have dwindled to 30-50 on Game Days. They still have pierogies and cater to Steelers fans. Earlier in the season, Ray Seals (1994-1996) made an appearance and signed autographs and watched the game with the fans. The hope is that when the construction is complete the crowds will pick up again.

As we left the Tap Room we heard a familiar phrase from Josh, "Man, I could go for some ice cream right now." We were in luck. There was an ice cream shop right in the mall. We started chatting with the server as he was putting our order together and discovered another amazing coincidence. He was from Steubenville, Ohio, and was a huge Steelers fan. We asked why the Steelers instead of the Bengals or Browns. He told us that he had attended college with none other than Mr. Lambert himself. Steelers fans are everywhere!

✦ ✦ ✦
COOTER'S RESTAURANT & SPORTS BAR

423 Poinsettia Ave
Clearwater Beach, FL
(727) 462-2668
www.cooters.com

Our next stop in Tampa was Cooter's Restaurant & Sports Bar. Cooter's is located right on the water and the smell of salt water was refreshing as we entered the large restaurant. The Steelers hangout is in the sports bar section, all the way to the left. The Black & Gold painted walls and Steelers memorabilia made a very good, very loud statement.

There is not an organized Steelers fan club at Cooter's, but each week it is packed with fans. The owner is from Pittsburgh and he caters to his patrons with buckets of Yuengling each week. Cooter's has a number of special and unique pieces of memorabilia from the '70s and '80s. This place reminds me of "man caves" in Pittsburgh. Given that there are no

basements in Florida, this must be the next best thing for Steelers fans.

We noticed that there were fried gator bites on the menu. We had to try them. While waiting for our order, we watched the Pens game. If it were not for the 70-degree weather (and eating alligator instead of, say, mozzarella sticks) at 8 p.m. we might be at a bar in Pittsburgh. This is a great place to spend an evening. And the gator bites were okay.

As we were getting ready to leave, George started cleaning out one of the plastic containers that held the dipping sauce for the gator bites. Turns out George wanted to gather some sand from the beach to take back to Pittsburgh. We are all tired of the Polar Vortex back home.

♦ ♦ ♦
RUDY'S SPORTS BAR

11100 66th Street
Largo, FL 33773
(727) 546-2616
www.rudyssportsbar.com

We proceeded down the west coast of Florida to the next stop on our Journey, Rudy's Sports Bar. All day, Steelers fans had been asking if we were going to Rudy's. Now we understood why. Rudy's is a huge Steelers hangout. Not only does it have the capacity to host over 300 Steelers fans each week, but the memorabilia is out of control. It is rumored that the tailgating starts at 9 a.m. on Game Day to ensure that fans get a seat when the game starts at 1:00.

There are full size Fatheads and custom paintings on the walls along with jerseys and signed photographs from every era of Steelers players. As we spoke to the manager, we realize that the current "Rudy" is the third generation owner of the bar, and that it has been dedicated to serving Steelers fans since the day it opened the doors. Every Game Day, they serve Iron City and IC Light, with the Steelers game showing on every TV – no other team or game matters at Rudy's. Every time the Steelers score, a huge gong echoes throughout the bar.

Two fans approached us as we gawked at the memorabilia. Ramona and Marlene had waited all evening for us to show up, eager to meet Josh and get his autograph. They showed us their matching tattoos. Of course, they were drinking Iron City. They told us of their road trip to Las Vegas and how they transported 10 cases of Iron City to Steelers fans at Noreen's (a local Steelers hangout in Las Vegas) because they are unable to get any. We think Vegas now has to be on the list for the next Journey as well.

I noticed that the entire bar top was covered with sports memorabilia – things like Sports Illustrated covers, pictures of players. The majority of it was Steelers stuff and coated with a laminate or acrylic so you could put your drink down and not worry. Pretty cool.

Beer Note: I ordered a Magic Hat #9 from Burlington, Vermont, and it was served in a Magic Hat #9 pint glass. Kudos to Rudy's for following the European tradition of serving each beer in its own unique glass. The #9 is a beer without a defined style. The folks at Magic Hat refer to it as "not quite a pale ale" and that is a good place to start. This beer has a very fruity aroma but is balanced with enough of a hop profile to provide a crisp, clear finish. Overall, this is a very good, unique beer. A "3."

Open 11-close...7 days a week. We initially thought it should not be included in the book because we didn't go inside, but we could tell by visual inspection alone that this was truly a Steelers hangout. But don't just take our word for it. One reviewer on TripAdvisor called Great White Grill "a Pittsburgh style neighborhood bar and grill." A Yelp reviewer posted: "It was fun to come to this 'Pittsburgh' bar complete with Steelers flag, neon sign AND I.C. Light beer!"

◆ ◆ ◆
GREAT WHITE GRILL
2440 Palm Ridge Road
Sanibel, FL 33957
(239) 472-0212
www.greatwhitegrill.com

The day was so successful that we were way behind schedule by the time we reached the final stop of the night, the Great White Grill. The Great White Grill has tons of Steelers items on the walls – including a Steel Curtain jersey. We also noticed the bar chairs upholstered with Steelers jerseys. The Grill is not a big place, but there is ample room to watch the game. And it boasts the largest tap selection on the island. The biggest drawback to the Grill is that it closes too early on a Saturday night. We had heard good things about this place, but we didn't know that they had non-specific closing hours. By the time we got there it was closed for the evening. Then we checked their website and saw their hours of operation listed this way:

Tampa was a Big Board game at the one and only Beef "O" Brady's. This was one of our bigger and better filmings. Our biggest question every time we do a recording for the Big Board is will we have enough people that show up? Well, we didn't have to worry about that in Tampa. We were dealing with the Three Rivers Club at the Villages. This was a group of seniors. I'm not talking about seniors in high school or seniors in college. I'm talking about seniors in life. In the Villages, there are two other Steelers fan clubs, each one with 500 members. We got in contact with one of the groups and they told us if we went to Beef "O" Brady's they would show up. All of them. I wish all our filming went this smooth. We must've had over 200 senior citizens wearing Black & Gold showing up two hours before kickoff. It was raining seniors, hallelujah. The leader of this group was Len. He would point and yell and everyone would go in that direction. It was truly something to see. I wish Len would've been with us on the entire Journey. Georgie Boy was able to work his magic with the camera and our Always a Home Game girl Abbey Way did her thing as well. Watching 70-year-old men flirt with a twenty-something girl is always entertaining. As I recall, the taping that we sent back to Heinz Field was one of our best ever. I think the message was real loud and clear. It doesn't matter what generation you are from, a Steelers fan can be found at any age. We just happened to find 500 of them that live in a 50+ living retirement community.

I must've signed over 100 Terrible Towels, told 45 different Steelers stories and had to explain the difference between Coach Cower and Bill Belichick 50 times. I loved every second. Some of the nicest people we've come across on the Journey can be linked back to our time in Tampa Bay at Beef "O" Brady's.

Next up was Cooter's. This place was very cool. It was located on the water which meant an awesome ocean breeze would find its way underneath your skin, followed by that beach smell that you can't quite describe but that makes you smile every time it greets you. I love restaurants on the water, and now here was a Steelers bar on the water. It was maybe 8,000 square feet, with (I'm guessing) 1,500 feet walled off for Steelers fans only. Obviously, the owner was a Steelers fan and needed a little section for his team. It was painted Black & Gold and had incredible sports memorabilia wherever your eye wandered. I could be a regular here. Everything on the menu was swimming in water that morning, including the gator bites. Just an awesome place to watch a game or hang out with your friends. I will go out of my way to visit Cooters next time I'm in town.

Great White Grill, our paths will cross again. We've traveled over 3,000 miles checking out Steelers establishments throughout the country. I regret not getting the opportunity to hang out and hear the story of the Great White Grill.

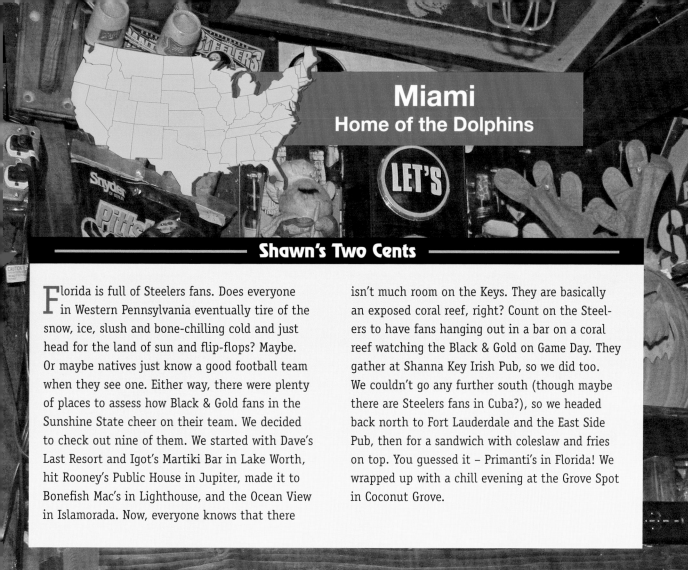

Miami
Home of the Dolphins

LET'S

Shawn's Two Cents

Florida is full of Steelers fans. Does everyone in Western Pennsylvania eventually tire of the snow, ice, slush and bone-chilling cold and just head for the land of sun and flip-flops? Maybe. Or maybe natives just know a good football team when they see one. Either way, there were plenty of places to assess how Black & Gold fans in the Sunshine State cheer on their team. We decided to check out nine of them. We started with Dave's Last Resort and Igot's Martiki Bar in Lake Worth, hit Rooney's Public House in Jupiter, made it to Bonefish Mac's in Lighthouse, and the Ocean View in Islamorada. Now, everyone knows that there isn't much room on the Keys. They are basically an exposed coral reef, right? Count on the Steelers to have fans hanging out in a bar on a coral reef watching the Black & Gold on Game Day. They gather at Shanna Key Irish Pub, so we did too. We couldn't go any further south (though maybe there are Steelers fans in Cuba?), so we headed back north to Fort Lauderdale and the East Side Pub, then for a sandwich with coleslaw and fries on top. You guessed it – Primanti's in Florida! We wrapped up with a chill evening at the Grove Spot in Coconut Grove.

DAVE'S LAST RESORT & RAW BAR

632 Lake Avenue
Lake Worth, Fl 33460
(561) 588-5208
www.daveslastresort.com

Dave's Last Resort & Raw Bar was our first stop on the East Coast of Florida. It gave off a distinct Florida vibe with a fishing motif and other beach decorations. Upon closer inspection, however, we knew it was a Steelers hangout. There were Steelers banners and signs hanging throughout the place.

The first person we met was Wes, the executive chef. He apologized for Dave's absence. Dave had flown to Pittsburgh for the game. No apologies necessary! Wes told us that Dave was originally from Aliquippa and that his partner, Mark, was from Moon. Dave's Last Resort has been a Steelers hangout for the past 14 years and the crowds continue to grow.

We asked Wes what he thought the most interesting piece of memorabilia was. He directed us to a very old

Terrible Towel hanging on the wall. A friend of Dave's had done some work on Art Senior's car in the 1980s. After completing the work, he detailed the car and found a Terrible Towel tucked under one of the seats. Mr. Rooney gave the towel to Dave's friend when he finished the work. Now it is proudly hanging on the wall at the Last Resort.

When we were ready for food we asked Wes for his recommendation. He had created the menu and he advised us to go for the seafood casserole. We did, and have to say it was incredible.

Beer Note: To go with the meal, I ordered a Category 3 IPA from Due South Brewing. I was not familiar with the Due South, located in Boynton Beach, Florida, but after the Category 3, I am eager to learn more. This is a very good IPA (rating – "4") and can see why it is popular. I later learned that this was the first beer produced by Due South and leads the strong lineup from this brewer.

"Martiki" aptly describes the place. It is a combination of a martini bar and a tiki hut, with a very South Pacific design and a completely open-air bar. You've got to like the fact that you can head to Igot's Martiki and Dave's Last Resort and, no matter what kind of Steelers fans are in your group, Dave and Mark have got you covered!

✦ ✦
IGOT'S MARTIKI BAR

704 Lake Avenue
Lake Worth, FL 33460
(561) 582-4468

As we looked across the street while sitting in Dave's Last Resort we saw Igot's Martiki Bar and noticed that a large man behind the bar was wearing a Steeler's jersey. We asked and were told that Dave and Mark owned Igot's as well and that Steelers fans also hang out there to watch the game. Igot's does not have a kitchen, but it does have menus. The orders are sent across the street to Dave's, where Wes and his team prepare all the food and deliver it back across the street to the patrons at Igot's.

So why have two places right across the street from each other, both of which cater to Steelers fans? Well, Dave's Last Resort is a family friendly place. Igot's is 21-and-over only and allows smoking. And Igot's is open later so Steelers fans can celebrate into the early morning hours.

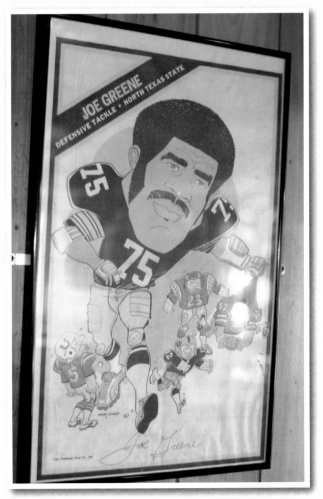

Beer Note: Of course we ordered Rooney's Old Irish Ale, and it tasted much better sitting in the pub than it did in the parking lot in Jacksonville. I think the difference is that this style of beer works when it is served on draft at the proper temperature. Too many bottled beers are kept on ice and served immediately, while they are too cold. Many beers, especially Irish ales, should be served at cellar temperature (i.e., the temperature in a cellar) – between 54 and 57 degrees. The rating is still a solid "3," but I recommend a draft.

We sat in an alcove off the main bar and it could be the best place we've found on our trip to watch the game with just a few friends. There was a big, heavy wooden table that would seat 6-8 people and a fireplace and your own private TV. It was perfect... until the baby lion appeared. As we watched the game we noticed that every few minutes the picture would disappear and the logo of the TV manufacturer (in this case, a baby lion) would appear. The hostess apologized and just gave us the remote. We just needed to press a button every few minutes to keep the lion away. There's got to be a metaphor in there somewhere, but I'm not sure what it is.

✦ ✦ ✦
ROONEY'S PUBLIC HOUSE, THE GASTROPUB

1153 Town Center Drive
Jupiter, FL 33458
(561) 694-6610
www.rooneyspublichouse.com

This stop was one we'd been looking forward to for the entire Journey. We were headed to Rooney's Public House, the Gastropub. As with most Irish pubs, Rooney's has a warm and inviting atmosphere and an incredibly friendly staff. The Steelers décor is understated, but the items on display are very cool. One entire wall is dedicated to The Chief – Art Rooney, Senior. There are original photographs and other unique memorabilia from the era when he made the Steelers great. This includes the first team picture of the Pittsburgh Football Pirates.

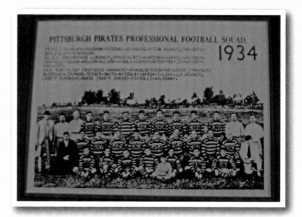

atmosphere on this afternoon. Fans from both sides were very loud in their support of their teams and it was a fun time. Bonefish Mac's has been a favorite Steelers hangout for the past 10 years, even though there isn't an organized fan base there.

As we were watching the game, we started up a conversation with the couple at the next table. They were both decked out in their Sunday best – Black & Gold. I asked Ken where he was from. He originally hailed from Lower Burrell but had retired in Florida. Because our neighbor Don (our guest on the trip to Buffalo) has one of his offices (Lamparski Orthodontics) in Lower Burrell, I figured I'd ask Ken if he knew Don. As it turns out, Ken was a golfing buddy of Don's father. An amazing coincidence, but the story got even better: Ken was a real estate agent in Lower Burrell and had sold Don and his wife Alycia their first home. Crazy. Pittsburgh is such a small city with such a huge reach. Ken then asked us if we were going to the OV. He said it was a must-see in the Keys. We told him that was our next stop and we headed out the door.

◆ ◆
BONEFISH MAC'S SPORTS GRILLE

2002 East Sample Rd
Lighthouse, FL 33064
(954) 781-6227
www.bonefishmacs.com

The next stop in the Sunshine State was Bonefish Mac's Sports Grille. Bonefish Mac's has an outstanding outdoor bar area that is perfect for watching the game. For those Pittsburghers not yet used to the sun, there is also a large indoor circular bar and dining area. The bar seemed to be split equally between the Dolphins and the Steelers, which made for a great

THE OCEAN VIEW PUB

Mile Marker 84.5
Islamorada, FL 33036
(305) 664-8052
www.theocean-view.com

Heading south, the first thing we noticed was the strange address of the Ocean View as we tried to enter it into the GPS – a mile marker. We figured that since there is only one road in and one road out of the Keys we'd be able to find it.

The Ocean View Pub, or the "OV" as the locals know it, is owned by former Steelers player Gary Dunn (1976-87). For those of you who are as GPS-challenged as were we, it's on the right hand side as you head south through the Keys. As you pull up, notice the sign outside the bar stating that it was the first establishment in Monroe County to be granted a liquor license. Head through the doors and you will see the connection to the Steelers right away, with all the

cool pieces from the '70s and '80s adorning the walls. The bar seemed very empty, then we realized that the inside bar was not the main bar at the OV. Out back there is a covered porch with a second bar. Given the great weather and fresh air in the Keys, this is where all the cool kids sit. We pulled up chairs and nobody kicked us out. The OV also has a few guest rooms, a pool and an outdoor fire pit. And there's a small stage with a high top table. Gary hosts a "live" weekly radio show. He invited Josh to stay for the show but we needed to press on with our Journey.

One of the patrons at the bar, Captain Dennis, told us an amazing tale about the OV. We had noticed that the OV was on the Gulf side of the road and that there was no discernable view of the ocean. Captain Dennis said that Hurricane Donna, which hit the Keys in 1960, was so powerful that it actually lifted the OV structure and pushed it across the road to the Gulf side. Rather than move it back, a few repairs were made and the OV had a new home and a new Gulf view. Nobody bothered to change the name. We did not Google the story to check its veracity. Why destroy the romance?

✦ ✦ ✦
SHANNA KEY IRISH PUB

1900 Flagler Avenue
Key West, FL 33040
(305) 295-8880
www.shannakeyirishpub.com

After the stop in Islamorada, we continued south to Key West. Never doubt that Steelers fans can be found even on the southernmost point of the continental United States. For the past 10 years, the Shanna Key Irish Pub has been home to Steelers fans in Key West. Fair warning though, the pub also caters to another type of football fan – European football. Leeds United is the favorite side.

We were surprised to discover that, unlike so many others, the owner of the Shanna Key did not have a personal connection to Pittsburgh. Instead, it was his customers who fostered the connection with the Steelers. The owner is originally from Ireland and is also a fishing boat captain. Many of his charter clients were either from Pittsburgh or supported the Steelers. When he opened the Shanna Key, naturally

he created a place for his fishing clients to watch the games. Word spread and more fans started showing up. On Game days, they now have 50+ fans for the games. It's the only place to be in the Keys. As we spoke he made a comment that really resonated with us after spending time with so many Steelers fans on our Journey. He said, "Pittsburgh is a lot like Ireland. Everyone becomes a bigger fan of the place after they leave."

Once you get past the Leeds United flag, there are Terrible Towel flags lining the walls, all signed by former Steelers players who have stopped in to see how fans in Key West enjoy the games. As we approached the bar, there was a towel and pen waiting for Josh to add his signature to the list.

The other interesting aspect of the bar is the little "room" at the end. It's almost as if someone wanted to have a living room in the bar. There are three walls and a doorway leading to a comfortable sitting area. Of course there is also a window where drinks can be handed in directly from the bar. Perfect!

♦ ♦ ♦

EAST SIDE PUB

2376 N. Federal Hwy
Ft. Lauderdale, FL 33305
(954) 566-0001
www.eastsidepubfl.com

After hitting Key West, we headed back up to Fort Lauderdale. Like many places in Florida, Fort Lauderdale is covered with huge strip malls so we weren't sure what to expect from this Steelers hangout. We were reassured once we walked in the door. It was like being transported back to the 'Burgh (with better weather). Right inside the door is an enormous collage of Steelers fans proudly sporting the Black & Gold. The Steelers memorabilia does not stop there. Almost every inch of wall space is covered with unique items celebrating the proud Steelers tradition, with a few notable exceptions. The owner Michelle is a rock 'n' roll fan. If you visit the East Side Pub, take note of the Led Zeppelin and Tom Petty pieces, as well as the Rolling Stone guitar.

The large center bar creates a very friendly atmosphere and we joined the locals for an afternoon beverage. The beer selection was adequate but lacking in craft beer. Settling for a Yuengling ("3"), this visit was more about the memorabilia and the fans. Jackie, the bartender, told us we were lucky to come on a non-Game Day. Lucky? She said that it is so crowded during games that we would not have gotten a seat and no one would have any time to talk to us, they would all be too busy serving the fans.

Then we saw one of our favorite items on the trip. On a shelf high over the bar stood the bust of Darth Vader. Sort of. This one donned a Polamalu wig and a Steelers hard hat. It was one of the coolest creations we have seen.

Feeling like insurance salesmen, we ended the visit in typical fashion – asking for referrals. A guy across the bar spoke up. He said he was not from Pittsburgh but was a Steelers fan. It turned out that his disclaimer was entirely unnecessary after his next comment. He told us that we should go to "Pre A Montes." Being the fastidious note taker, I just spelled it phonetically and asked for directions. He told us that all the Pittsburghers hung out there. We were shocked that we had not discovered this place on our own. Of course, when he described the specialty sandwich served, we knew exactly the place he was talking about. Primanti Bros. It was already on our list.

◆ ◆ ◆
PRIMANTI BROS.
901 North Atlantic Blvd.
Fort Lauderdale, FL 33304
(954) 565-0605
www.primantibros.com

We laughed about the odd South Florida pronunciation of the famous Pittsburgh sandwich shop. Then it occurred to us that we needed to be careful about making disparaging remarks about regional speech patterns. Pittsburghers had their own problems with non-English words: "North Versailles" and "Dubois" immediately come to mind. There are three Primanti Bros. in South Florida and we were aiming to hit the one right on the beach.

We grabbed a table by the window. It was a gorgeous, warm sunny day in December. We ordered the # 2 Best Seller (The Pitts-burger) and of course had to wash it down with the #1 Best Seller (Iron City – rating "2"). The sandwich was perfect! The beer... not so much. On this trip we've been fortunate enough to sample some of the best beers in America, if not the world. Each city has its own unique breweries and we've been able to enjoy quite a few. Consequently, I might be spoiled, which might account for the lower rating for Iron.

While we were enjoying a taste of Pittsburgh, we asked about the Steelers fans and Game Days. As one might expect, it's standing room only. The beach location is not as large as Primanti's other places; so many of the regulars opt for the larger venues with better viewing options. That said, there is something about watching the Steelers on TV while having the ocean breeze blowing over your shoulder. You can't lose in any case.

We have experienced a number of "Primanti" style sandwiches on our Journey, but this is the first time we've had the real thing. We found out that the owner, Eric, was a longtime employee in Pittsburgh. He took the entire experience south for the winter and decided to stay. We are grateful that he made such a wise decision (and so are all the other Steelers fans in Florida).

other quality craft brews on tap). This was the point where The Grove Spot went from a nice bar to a great one. The beer was served in a Laguntias mason jar. In my opinion, any establishment that serves beer in the proper glass (style and branding) is head and shoulders above the competition. The beer is rated a "4" but The Grove Spot gets a "5" for serving it in the right glass at the correct temperature. Cheers!

In talking to the bartender, we had to ask, "How did a nice place like this become a Steelers hangout?" As with many movements throughout history, it takes just one person to start a revolution. One of the longtime patrons, Amy, was a die-hard Steelers fan. She would come in every week and insist that the game be put on the TV. Eventually, more and more Steelers fans started to show up to watch the games. Now the game is on every TV in the place on Game Days.

✦ ✦
THE GROVE SPOT

3324 Virginia Street
Coconut Grove, FL 33133
(305) 774-6696
www.grovespot.com

The final stop in Miami was The Grove Spot in Coconut Grove. The Grove Spot has a simple elegance to the place. Of course, as with many other bars we've visited on this Journey, it also has a real neighborhood feel to it. While we were sitting at the bar, a regular came in and his drink was waiting for him. He was from Pittsburgh (the South Hills) and was as friendly as one would expect.

Beer Note: As you know by now, I have a weakness for Lagunitas IPA. When I saw that it was on draft, it was a simple selection (although there were

The Grove Spot has created a new category of Steelers hangout. This is the #1 Steelers Date Night/Afternoon Bar – a perfect place to hang out with your significant other!

Dave's Last Resort & Raw Bar set the mood for this East Coast Florida swing. It was tropical, with pastel colors everywhere and seashells and sand splattered all over the walls. But there was Steelers memorabilia on the walls too, as if they had been washed up by the sea and just landed there. There were old Terrible Towels, faded Steelers jerseys and plenty of helmets that looked like they'd spent years inside a whale's belly. I'd loved this place the moment I'd stepped into it 10 years earlier. I've had a home in Florida for about 15 years, about 20 minutes from this place. I spent a few afternoons and had too many Loose Gooses there over that period of time. Of course I learned something new, that the same guys owned Igots Martiki Bar across the street. Igots is adults only whereas Dave's is family friendly. That explains why I never made it to Igots – I always had a child in hand and my beautiful wife by my side. This is definitely one of the better places on the planet to watch the Steelers in flip-flops.

Rooney's Pub. I've visited Rooney's a number of times; it's within walking distance of my home. Not a better place to watch a Steelers game than in Rooney's. I mean, think about it, the Rooneys own the Pittsburgh Steelers – how can you not think this is the best place to watch a game? It's like watching a game in their home. Obviously, this place is covered with sports memorabilia that only an owner would be able to get his hands on. You will find Steelers fans here wall to wall. (The food

is great and, again, win or lose, there's a beautiful sunset and the weather is 70 degrees. Everyone walks or stumbles away happy.

Bonefish Mac's was a pleasant surprise. Not only did I have something on a Kaiser roll that was swimming an hour and a half ago, but I also had one of the best Loose Gooses on this Journey. And we were in yet another Florida bar packed with Steelers fans. We're finding that Florida has the largest number of Steelers fans of any other state. They are the same kind of fans we find everywhere else, but the Florida Steelers fan has no problem wearing flip flops and is usually wearing a jeans shorts and a sleeveless shirt (the kind with ripped sleeves) or a Hawaiian shirt. And even if they've lived in Florida for a number of years, they are usually red and burnt rather than tanned.

The Ocean View – now we were sneaking into the Keys. Not a bad place to sneak into. Chain restaurants and chain hotels are not welcome in the Keys. Everything is mom and pop stores. This is the place where people can be worth $8 or $40 million and you would never know the difference. Islamorada is the start of the Keys and you may ask yourself how there could be a Steelers place there? Well it's the simple business mantra – supply and demand. A ton of Steelers fans live and vacation in the Keys. Former Steeler Gary Dunn loved the Keys so much that he bought the Ocean View. The OV has a very laid back feel to it. It's got great sports memorabilia on the walls but the main attraction is out back – two great bars with a huge fire pit built into the sand – with TVs hanging underneath tiki hut rooftops. If you blink, you've lost four hours of your life. This place was in my top five of enjoyment.

We are trekking through Florida while it snowed 18 inches in Pittsburgh; what's not to love? I've been waking up and going for nice long runs on the beach. The Shanna Key Irish Pub – Key West was a memorable visit. They cater to Steelers fans and anyone from Ireland. Needless to say that drinking and having fun are top priorities for anyone who walks through the doors. Like any other great Steelers place, the sports memorabilia was second to none and the service was fantastic. I do remember a story our bartender told us while we were there. I think it describes the Keys perfectly. She told us about a patron that hadn't worn any kind of shoes in the last eight months. Apparently, he has one pair and he only puts them on when someone dies and he has to wear a suit and go to a funeral. So there you have it, welcome to the Keys.

Cincinnati
Home of the Bengals

Shawn's Two Cents

We headed to Cincinnati in mid-December. The air was turning cold, winter was upon us and it felt like football weather. We had three bars to check out, the Fox and Hound, O'Malley's in the Alley and Martino's on Vine. We were looking forward to an easy drive and I was excited to check out the craft beer in Cincinnati. We had a full crew – Georgie Boy and Abbey were along for the ride.

We were filming for the Big Board.

Of course we were driving the RV. We wanted to make sure that everyone in Cincinnati saw that the Black & Gold and Always a Home Game crew were rolling into town. Let's just say that the Bengals fans noticed us and did not greet us with open arms. Perhaps they sensed impending doom: by day's end, the Steelers defeated the Bengals 30-20.

WEEK 1	SEP 8	TITANS	1:00pm	WEEK 10	NOV 10	BILLS
WEEK 2	SEP 16	@BENGALS	8:40pm	WEEK 11	NOV 17	LIONS
WEEK 3	SEP 22	BEARS	8:30pm	WEEK 12	NOV 24	@BROWNS
WEEK 4	SEP 29	@VIKINGS	1:00pm	WEEK 13	NOV 28	@RAVENS
WEEK 5		BYE		WEEK 14	DEC 8	DOLPHINS
WEEK 6	OCT 13	@JETS	1:00pm	WEEK 15	DEC 15	BENGALS
WEEK 7	OCT 20	RAVENS	4:25pm	WEEK 16	DEC 22	@PACKER
WEEK 8	OCT 27	@RAIDERS	4:05pm	WEEK 17	DEC 29	BROWNS
WEEK 9	NOV 3	@PATRIOTS	4:25pm			

✦ ✦
FOX AND HOUND

5113 Bowen Drive
Mason, OH 45040
(513) 229-7921
www.foxandhound.com

The first stop in Cincinnati was the Fox and Hound (definitely the most popular of the national chains of sports bars for Steelers fans.) The Fox and Hound is very large and has separate viewing areas. As we started to run through our drink order and Josh was asking about the quality of their Loose Goose, the server stopped Josh in mid-sentence. She said that she did NOT make a good drink, but she knew who could. She introduced us to Carley (aka Culinary Carley), saying she made the best Loose Goose in town. Guessing by the look on Josh's face and the fact that he quietly enjoyed his drink, he must have agreed! One more indelible memory along our Journey.

Beer Note: The craft beer scene in Cincinnati is thriving – unlike their NFL team. Rhinegeist Brewery

leads the way. Rhinegeist means "ghost of the Rhine" and refers to the physical modern brewery that was built within the skeleton of the old Moerlein bottling plant (built in 1895) in the historic brewery district in the Over the Rhine neighborhood of Cincinnati. At the turn of the century, the neighborhood had nearly 45,000 inhabitants, most of them of German descent. There were 38 breweries. As a hophead, I love their brewing philosophy, which is to brew hoppy/sessionable beers where "the first sip calls for the third." I ordered the Truth IPA (not exactly a session beer at 7.2% ABV). This is a very aggressively hopped IPA, but not so much that you feel like you've been punched in the face with a handful of grass. Nicely balanced with a smooth finish. Rating – "4." The distribution is limited, so if you see one, order it.

The Fox and Hound gives the faithful Black & Gold fans a private viewing room for the weekly games. As it turns out, Cincinnati is one of the "angriest" cities on our Journey, and there are routinely conflicts in the city – not just in the Fox and Hound, but everywhere when the game is on the schedule. Our server felt that the Bengals fans want a rivalry, but the team is not good enough to merit such hostility from Steelers fans. She told us something that we heard time and again. Steelers fans are very serious when it comes to watching the play. They arrive wearing Black & Gold (Pittsburgh fans wear more branded merchandise than fans from any other team, regardless of the sport) and they do not like to be disturbed during the game. The servers only go to the tables during commercial breaks and respect the fans...just like the fans respect the team. Come Game Day, tables often have three generations of fans gathered together.

that we were #1. As one would expect from Bengals fans, just like the Ravens fans, they just weren't smart enough to use the correct finger. The second thing, there were hundreds of Santa Claus lookalikes wandering the streets.

It seems there was a Santa pub-crawl going on this weekend. Apparently it is a national event done to raise money for a charity – and a perfect opportunity to sing X-rated Christmas carols. This is not an event for children!

It made for an interesting visit to O'Malley's in the Alley. It literally is in an alley, just off one of the main streets in downtown Cincinnati. A few dozen drunken Santas joined us as we headed inside. That's when we discovered the Christmas carols. The small bar was packed, but we spotted the Steelers fans in the crowd. There were a number of "elves" dressed in Black & Gold caps and they welcomed us into the holiday chaos. They explained that the group of Steelers fans at O'Malley's is not large, but are among the most loyal (and apparently festive) fans in the city. After a brief conversation, and feeling like we were in the middle of a crazy nightmare, we quickly moved on to Martino's on Vine.

✦ ✦
O'MALLEY'S IN THE ALLEY

25 Ogden Place
Cincinnati, OH 45202
(513) 381-3114
www.omalleysinthealley.com

As we headed from the safe confines of Mason to the downtown area we couldn't help but notice two things on our jaunt around Cincinnati. First, Bengals fans really do hate the Steelers. We drove the RV around the streets of downtown and were told, once again,

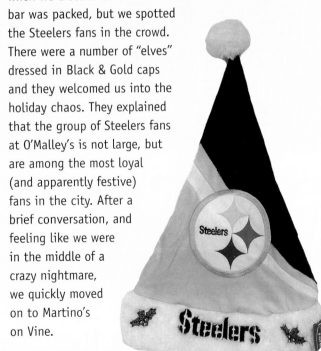

--- ◆ ◆ ◆ ---
MARTINO'S ON VINE

2618 Vine Street
Cincinnati, OH 45219
(513) 221-8487
www.martinosonvine

Martino's has been on our radar for months now and we were excited to have finally arrived on "short Vine" in the Uptown area of the city. We had learned about this Steelers hangout from Kim Marie Angiulli, a Pittsburgh Realtor. She said her family ran one of the best Steelers restaurants in the country and that when we got to Cincinnati, we needed to find Martin. After getting to Martino's we realized the problem with her tip – she didn't specify which Martino. All three Martys were there to greet us at the door. For the record, this would be Martin II, Martin III and Martin IV – like European royalty, right? But after visiting Martino's, you will realize that it is actually Black & Gold royalty.

Walking into Martino's is like walking into a Steelers memorabilia shop. Every wall is covered with Black & Gold, displaying over 40 years of dedication to the Steelers, with signed pieces from every generation of Steelers teams – from the Steel Curtain to the Super Bowl XLIII Championship Team of 2008. When we commented on the collection and its amazing diversity, Marty II quickly told us they only had room for a fraction of the collection. It would take days to see the entire collection stockpiled upstairs.

Beer Note: Our visit to Martino's coincided with another Big Board video, so the place was packed. After fighting through the crowd to get to the bar, I ordered a beer from Cleveland, The Great Lakes Elliott Ness Amber Lager – a great example of the Amber Lager. This beer has won no less than 12 medals at international beer festivals, including 9 gold medals at the World Beer Championships. Though it is not a local Cincinnati beer, I could not pass up the opportunity to enjoy this excellent lager. Rating – "4."

Sitting down with Martin II, we asked about the restaurant and how he ended up in Cincinnati. He explained that the family has another restaurant in Ford City, PA, which is also a great place to watch a Steelers game. When Martin III attended the University of Cincinnati, the family spent years traveling to the "Queen City." Marty IV was conceived in the Queen City and the decision was made to make the move to the Queen City permanent. It was in need of a fine Italian restaurant, and a great place for Steelers fans to congregate. Martino's on Vine was born.

Off to Cincinnati for a Big Board game. We had Georgie Boy and Abbey Way along. The entire Always a Home Game team was locked and loaded in the RV that we have grown to love and hate. I am sure Cincinnati is a wonderful place to live and raise a family. I'm also quite positive that Cincinnati has beautiful places. On the other hand...I can't tell you how many NFL games I've played in Cincinnati, but I can tell you whatever that number is, I have never been more verbally abused in any stadium than here in sweet old Cincinnati. I would get crushed from pre-game all the way to the end of the game. It was as if the city would make announcements all week reminding Cincinnati Bengals fans, "If you're going to the game, please don't forget to verbally abuse Josh Miller. He'll be wearing number 4 and hanging out by his kicking net." It was really something. I remember a game in Cincinnati where this guy wouldn't stop yelling, screaming and cursing at me all game long. Usually, after they get a couple F-bombs off their chest they will go back to watching the game. Then after our offense stalls and I punt the football on 4th down, it would remind

them again to start yelling at me. There was one day, though, that was different than most other days. This guy didn't stop the entire game. I finally turned around, because that's usually what they want you to do – and I was shocked. This guy had his 10-year-old son by his side the entire game. Wow, talk about your role models. I do remember going up to the kid with two minutes left in the game and handing him a football. I told him, "When you're 17 you can move out, you know." I also told him, "You're better than that."

Anyway, it's a Big Board game today and I will be among the Black & Gold. We first hit Fox and

Hound, a normal sports chain restaurant, not really a Steelers-only destination, but sometimes it's best to travel in numbers. That's exactly what they do at the Fox and Hound. Steelers fans gather like a swarm of bees and take over this place and then vanish after the game. I also will say that I had one of the better Loose Gooses and that always scores points with me.

O'Malley's in the Alley was a pretty cool bar, but it was a strange experience for me. Being a little Jewish kid from New Jersey and not really celebrating Christmas until I got married and got my kids christened, I now found myself in a weird dream. There must have been 700 Santas inside, outside and all around O'Malley's. Talk about being outnumbered. I felt like a Jewish spy flying under the radar, hoping I wouldn't be detected. It was crazy but it seemed like fun. O'Malley's in the Alley was definitely a Steelers joint. Any time they give you your own floor, whether it's downstairs in the basement or upstairs in the attic, it's a win. It just

shows you, no matter what city you're in, there will always be safety in numbers if you're a Steelers fan. They certainly had numbers at O'Malley's.

Finally, Martino's on Vine. This was the reason we traveled to Cincinnati in the first place. Not only was this a Big Board game, it was also a nationally televised game. We needed an electric atmosphere, tons of Steelers fans in a place that looked like it was on the North Shore. We needed to make a statement on the national stage. We needed everybody to be on his or her "A" game to get some great film to send back to Heinz Field. We found it at Martino's on Vine.

Martino's could very well be in the top three in sports memorabilia. Talk about one-of-a-kind type of items that are signed by the player or coach – this place had everything. And it had great fans. We handed out towels to everybody and we didn't have to ask twice to get the group fired up and loud. That's the good thing about night games or even late afternoon games. Everybody's been sitting around the house all day looking forward to cheering on the Black & Gold.

Martino's had it all. Great food, great atmosphere, friendly and knowledgeable Steelers fans, and the topper – great ownership from top to bottom. It almost made me forget how much I didn't like Cincinnati...until we made it back to our Steelers RV and someone drove by and told us where we could drive that RV. Can't get home quickly enough!

Green Bay
Home of the Packers

Shawn's Two Cents

Trying to fit all the NFL cities into one NFL season without the luxury of a team plane is a bit difficult. It makes for long road trips. As our Journey was winding down, we prepared ourselves for one that made more sense when we were planning things in August when it was sunny and hot than it did now in the last days before Christmas. We drove from Pittsburgh to Green Bay and its surrounding areas, then to Minneapolis, then back to Pittsburgh, all in three days and all in blizzard conditions. I think we covered more than 2,000 miles. I can't even begin to calculate how many cups of coffee we drank. I know that as soon as we got back to Pittsburgh in the early hours of Monday morning, Josh had to go on the radio and I had a job interview (thankfully, I did NOT smell like a bar) – then I was driving to South Carolina for Christmas vacation (okay, so I slept and my wife drove).

As much as we griped about the drive on our way to Green Bay, we had a great time at Quaker Steak, Wilson's Bar and the Capitol Center. We found really down to earth people, some great hangouts and, oh yeah, snow.

✦ ✦ ✦
QUAKER STEAK & LUBE

4900 S. Moorland Rd.
New Berlin, WI 45151
(262) 754-9090
www.thelube.com

One of the questions we are constantly asked on this Journey is, "Do you think every NFL team could write the same book?" The answer is a resounding "NO," with one exception. There are a number of factors that make the Steelers fans one of the greatest in the world. The team has a tremendous winning tradition. The region was a stronghold of industry for decades, but as the country moved away from heavy manufacturing the region slipped economically (of course, we've come back, baby!), fans dispersed across the country spreading Black & Gold fever. Finally, the weather is not so great... many fans have opted to move to different regions for nicer weather or other employment opportunities. One thing is clear – wherever they go they take their love of the Steelers with

them. All of these factors can be said for the Green Bay Packers too. It's the only team that maybe has as widespread a fan base as the Pittsburgh Steelers, though clearly a distant second.

Understandably, then, Wisconsin was the most difficult region in which to find Steelers fans. They were there; we just had to look a bit harder. The first stop was at another Western Pennsylvania favorite, the Quaker Steak & Lube. Early on a Sunday morning, we showed up to a tremendous buffet. Josh suggested that they rename the buffet the Loose Goose buffet. Everything you can imagine to make a great morning cocktail was available.

Beer Note: The beer was also special. When most people think of beer from Wisconsin, they think

Milwaukee and mass-produced, watered-down lagers. Growing up, I always though Laverne and Shirley inspected every beer made in Milwaukee! Yet Wisconsin is home to New Glarus brewing, an award-winning brewery that espouses that beer should be served fresh and made with local ingredients. New Glarus only sells beer in the State of Wisconsin. The marketing tag line is "Drink Indigenous, Only in Wisconsin!" The "Beer of the Day" – a great marketing promotion at Quaker Steak & Lube – was the New Glarus Spotted Cow, a Cream Ale reminiscent of cask-conditioned farmhouse ale. The brewer leaves some of the yeast in the bottles, making for a cloudy, or creamy appearance and enhancing the flavor of this lightly hopped ale. Not being a tremendous fan of this style, the rating is a "3," but I expect that anyone not a hophead would love this light fruity beer. One of the recommended pairings for the beer is wings and we were in the best spot in town for those.

In an attempt to fight the bitter Wisconsin weather, we opted for some dusted habañero wings. They were excellent and brought a little fire to a cold morning. After paying, we went in search of the Steelers Room. The "garage" is an area where the windows (roll-up garage doors) can be opened in warmer weather. Hanging from the ceiling was a huge Steelers flag and there was memorabilia on every wall.

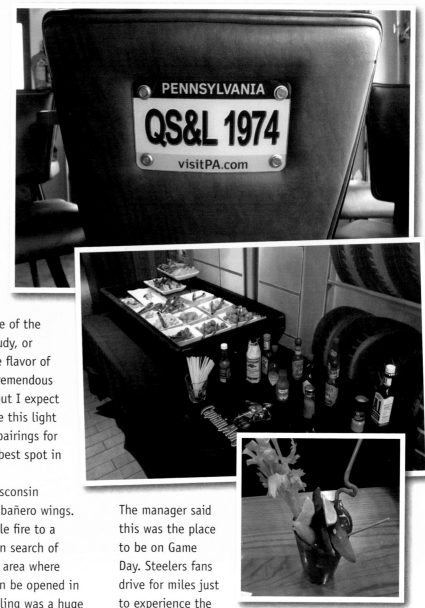

The manager said this was the place to be on Game Day. Steelers fans drive for miles just to experience the camaraderie of watching the game at Quaker Steak.

The next stop on our way to Green Bay was Wilson's Bar. Wilson's is a combination college bar and neighborhood bar. The slogan reads, "Where everyone knows your name." Wilson's has been a Steelers hangout since the days of the six-foot satellite dish. Back when Wilson's opened in 1985, the Steelers were struggling, yet the fans still showed up in huge numbers to watch the games. Today, there are a lot of Packers fans here, too, but the Black & Gold supporters are just as loud and just as passionate. According to the owner, no other team comes as close to the out-of-town support that the Steelers get.

Beer Note: The beer selection at Wilson's was excellent and we decided to enjoy a few pints. The first was Kiss the Lips IPA from Lake Louis Brewing Company. Lake Louis is located in Arena, WI. Kiss the Lips is a traditional American IPA and deserves a rating of "3." The bartender told us that the beer was named after a classic Vince Gill country song, "It's Hard to Kiss The Lips At Night That Chew Your Ass Out All Day Long." Almost enough to change the rating to a "4," but not quite. Now if it was named after a Donny Iris or Joe Grushecky song... The next local beer selection was Hopalicious from Ale Asylum in Madison. This beer reminded me of one of my favorite Pale Ales, Dale's. A "4." Wanting to learn more about the brewery and this excellent Pale, I went to the website and read the following description. They called their Hopalicious "unique enough for the connoisseur, approachable enough for the novice, and drinkable to everyone."

The owner came out from behind the bar to sit with us and tell stories of the Steelers fans. The Steelers fans were great people, he said – passionate about the team, but did not hate other teams. They are just educated football fans that love the sport and, win or lose, they bleed Black & Gold. It seems to us he knows the Steelers fans quite well.

✦ ✦

CAPITOL CENTRE

725 W. Capitol Drive
Appleton, WI 54914
www.capitolcentreonline.com

Green Bay gives off a friendly, down to earth impression very similar to that of Pittsburgh. We've been greeted very warmly, regardless of our NFL affiliation. The Capitol Centre was no exception. We arrived later in the evening when the bar was full of locals. They were all interested in the book and started telling us stories of the die-hard Steelers fans that frequented the establishment every Game Day.

There was one about a Steelers fan who started attending games and quickly became one of the leaders of the group. Then he started bringing a girl with him to watch the games. This was great until one day when his wife decided to pay a visit to the Capitol Centre during a game. Quite an argument ensued. The best part of the story was that the other Steelers fans told the couple to go outside and argue – the game was on!

Beer Note: I asked about the local beer and the answer was immediate and unanimous. We needed to sample something from Capital Brewing in Middleton, WI. Capital was awarded 9 medals at the 2013 World Beer Championships, so we decided to go with the flagship beer, the Wisconsin Amber. This is a clean, crisp Amber lager with a strong malt profile and a touch of caramel – definitely a beer that tastes better as the temperature of the beer rises. When served too cold, the richness of the malt is hidden. In most cases, letting the beer come to room temperature is necessary to appreciate the fullness of a beer. Rating – "3."

We started talking about our plans for the evening and the next day. We were going to spend the night in Green Bay and start out for Minneapolis in the morning. But the talk turned to the weather and the projected snowfall. We debated the accuracy of the forecast and the best way for us to make a safe trip across the state. The consensus was that the Green Bay area was going to get 12" of snow and we would be better served to leave immediately and stay ahead of the storm. Directions in hand (we were told not to follow a GPS in this part of Wisconsin), we took off across the frozen tundra.

Driving from Pittsburgh to Green Bay and Minnesota in the summer months would be considered a pain in most people's backsides. Let me now expand your imagination as to what it would be like in the dead of winter. Not to mention of course that I had to be back Monday for my radio show. Out of all our road trips, I would have to say that this one was dangerously close to being dangerous. We drove through the night taking two-hour shifts and getting coffee. Two hours sleeping followed by two hours of driving. When I ask myself, would I let my kids do this? The answer is no way in hell. But that kind of shows you how stupid it was. Oh well, we made it. Shawn and I really built a lot of trust between each other. It doesn't mean much if you die side-by-side, I understand that. Because we didn't, however, I can honestly say that I trust this guy with my life. That trust was tested more than a couple of times on this Journey through Steelers Nation.

I almost played in Green Bay two different times in my career. First time was in 1992. I was a first-team All-American right out of the University of Arizona. They didn't draft me but I signed up as a free agent right after the draft. I showed up in Green Bay scared to death. I remember taking a shower and in came the late Reggie White. I was thinking to myself, please don't let me say anything stupid and please don't let him mistake me for a bar of soap. He is a gigantic man. I got the hell out of there as quick as I could. Green Bay

wasn't meant to be because they cut me 10 days later. So much for first impressions. The second time I almost played for them was 2003. That was when the Pittsburgh Steelers were going to trade me to Green Bay for a seventh round pick. Of course it didn't go down like that. I ended up in New England and moved back to Pittsburgh a few years later. Okay, now let's go back to Green Bay and find out if there are any Steelers hangouts.

Quaker Steak & Lube was a pretty good showing for a chain restaurant. They allowed Steelers fans to take over the patio, which had Steelers signage that they put up regularly. Of course, we are talking about Green Bay and it's 3 degrees outside. They do have heaters, and again, it shows how tough the Steelers fan is.

Wilson's Bar – this was definitely a Steelers place. It reminded me of a secret place to go. I guess you have to keep things secret in this town if you aren't going to be a Packers fan. Everyone in Wilson's stared when we walked in, as if they were making sure we could be trusted before they went on with what they were doing. They were very nice and we ended up spending more time there than we should have.

I'm not sure Capitol Centre was a Steelers hangout, except that people watch Steelers games here – but the owners and regulars we met that freezing night were some of the nicest people we met on this Journey. Lots of laughs and great debates.

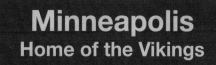

Minneapolis
Home of the Vikings

Doing research for this trip, I learned that Minnesota's name comes from the Dakota word for "clear water." Sounds like Josh's kind of beer.

Usually, when we are doing research on the places Steelers fans gather to watch games, we come across three or four contenders. We try to vet them before the road trip and get a sense of whether they merit a stop by the Always a Home Game crew. In Minneapolis and St. Paul, we had a tough time finding any watering holes for Steelers fans other than Patrick McGovern's Pub. We were worried that we had finally met our match. Maybe our hypothesis – that the Steelers could find fans ANYWHERE they traveled, thus making every away game a home game – was about to be turned on its head. Minnesota was going to defeat us. Then we actually went to Patrick McGovern's Pub. Well, we learned that there was a reason there is only one place that Steelers fans in the area call home. Patrick McGovern's was everything they needed. We left feeling relieved. Our hypothesis was still intact.

♦ ♦
PATRICK MCGOVERN'S PUB

225 7th St. W
St. Paul, MN 55102
(651) 224-5821
www.patmcgoverns.com

The drive from Green Bay to Minneapolis took most of the night, but when we saw the snow during the Steelers pre-game warm-up, we knew that we had made the right decision. Having arrived hours ahead of schedule, we had a few hours to kill that morning. We were lured by the Mall of America (it was across the street from our hotel)! It is even larger than you can imagine. Neither of us are shoppers, so we do not feel qualified to describe the shopping options, but suffice it to say that there were five (that we counted) Foot Locker stores – one of which was specifically designed to sell only basketball shoes. There was also an indoor roller coaster. Although it's slightly embarrassing to admit, it was a pretty cool place.

When it was finally game time, we headed to Patrick McGovern's Pub. As with many of our visits, we were warned that many of the regulars had made the reverse drive the night before and were in attendance at the game. Yet even with the traveling fans, the place was still packed. Signs led us up to the second floor bar area where it was 100% Pittsburgh Steelers. Every table that was not full of fans sporting jerseys from all years had custom made signs reserving the table or barstool for a longtime club member. The Steelers Fans of Minnesota president was away at the game, so we were welcomed by Carla, who explained to us that this was a strong and proud club. She showed us the items available for raffle – what a collection! It was like this for every game, she said. (We donated a few Always a Home Game T-shirts. They offered a special prize (free appetizer) for the person that correctly answered the weekly trivia question. Carla smiled at Josh and asked him if he would be willing to read the question at halftime. Always obliging, Josh agreed, but we needed to visit the bar first!

It was time to see how a Loose Goose was made in Minnesota. It arrived alongside a small beer. At first I thought Josh was playing a trick on me with such a small beer. Then we learned that this was a "snit." In Minnesota, it is customary to serve a snit with a Loose Goose. When in Rome...

Beer Note: I asked about my favorite Minnesota brewery, Surly Brewing Co. When in Denver for the Great American Beer Festival, I sampled Surly and really enjoyed the beer lineup. I was equally impressed with the marketing tag line, "Beer for a glass, from a can." This won me over and I search out Surly whenever possible. I selected Furious, the American IPA.

This is a tremendously hoppy IPA that is balanced quite nicely with a strong malt base. Furious is a "4" (oh so close to a "5"), and should be on everyone's "beer bucket list."

We then tried an open-faced turkey sandwich, one of the house specialties. It was fantastic! Next, we were given a bowl of wrapped chocolates, each in a different Black & Gold design. We would have eaten and drunk ourselves into oblivion, but we had not only a 13-hour drive home (quite a task after the late kickoff and losing an hour due to the time zone change), but

it was almost halftime. Josh was handed the question and immediately he looked uncomfortable. Josh is never one to speak of his accomplishments. He could be getting a huge award for something and he won't tell anyone. You can imagine, then, his discomfort when he was asked to read the following: "What Steelers passing record does Josh Miller hold?" Of course, the answer is that Josh holds the record as the longest touchdown pass by a non-quarterback. The entire crowd got a kick out of Josh reading his own trivia question, but the real surprise came when someone asked the following question, "If the play was so successful, why was it that Coach Cower never called the play again?" In his typical dry sense of humor, Josh replied, "He did, I just changed the play at the line of scrimmage because I did not want to wreck my perfect passer rating."

As the table was cleared during the raffle, we noticed a large trophy/plaque still sitting there. This was the award for the group that raised the most

money for a local food bank. The story goes that another NFL team's fan club (the name will go unmentioned so as to save them from embarrassment in their own backyard) had challenged the Steelers Fans of Minnesota. In line with the proud tradition of the Pittsburgh Steelers, the Steelers Fans of Minnesota rallied and crushed the rival club. They still collect for the food bank on an annual basis. When it comes to giving to charity, the Steelers fans are second to none.

The club has ties to Pittsburgh. It was started by a group of airline mechanics and service personnel that had trained in the Pittsburgh area and then moved back to Minnesota. Of course, the passion for the Steelers still remains. The mailing list is close to 1,000 members and there were 600 members in person for the Super Bowl XVIII victory. The club has been meeting at Patrick McGovern's for six seasons and expects the tradition to continue for many years to come.

Patrick McGovern's Pub was our only stop in Minnesota. We were there to visit Carla and the members of her club. During this Journey we have constantly been reminded of this fan club in Minnesota. They would call, text, tweet and email to make sure we were still coming out and make sure we knew that it would be a worthwhile stop. This had been going on for months so we were anticipating a great visit with Carla and a lot of her happy, thousand-plus Steelers fans. To be honest with you and Minnesota, I was tired at this point in our Journey, but I knew we that if we got there alive and in one piece, it would be worth it. Of course, getting there would be the tricky part. Even Shawn was tired of being positive. Shawn is a few years older than me and he always has a way of turning things around and putting a positive spin on it. No matter what the situation was, there was Shawn spinning it just enough to where it made sense to me in a positive way. God, I hated that. It's a gift, not everyone can do it. And yes, on this trip Shawn was tired as well. But we were glad we persevered.

We were both pleasantly surprised by how cool Patrick McGovern's Pub really was. We walked into a packed house. There were Steelers fans all over the place wearing their favorite players jerseys, eating, drinking and laughing as they've been doing every Sunday for a handful of years. Shawn and I were simply invited to witness a Sunday ritual.

I also love when a Steelers fan club goes out of its way to help others. Whether it's some kind of cook-off or raising the most food for the food bank, the Minnesota Steelers fans seem to answer the call year in and year out.

I'm glad we decided to drive the 13 hours to see these Steelers fans get down in Minnesota on Game Day. This was one of the best bars and fan bases we've come across. This group has an impressive following, a great tradition and a very high football IQ. Educated football fans along with great food and a Loose Goose? Are you kidding me, this was an amazing stop. I could've stayed here all night, but again, Shawn did the math and reminded me that if we didn't leave I would miss my radio show the next day. So long, Minnesota, it was worth the wait and you surpassed my expectations. Thank you and hope to see you guys again soon.

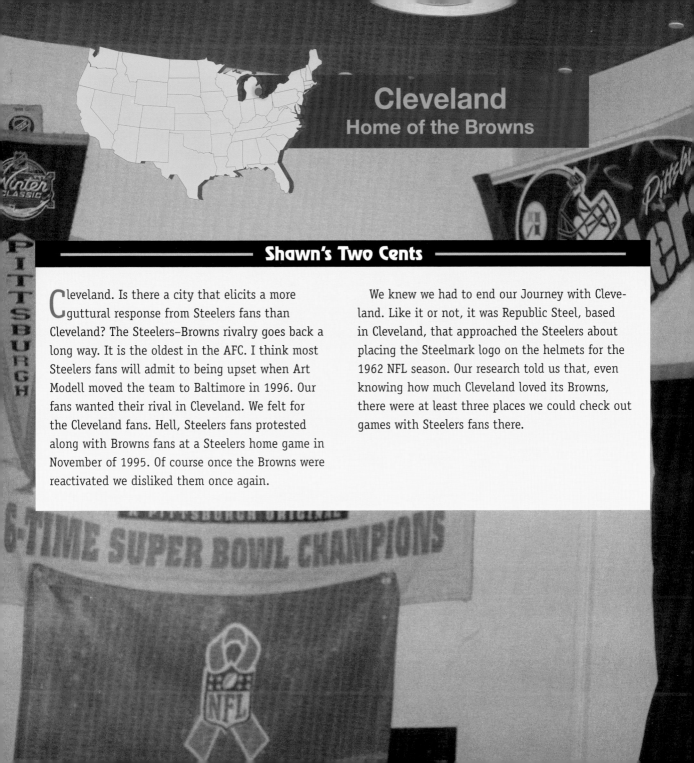

Cleveland
Home of the Browns

Shawn's Two Cents

Cleveland. Is there a city that elicits a more guttural response from Steelers fans than Cleveland? The Steelers–Browns rivalry goes back a long way. It is the oldest in the AFC. I think most Steelers fans will admit to being upset when Art Modell moved the team to Baltimore in 1996. Our fans wanted their rival in Cleveland. We felt for the Cleveland fans. Hell, Steelers fans protested along with Browns fans at a Steelers home game in November of 1995. Of course once the Browns were reactivated we disliked them once again.

We knew we had to end our Journey with Cleveland. Like it or not, it was Republic Steel, based in Cleveland, that approached the Steelers about placing the Steelmark logo on the helmets for the 1962 NFL season. Our research told us that, even knowing how much Cleveland loved its Browns, there were at least three places we could check out games with Steelers fans there.

♦ ♦ ♦

LAKE EFFECTZ

6710 Lake Rd
Madison, OH 44057
(440) 428-5400
www.facebook.com/lake.effectz

We planned to charter a bus to bring Steelers fans to Cleveland to celebrate the final stop on the Always a Home Game Journey. Knowing that the day would be filled with drink and merriment, we decided that bringing the group to more than one bar was perhaps not the best idea. Plus, it's hard to talk to the owners and bartenders and get the skinny on why someplace is a Steelers hangout when you're mobbed by a busload of friends. So...before taking that LAST trip, Josh and I figured out a way to visit a couple of Cleveland bars on our own. We dropped in on our way out to Green Bay (this would sound weird in any other context, but on this Journey, it seemed perfectly acceptable).

In a classic case of erroneously relying on the GPS, we ended up on a dark country road somewhere between Pittsburgh and Cleveland. Out of nowhere, we see a box of reflective tape on the side of the road. Then a number of white lights are bobbing along the road, rapidly approaching. After briefly considering the possibilities that a UFO had landed in the farmland, we remember that we are in Amish country. The reflectors were nothing more than a horse and buggy and the white lights were kids walking along the side of the road with spelunking headlamps. We've been spending way too much time driving.

The first bar was Lake Effectz, and it was a cool Steelers hangout. The circular bar has a huge fireplace and is very inviting. Matt, the bartender, offered up one of the great beers from Cleveland. Steelers fans might think that great beers (and the Rock and Roll Hall of Fame) are one of the only positives to come out of the "Mistake on the Lake." I thoroughly enjoyed the Great Lakes Burning River Pale Ale, an award-winning Pale Ale (11+ medals at beer conventions). It was named for the infamous 1969 burning of the Cuyahoga River.

As we tipped back the fine ale, we noticed all of the Steelers memorabilia on the ceiling behind the bar. No doubt this is a Steelers joint 24/7/365. In addition to the memorabilia on the ceiling, there is a huge logo painted on the wall. Jason, the owner, is from Pittsburgh and has proudly catered to Steelers fans for 10 years.

palate. Lots of beer on tap, including a nitro system for pub-style ales.

In talking with the Steelers fans, we were told that the Winking Lizard doesn't put any memorabilia on the walls because of vandalism. Yet a good crowd gathers every week on Game Day. This is also a popular pre-game hangout for Steelers fans in town for the annual game against the Browns.

After visiting these two Cleveland two bars, we continued our trip to Green Bay, knowing we'd be back here again, but this time with a busload of superfans!

✦ ✦
WINKING LIZARD TAVERN
811 Huron Rd E
Cleveland, OH 44115
(216) 589-0313
www.winkinglizard.com

Our visit continued with a trip to the Winking Lizard in downtown Cleveland. Believe it or not, Steelers fans gather in the shadow of the First Energy Stadium (in case you missed it, this is the new name for the Mistake on the Lake). Unfortunately for us, our visit coincided with the ending of a Cleveland Cavaliers basketball game and the Winking Lizard is next to the basketball arena. The place was packed with basketball fans, but we found a few Steelers fans sporting the Black & Gold in the crowd.

The Winking Lizard is a bar for the beer lover. There are hundreds of different beers displayed in huge glass-fronted coolers. The selection is dominated by craft beer, and there is something to please every

✦ ✦
FOX AND HOUND

1479 Som Center Rd
Mayfield Heights, OH 44124
(440) 646-9078
www.foxandhound.com

his friends opened the shop conveniently located for us right in the North Hills on the way to the Turnpike! After enjoying a tremendous breakfast wrap, we rounded up our hardy fans and boarded the charter bus for Cleveland. Because it was still early, it seemed appropriate to begin the day with a Mammamosa (rating – "4"). This is a twist on a traditional mimosa by mixing orange juice with Mamma's Little Yellow Pils (the most excellent pilsner from Oskar Blues Brewing in Longmont, CO). The black and yellow can is the perfect way to begin a trip to Cleveland.

A few hours later, we rolled off the bus and headed into the Fox and Hound to meet up with the Heart of Steel Family – Steelers Fan Club of Northeastern Ohio. We met Erika through the Steelers fan club in Atlanta, Steelciti. Shawnee and Erika connected on Facebook and communicate regularly to share ideas and promote the love for the Pittsburgh Steelers. They also connected with the club in Memphis, which, because it doesn't have an NFL team, we weren't lucky enough to visit on this Journey.

Finally, we were ready for the last trip of the Journey. We began the road trip to Cleveland at the best coffee shop in Pittsburgh, Generoasta Coffee. Generoasta actually has a connection to the Pittsburgh Steelers. Eric Ravotti (Freeport, Penn State) played for the Steelers from 1994-1996. He gives back to the community in countless ways, including coaching football both at the youth level and at Fox Chapel High School. Being obsessed with coffee, he came up with the idea of opening a coffee shop as well. Eric's idea was that a portion of profits goes to local charities – showing the same sort of generosity that so many Steelers players and fans continuously demonstrate, So he and

The Heart of Steel Family has been meeting at the Fox and Hound for two years and they welcomed us to the City with free appetizers. The back room is designated for the Black & Gold and set up with a large

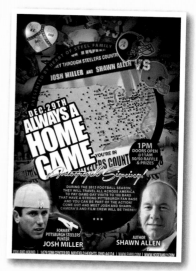

projection TV and has plenty of seating and a private wait staff. We also noticed a number of yellow and red flags. These flew at the screen in "good natured anger" as the game progressed. At one point, a few Cleveland Browns fans ventured into Steelers territory. They were greeted with boos by our compatriots and forced to retreat to safer confines to watch the game in a small booth in the main bar. Fox and Hound was a perfect setting.

Beer Note: Because we were in Cleveland, I felt compelled to drink a beer from their best brewery, Great Lakes (maybe the best thing to come from Cleveland). Feeling in a festive mood, I selected the 2013 Christmas Ale. This is a winter warmer-styled beer characterized by a heavy malt flavor, very few hops and lightly spiced with holiday aroma. The Great Lakes is one of the best winter warmers, but I made a huge mistake...the server suggested that this beer be served in a glass with the rim coated in a seasonal spice mix (similar to the salt on a margarita glass). I thought ordering the Kona Big Wave in Boston was a mistake, but this made that one seem inconsequential. The cinnamon sugar concoction on the glass ruined the beer – rating "1." That said, I am a very resourceful guy when it comes to a good beer. I grabbed an empty glass from behind the bar and transferred the beer to the new glass. What an improvement! It went from something I could not finish to a solid rating of "3."

Erika then told us of all the activities sponsored by the club. The club makes an annual trip to the NFL Hall of Fame and expects to have a huge crowd when Jerome Bettis gets in. They also travel to Pittsburgh in April for the Steelers Fan Blitz. As suggested by the name, the club also has strong ties to charity. Throughout the year, the club volunteers for many local charities. Not only do they collect for donations but also they give their time to help out those in need. Again, this is something we've seen time and time again with the Steelers fans across the country.

After another hard fought victory, we headed back to Pittsburgh. Everyone was pretty tired but having fun reliving the moments of the game. Then to our shock and dismay, Don (yes, Don of the Buffalo trip fame – possibly the "most valuable" non-AHG-staff Journey road tripper, certainly the most entertaining) grabbed the microphone from the bus driver. If we knew this was going to happen, we would have stopped it. But it was too late. We were serenaded home by the worst rap song in the history of music.

Finally, the day was here. I woke, had a breakfast wrap and a gigantic cup of coffee. I then kissed my wife and said, "Baby, after today you will have me back on the weekends." Truly unbelievable that this road trip to Cleveland and the Fox and the Hound would be our last trip on this Journey. The last NFL market we had to visit was in Cleveland. We rented a big cozy bus to go out in a blaze of glory. Not sure about the glory, but we did have a couple of people who got blazed.

Off to the Fox and Hound. We had to meet Erica and the Heart of Steel Family. They are on their "A" game 24/7 and it shows. You can tell this is also a tough group. If you live in Cleveland and you're a Steelers fan, you'd better be tough. I remember two gigantic Cleveland fans came in and they got bounced out fast.

Can't tell you how many times we Steelers rolled into Cleveland Stadium and had things thrown at

us on the sidelines. I remember all the stories of hearing about "the dog pound this and the dog pound that." Well, they're all true. It's amazing how I married a girl from Canton, Ohio. That move alone divided my family in half.

Rivalries are great. Every sport has it and every team needs one. When I was playing football for the Pittsburgh Steelers, the Cleveland Browns were the big one. It was a mean, nasty, physical football game. It didn't matter what the records were, both teams hated each other and winning the game made their season. Come on Cleveland, get your act together and get a football team that can compete so your fans don't have to wear bags over their heads during games. Truth be told, that is a loyal fan base over there in Cleveland and all they want is what Pittsburgh has. I can't think of another franchise that has endured so much pain over the last 15-20 years. The good news is that they are in our division and that usually means a win every year.

Anyway, back to the Journey. It was a good time. It was something that we've seen 99 other times: a group of people who all leave their egos and problems at the door. They put on their favorite Steelers jersey and join everyone else in the fan club. No matter what hand they are dealt in life they are always among friends when they gather to watch the Black & Gold. They share laughs, stories, food and of course a love for a great football team.

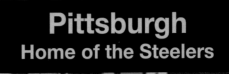

Pittsburgh
Home of the Steelers

Pittsburgh. Where it all started. Home to the rivers that protected frontier forts, forged iron and steel, and framed the past and present stadiums of the best football team in the NFL. The bars and the fans here set the standard for what it means to bleed Black & Gold. So many places are worthy of inclusion in this book. Where better to start our Journey than along the North Shore, in the shadow of Heinz Field. We made it to the Tilted Kilt during a preseason home game. The Steelers Alumni created just the stir we needed to kick off the Always a Home Game party. Then we hit the road, D.C. through Philadelphia. Time for some hometown love. Seeing fans across Steelers Nation is fantastic, but there's nothing like seeing the Pittsburgh skyline once again and mixing with the locals. This time we checked out Sharky's in Latrobe – the place to go during training camp – and Mullen's on the North Shore. The Steel City

Mafia at Mullen's and the stories we heard at Sharky's armed us with the fortitude to hit the road for Baltimore (love the city; the Ravens – not so much).

Seven cities later, we were feeling a bit homesick. We needed to reconnect with our hometown and ground ourselves in what it means to be from Western PA and love the Steelers. So we headed up to Billy's Black & Gold in Sharon on our way to Detroit. Any true Steelers fan must visit Billy's. After wrapping up the Journey in Cleveland, we needed to bring it back home to Pittsburgh. We made it to Bubba's for the best burger of the Journey, Sunny Jim's, the Clark Bar (home of some seriously dedicated fans) and Jerome Bettis Grille 36 (the BUS!). We've met people across the country and raised our glasses in some amazing places. We hope to visit many of them again. But there's nothing like the places in your own backyard.

The plan was to shoot the first Big Board video there. We wanted to make sure it was really good. We decided to call in some "talent" to help get us started. Between Josh Miller, Dwayne Woodruff, Marv Kellum and Louis Lipps we had four Super Bowl rings. Now that is talent!

The crowd was so loud and crazy – everything you expect from Steelers fans. It was all perfect until we tried to upload the file to the server. There were so many Steelers fans accessing the Internet that we were unable to upload the file. We were 15 minutes away from the premiere of Always a Home Game on the Big Board at Heinz Field and there was nothing to show. Thinking quickly, we loaded the file onto a flash drive and Josh took off sprinting for the stadium. In the end, Josh made it and the video played 10 minutes before kickoff as planned.

◆ ◆ ◆
TILTED KILT PUB & EATERY

353 N. Shore Dr.
Pittsburgh, PA 15212
(412) 235-7823
www.tiltedkilt.com/locations/northshore

We wanted to play it safe for our first stop on the Journey so we did not venture far from home. We made it only a few hundred yards from home, to be precise. With a good wind and a lucky bounce, Josh could kick a ball from Heinz Field to the Tilted Kilt Pub. We were a little hesitant to start our Journey in a chain restaurant, but the atmosphere on the North Shore sets it apart from every other Tilted Kilt location.

The Tilted Kilt sits equidistant between Heinz Field and PNC Park and is a great place to watch the away games or stop by before a home game. Of course, for most home games, you'd better plan on getting there early. There is a line at the door and the place is packed to capacity. Steelers' flags and banners hang from the ceiling and you will find memorabilia throughout the bar.

✦ ✦ ✦
MULLEN'S PITTSBURGH

200 Federal Street
Pittsburgh, PA 15212
(412) 231-1112
www.mullensbarandgrill.com

Our next stop in Pittsburgh was also on the North Shore – Mullen's Pittsburgh. This visit was special because it was the annual gathering in Pittsburgh for the Steel City Mafia, arguably the largest and most organized Pittsburgh Steelers Fan Club in the country. It boasts over 10,000 members and 15 "bosses" that organize events and gatherings everywhere. I think the club's motto speaks to the commitment of these fans – One World, One Team, One Family!

The Steel City Mafia began back in the days of MySpace and has been leveraging the power of

social media ever since. One of the original founders, Shawn, joined us at Mullen's sporting what can only be described as a Steelers' zoot suit. We also had the pleasure of meeting one of the fast-rising stars in the organization, Boss Jen, and her custom Steelers heels. One thing we learned is that the Steel City Mafia members take their game day outfits very seriously. If Jen keeps organizing events such as this one, she is well on her way to becoming a "Don."

Hanging with Greg Lloyd was one of the highlights at Mullen's. Greg and Josh spent hours talking to fans, signing autographs and enjoying the Game Day experience. Greg even helped us to sell our Always a Home Game shirts (get yours at www.alwaysahomegame.com) and ingeniously aided a fan who need a triple XL by adding a third "X" to one of our XXLs.

Beer Note: Stepping to the bar, we met one of the managers, Jake. He suggested that I try one of the seasonal beers, Blue Pumpkin Ale. I was underwhelmed by this beer. Rating – "2." As the rating suggests, it did not suck but the pumpkin flavors were muted.

♦ ♦ ♦

SHARKY'S CAFÉ

3960 State Route 30
Latrobe, PA 15650
(724) 532-1620
www.sharkyscafe.com

Sharky's Café in Latrobe is legendary for its Game Day atmosphere and Steelers fans. It's not uncommon to go to Sharky's during training camp and see current and former players enjoying the food and maybe even shooting a game of pool. On Game Days the atmosphere is electric. Steelers' memorabilia is all over the place and if you look closely you will notice one-of-a-kind pieces created by fans in Latrobe. They also have an incredible deep fried cheeseburger on the menu. If you order many of these, you may need Greg Lloyd's help with the sharpie to make our shirts XXXL. They also feature a great Loose Goose bar on Sundays.

Beer Note: The beer selection was good, but the list of craft breweries was limited. Time to go for an original craft beer – Sierra Nevada Pale Ale. This beer was first produced in 1980 and is a pioneer in the craft brewing movement. The Pale is bottle conditioned, which means that some of the fermentation takes place after the beer has been placed in the bottle. This allows for the flavor of the yeast to be prominent in the flavor profile, giving Sierra Nevada a fresh taste; rating – "4." I think some of the great beers that have been around a while get overshadowed by fancy labels or advertising. The fact of the matter is that Sierra Nevada is a great beer – order one!

To prove the popularity of the Steelers hangouts, the listeners of a local radio station voted Sharky's as the best bar in Pittsburgh in the annual Bar Bracket Challenge.

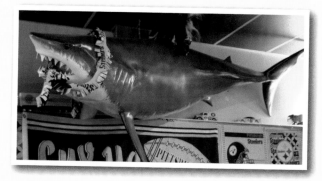

♦ ♦ ♦

BILLY'S BLACK & GOLD

514 Sharpsville Ave
Sharon, PA 16146
(724) 981-2030
www.billysblackandgold.com

We visited Billy's Black & Gold on our way to Detroit, so check out that chapter to get the scoop. It is a fantastic place and a Steelers must that you don't want to miss.

★ ★ ★
BUBBA'S GOURMET BURGHERS AND BEER

3109 Washington Pike
Bridgeville, PA 15017
(412) 654-5638
www.bubbaspgh.com

Much like Josh, Bubba is a popular radio personality on the Pittsburgh airways. This has allowed Bubba to create unique relationships with many Pittsburgh athletes, particularly Steelers. He told us that many come in to the restaurant for a great "burgher." The connection is so tight that he even has the grandson of former Steelers coach Tom Moore (receivers coach for Super Bowl XIII and Super Bowl XIV) on staff.

Not surprisingly, Bubba's features "burghers." Working with Big Ed – Bubba's father and a former butcher – they developed a special patty, which is a proprietary blend of brisket, prime meat and short ribs ground fresh daily. The burgher is second to none – just like the Steelers. There is no freezer on site. Everything is made fresh daily, no antibiotics, and no steroids.

On Game Day the TVs are dedicated to the Black & Gold. The menus also carry a few special items. One of the mainstays is the Black and Gold Burgher. The patty is coated with a special seasoning and then cooked at a higher than normal temperature, which produces a delicious black burgher that is topped with golden cheese. Some of the other specials are not quite as straight forward. For Raven's games, Bubba's cooks a special bird – CHICKEN! Bubba is very passionate about the Steelers and the experience on Game Day. Extensive efforts are made to mimic the experience at the stadium. Steelers-themed music is pumped through the audio system during all game breaks; there are weekly giveaways and numerous drink specials.

One of the more unique items on the wall is a sign where all of the letters are images from famous public signs around Pittsburgh. How many do you recognize? Stop by and check it out. Test your local knowledge.

Beer Note: The beer selection was good, and one of the featured drafts was Victory Prima Pils from Dowingtown, PA. This is a great German Pilsner, ideal for someone who wants to try a craft beer that is not too hoppy; rating – "3." One of the great lawnmower beers; nothing tastes better on a hot summer afternoon.

♦ ♦ ♦
THE ORIGINAL CLARK BAR & GRILL

D.L. Clark Building
503 Martindale St.
Pittsburgh, PA 15212
(412) 231-5720
www.thepipagroup.com/clarkbarandgrill.html

The Clark Bar has been a part of pre-game celebrations in Pittsburgh for decades. Opened in the late '80s, the Clark Bar was just a few yards away from Three Rivers Stadium. The memorabilia throughout the bar is amazing (we even found a signed picture of Josh kicking in his prime). They have one of the best collections of signed footballs we've ever seen. Joe told us stories of how the team used to practice at Three Rivers as well. On many occasions the players would stop by for a quick meal and to enjoy the atmosphere of the Clark Bar. The Clark Bar also has a segregated Cigar Bar – a unique Game Day experience for those fans who prefer a fine scotch and cigar while watching the Steelers.

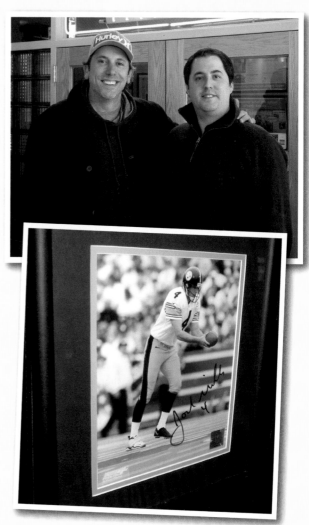

★ ★ ★
SUNNY JIM'S TAVERN

255 Camp Horne Rd.
Pittsburgh, PA 15202
(412) 761-6700
www.sunnyjimstavern.com

Choosing Steelers hangouts in Western Pennsylvania is a difficult thing to do. Every bar and restaurant in the region is a gathering spot for the fans. But when we saw the Sunny Jim's Tavern T-shirt at the Always A Home Game trip to New York, we knew this was a place we had to go.

We didn't make a game night, but we were fortunate enough to catch wing night. In talking to Mike, he told us that Sunny Jim's has been a Steelers hangout for over 36 years. There are over 200 fans for the away games. The home games are a different story. Many Steelers fans gather for pre-game festivities at Sunny Jim's, then carpool to the game. When the Steelers are victorious, the celebration continues at the Tavern long into the night. Mike said one of the reasons Sunny Jim's has been so successful is the consistent winning record of the Pittsburgh Steelers!

A unique game day feature is the 23' outdoor projection TV – the largest outdoor TV in the city. The two outdoor seating areas remain packed as long as the weather is tolerable. Many of the tables and seats at the bar have been reserved for the regulars throughout the years. Mike told us of a great story about one of his regulars. Unfortunately, she had a heart attack during one of the Steelers games a few years back. The EMTs arrived and rushed her off to the hospital. The next week, her seat remained empty. Out of respect, nobody was going to sit there. Then, just before kickoff, she came back into Sunny Jim's and reclaimed her seat! The entire bar gave her a standing ovation. That is a dedicated Steelers fan!

Like many of the Steelers hangouts, Sunny Jim's patrons spend considerable effort working with charitable causes – specifically, Wounded Warriors. As we looked behind the bar, we saw another shared interest with other Steelers fans, a shot-ski. At first glance, we thought it was just like the one from Houston, and then realized our mistake. At Frank 'N' Steins, the shot-ski was a water ski, at Sunny Jim's it was a snow ski! Regardless of the weather, Steelers fans know how to celebrate.

around the world, 36 wines and 36 of the most unique martinis and specialty cocktails. I think you get the drift – it's all about 36.

The walls are covered in signed personal notes from many famous celebrities and more former Steelers players than you can imagine. One could spend hours remembering all the great plays these names made. The restaurant features one wall next to the central bar where the "Bus" is running over would-be tacklers. As one would guess, Grille 36 is completely packed for every Steelers home game with a first-come first-served policy. The line forms outside long before the doors open.

✦ ✦ ✦
JEROME BETTIS' GRILLE 36

93 N. Shore Dr.
Pittsburgh, PA 15212
(412) 224-6287
www.jeromebettisgrille36.g3restaurants.com

Just as Jerome Bettis ended his career by playing his last game in his hometown of Detroit, we ended our Journey where it began, in the shadow of Heinz Stadium, at Jerome Bettis' Grille 36. Grille 36 has been voted Pittsburgh's best sports restaurant every year since it opened. This Steelers hangout boasts 50 state-of-the-art high definition flat screen TVs and has an amazing sound system. As Jerome likes to say, Grille 36 is the home for everything Steelers, everything Penguins, everything Pirates, everything Panthers, everything Pittsburgh!!! Grille 36 is also the home of the famous succulent 36-oz bone-in NY Strip Steak. The bar features, what else, 36 beers on tap, a selection of 36 exceptional bottled beers from

Pittsburgh has so many great bars that cater to sports teams that we could devote an entire book to them. That being said, we had to get a sampling of a few that seem to stick out. Our first was the Tilted Kilt. I understand that it's a chain, but it's settled behind one of the end zones at Heinz Field. So you can throw the chain theory out the window. This is a big-time Steelers hangout on the North Shore. It also served as our launching pad for the Always A Home Game Journey. We had our first Big Board game there in the pre-season. It was our first chance to show Pittsburgh and Steelers Nation what we were about to do. We had an all-star cast to get things rolling. Dwayne Woodruff, Mark Kellum and Louis Lipps came to the party. I've been doing radio shows at the Tilted Kilt for a couple of years now before the game and I swear it seems like everyone in that stadium walks through this particular bar at some point before kickoff. We knew it would get loud and crazy. If this sounds like your scene, head to the Tilted Kilt.

Sharkey's Café in Latrobe: back when I was alive and playing for the Steelers, I can't tell you how many times I walked through those front doors. Players, coaches, reporters and fans alike head to Sharkey's. My relationship with Sharkey's is different than most. Every year when we had to report to Saint Vincent's, home of the Pittsburgh Steelers preseason training camp facilities, I would take the placekicker and especially the punter out for a night on the town. We made ourselves comfortable

at Sharky's. This was the only hazing I would do the entire year. Hazing is of course what veterans do to the rookies when they come into camp. I had a deal with the bartender – every half hour he would come over with four Jagermeister shots. After a handful of hours that would add up. Of those four, two would actually be filled with Diet Coke – one for the veteran kicker and one for the veteran punter. Hey man, any advantage I can get I was going to try. That trick usually took them two days to recover from. You would think that after all this time I would feel bad about that. You'd be wrong.

On to Bubba's. Other than my wife and kids, I can't think of anything else I love as much as a great hamburger. I am on a constant quest to find the best burger and am willing to drive for it. I understand how sad that sounds but it's true. Having a burger is a treat and I only have one a month. Why I do this I have no idea but it's a rule I've been following a long time. If we jump back to 1994 and replayed most of that year you will find that Bubba and I were pretty good friends and spent a great deal of time together. Norm Johnson, the place kicker at the time, introduced us and we remain good friends today. You can imagine my delight that Bubba opened up a place of his own (about time) and has the greatest burger in all of Pennsylvania, in my opinion. Yes, Bubba is a gigantic Steelers fan. But he loves the Pens and clearly the Pirates as well. If you head to Bubba's to catch a game you will enjoy a fantastic gourmet burger and you might just see Bubba in the house. Not only is he a great husband, father and friend, he is a great owner and makes sure that everyone that walks through that door has a great experience (and the best burger they've ever had!).

The original Clark Bar: this place alone could be its own book. No joke, the stories that took place at the Clark Bar are legendary, as are the celebrities that walk through those doors. If you ask Angelo Lamatrice, the owner, to tell you those stories he will tell you to "go take a walk." Loyal as the day is long best describes Angelo. He is one of the nicest and most generous men I have come across in all my playing days. There is not another human being on this wonderful planet that has a better Pittsburgh memorabilia collection than Angelo. The beautiful thing about the collection is that he didn't ask for any of it. When players were in town they would make the Clark Bar their first and last stop. They would come by and hold court with Angelo and give him some piece of memorabilia. Nothing was better than hanging with Angelo and his sons David and Joey after a

game. He would rope off a section and a bunch of Steelers would come by and enjoy the greatest ribs you could find in Pennsylvania. Talk about legendary – that's his relationship with the ballplayers. It was different back then. Players weren't so guarded as they are today. I swear to God there was a tunnel that went from Three Rivers to the Clark Bar. Some of my greatest memories of playing professional sports happened at the Clark Bar. Whether it was late nights with Angelo, David, Joey and Debbie and yes, even Cheeks, or the memory of them all coming to my wedding in about 17 inches of snow. What makes this place so special is the people running it.

WRAP-UP AND THANK-YOUS

When people ask us, "What were the Steelers fans like in _____ (fill in the blank)?", the answer is the same everywhere: they are passionate for the Black & Gold. Game Day at their favorite hangout is like a family reunion. Their commitment to the team is rivaled only by their commitment to the community. Steelers fans are simply the best.

Statistics from the Journey: We travelled 33,834 miles across Steelers Country while visiting 100 bars in the 32 NFL markets. We were greeted by 28 formalized Steelers fan clubs and met thousands of other Steelers fans who make their own journey each Game Day to their local Steelers hangout. Shawn enjoyed 78 different craft beers (Josh, not so much), and we had the opportunity to sample some incredible food. Most of all, we learned something important: we have a GIGANTIC family tree. That tree is Black & Gold.

First and foremost, we would like to thank our families. Carolyn and Angie, you were superheroes for 140 days (in particular, though for much longer in general) keeping everything running smoothly while we embarked on this epic Journey. Without your tireless efforts and support none of this would have been

possible. Olivia, Cal, Ava, Lauren and Mac, thanks for making the time home special, and not giving us too much crap for missing all the activities.

To the Pittsburgh Steelers: In our humble opinions, the Pittsburgh Steelers are the best run, most respected franchise in the NFL. Mr. Rooney, your faith in this project and willingness to support our Journey was incredible. Your family, and the entire organization, has created something truly special. The way you guide the franchise is reflected in the fan base. We saw passion and commitment to the team and community that can only come from superior leadership – all Steelers fans thank you. Tony, your guidance and assistance were invaluable. Rick and Rick, your time and skills allowed us to fulfill our dream of meeting Steelers fans throughout Steelers Nation. Although the deadlines were too close some game days, your flexibility and understanding were amazing. Finally – Lynne, you are an asset to the organization. Every player we met speaks so highly of you and your ability to make everyone feel a part of the family, even long after their playing days are over. The only team better than the one on the field is the one in the front office; we could not have done this without your support. Thank you.

To Carolyn Allen: You took our gibberish and turned it into a story that all Steelers fans can be proud of. Thank you for your patience as we missed deadlines and turned in chapters out of order. Your ability to organize our thoughts and make sense of this crazy Journey is commendable. This book would have never been made without you.

To St. Lynn's Press: Paul, you took a chance on two first-time authors with a harebrained scheme. I am sure you thought at times that we were crazy – and you still may – but you stuck with us and for this we are grateful. Cathy and Holly, it has been a pleasure working with you and we have seen what a truly talented team can do with our pictures and text. Your skill and craft have turned such ordinary content into this tremendous book. We are so lucky to have found such a great partner for our book.

To the Always a Home Game team: Domenic, George and Abbey. For the long hours spent on the road and the unrelenting dedication to the project – thank you. Not only did your efforts bring the book to fruition, but the constant pestering finally forced Josh to start his Twitter account – so the thousands of followers thank you as well.

To our interns: Kate, Adam and Tiffany. Your behind the scenes effort ensured we had a place to go each week and someone to greet us so warmly. I can only imagine your thoughts when we first met in the basement of the old office in Warrendale. My best guess is that you regretted the decision...we are grateful you stuck with us.

To our best traveling supporters: Don, Mike and Gooz. It is always special to meet someone new, but even more enjoyable when we see a familiar face.

Special mention to the entire Steward family for joining us in St. Louis, Chicago and Tampa.

To Joyce Allen: For the countless hours stitching together all of the T-shirts collected on the Journey into the incredible quilts that commemorate our adventure.

To our sponsors: Clem's Trailer, Sign-a-Rama South, Wilson Insurance, Lamparski Orthodontics and Pine-Richland Self-Storage. Every project needs financial support and you were there for us. We encourage every reader to support these fantastic businesses. Steve and Randy, the RV was incredible. We always made a grand entrance, thanks to you (additionally our families now want to vacation in an RV). Gary, thank you for the phenomenal wrap job on the RV – we turned heads in every city across Steelers Nation. It was also a pleasure to meet your son, a true American and we are proud of his service. Bob, I am glad we did not need to call you...although it was close in Buffalo. Don... the rap (not to be confused with the wrap on the RV) on the bus says it all. Thanks for all of your support and content for the book – we see your great work in our kids' smiles everyday. Finally – Trina, without your support we would have been hated by everyone in our neighborhood for parking the RV on the street...our thanks extends beyond the two of us.

To the fan clubs: You welcomed us on Game Day as if we were a part of your family. One thing we learned on this Journey is that the fan clubs are very similar across Steelers Nation, showing not only a dedication to the team, but also to the community. Keep up the good work, and thanks to each and every one: 408 Steel City Mafia, Atlanta Steelers Fan Club, Bay Area Black and Gold Club, Cajun Steelers Fan Club, Chicago

Steelers Club, DC Steelers Nation, First Coast Black & Gold, Fort Worth Steelers, Heart of Steel Family, Hwy 6-Burgh Steelers Nation, KC Steelers Fan Club, Northwest Steeler Nation, S.E. Pa. STEELERS Brigade, South Bay Steelers, Southern Steel Fan Club of North Texas, Space City Steelers Fan Club, St. Louis Steelers Fan Club, Steel City Crusade, Steelciti, Steelers Fans of Minnesota, Steelers Fans of Pinellas, Steelers Nation Fan Club - Fort Worth, Steeltown in Uptown, The Heart of Steel Family, Three Rivers Club, Virginia Black and Gold No. 1, West Houston Steelers Nation, Yinz in Boston.

To the Steelers hangouts: As it says on your certificate, we appreciate your efforts to carry on the proud tradition of the Pittsburgh Steelers, and we thank you for allowing us to share your stories and tradition with the rest of Steelers Nation. Thanks to: Austin Avenue, Beckett's Bar & Grill, Beef "O" Bradys (Wildwood), Big Al's Pub & Grubberia, Billy's Black and Gold, Bobby V's Sports Gallery Café, Bonefish Mac's Sports Grille, Brittany's Restaurant & Sports Bar, Bub's Dive Bar & Grill, Bubba's Gourmet Burghers and Beer, Buccelli's JJ Madwell's, Buffalo Wild Wings, Buxy's Salty Dog, Capitol Centre, Cheaters Sports Bar, Cheers Bar & Grill, Cooter Brown's Tavern & Oyster Bar, Cooter's Restaurant & Sports Bar, Dark Horse Tap & Grill, Dave and Buster's (Plymouth Meeting), Dave's Last Resort & Raw Bar, Delaney's Music Pub and Eatery, Durkin's, Eagles Nest Sports Grill, East Side Pub, End Zone Sports Bar & Grill, Fado Irish Pub & Restaurant (Seattle), Fitzgerald's Irish Pub, Fox and Hound (Mason), Fox and Hound (Mayfield Heights), Fox and Hound (New Orleans), Fox and Hound (Philadelphia), Francesca's Sports Bar, Frank 'n' Steins Bar and Grill, Fremont Dock Restaurant, Giordano Bros. (Mission), Giordano Bros. (North Beach), Giuseppe's Steel City Pizza, Great White Grill, Hammerhead's Seafood & Sports Grill, Harold's Cave Creek Corral, Helen Fitzgerald's Irish Pub & Grill, Hibernia Bar & Grill, Igot's Martiki Bar, Jerome Bettis Grille 36, Johnny's Tavern, Lake Effectz, Latitude 30, Lir, Lombardo's Tavern, Main Event, Malarkey's Tavern, Martino's on Vine, McGregor's Grill & Ale House, Mullen's Pittsburgh, Nickel Plate Bar & Grill, O'Brien's Irish Pub and Grill, O'Malley's in the Alley, O'Neal's Pub, Outta the Way Café, Pappa's Ice House, Patrick McGovern's Pub, Piranha's Bar and Grill, Pittsburgh Willy's, Pittsburgh's Pub, Primanti Bros. (Ft. Lauderdale), Prost!, Quaker Steak & Lube (New Berlin), Reservoir Bar, Roggie's Brew & Grill, Rooney's Public House, the Gastropub, Rudy's Sports Bar, Shanghai Kelly's, Shanna Key Irish Pub, Sharky's Café, Smith's Olde Bar, Southside 815, Spanky's Sports Bar, Sunny Jim's, Tampa Tap Room, Te Roma, The Blue Chip Sports Bar, The Cab Bar & Grill, The Grove Spot, The Irish Exit, The Library, The Locker Room Sports Lounge, The Mighty Pint, The Ocean View Pub, The Original Clark Bar, The Pittsburgh Inn, The Plantation, Pour House, The Rusty Bucket Bar and Grill, Tilted Kilt North Shore, Todd Conner's Bar & Restaurant, Vivio's Food & Spirits, Wilson's Bar, Winking Lizard Tavern and Woody's Tavern.

To the Pittsburgh Steelers fans: Without the support of the millions of Pittsburgh Steelers fan around the world, none of this would be possible. Your passion for the team, and compassion for your communities is unsurpassed by the fans of any other team or organization. It is your fanatical commitment that makes it all possible...and for the Black & Gold – it's Always a Home Game. ✦

INDEX OF THE BARS

Name	Street Address	City	St	Zip	Phone	Website
Harold's Cave Creek Corral	6895 E Cave Creek Road	Cave Creek	AZ	85331	(480) 488-1906	www.haroldscorral.com
Pittsburgh Willy's	1509 N. Arizona Avenue	Chandler	AZ	85225	(480) 857-2860	www.pittsburghwillys.com
Francesca's Sports Bar	2135 Old Middlefield Way	Mountain View	CA	94043	(650) 965-1162	www.francescasbar.com
Cheaters Sports Bar	3221 Folsom Blvd.	Sacramento	CA	95816	(916) 736-0563	
McGregor's Grill & Ale House	10475 San Diego Mission Rd	San Diego	CA	92108	(619) 282-9797	www.mcgregorssandiego.com
The Library	7459 Mission Gorge Rd	San Diego	CA	92120	(619) 583-5839	
Bub's Dive Bar & Grill	1030 Garnet Avenue	San Diego	CA	92109	(619) 270-7269	www.bubsdive.com
Shanghai Kelly's	2064 Polk Street	San Francisco	CA	94109	(415) 771-3300	
Pittsburgh's Pub	4207 Judah Street	San Francisco	CA	94122	(415) 664-3926	
Giordano Bros. - Mission	3108 16th Street	San Francisco	CA	94103	(415) 437-BROS	www.giordanobros.com
Giordano Bros. - North Beach	303 Columbus Avenue	San Francisco	CA	94133	(415) 397-BROS	www.giordanobros.com
The Blue Chip Sports Bar	325 S. 1st Street #190	San Jose	CA	95113	(408) 971-2898	www.bluechipsj.com
Buccelli's JJ Madwell's	26412 Main Street	Conifer	CO	80433	(303) 838-1440	www.jjmadwells.net
The Rusty Bucket Bar and Grill	3355 Wadsworth Blvd. Ste. G101	Lakewood	CO	80227	(303) 980-6200	www.the-rusty-bucket.com
The Mighty Pint	1831 M Street NW	Washington	DC	20036	(202) 466-3010	www.themightypint.com
The Pour House	319 Pennsylvania Avenue SE	Washington	DC	20003	(202) 546-0779	www.pourhousedc.com
Cooter's Restaurant & Sports Bar	423 Poinsettia Avenue	Clearwater Beach	FL	33767	(727) 462-2668	www.cooters.com
The Grove Spot	3324 Virginia Street	Coconut Grove	FL	33133	(305) 774-6696	www.grovespot.com
East Side Pub	2376 N. Federal Hwy	Ft. Lauderdale	FL	33305	(954) 566-0001	www.eastsidepubfl.com
Primanti Bros	901 N. Atlantic Blvd.	Ft. Lauderdale	FL	33304	(954) 565-0605	www.primantibros.com
The Ocean View Pub	Mile Marker 84.5	Islamorada	FL	33036	(305) 664-8052	www.theocean-view.com
Latitude 30	10370 Philips Hwy	Jacksonville	FL	32256	(904) 365-5555	www.latthirty.com
Rooney's Public house, the Gastropub	1153 Town Center Drive	Jupiter	FL	33458	(561) 694-6610	www.rooneyspublichouse.com
Shanna Key Irish Pub	1900 Flagler Avenue	Key West	FL	33040	(305) 295-8880	www.shannakeyirishpub.com
Dave's Last Resort & Raw Bar	632 Lake Avenue	Lake Worth	FL	33460	(561) 588-5208	www.daveslastresort.com
Igot's Martiki Bar	702 Lake Avenue	Lake Worth	FL	33460	(561) 582-4468	www.daveslastresort.com
Rudy's Sports Bar	11100 66th Street North	Largo	FL	33773	(727) 546-2616	www.rudyssportsbar.com
Bonefish Mac's Sports Grille	2002 East Sample Rd	Lighthouse	FL	33064	(954) 781-6227	www.bonefishmacs.com
Plantation Bar & Grill	3754 Roscommon Drive	Ormond Beach	FL	32174	(386) 615-8948	www.plantationbarandgrill.com
Giuseppe's Steel City Pizza	3658 S. Nova Road	Port Orange	FL	32129	(386) 761-4717	www.giuseppessteelcitypizza.com
Great White Grill	2440 Palm Ridge Rd	Sanibel	FL	33957	(239) 472-0212	www.greatwhitegrill.com
O'Brien's Irish Pub and Grill	15435 N. Dale Mabry Hwy	Tampa	FL	33618	(813) 541-6968	www.obrienspubstampa.com
Tampa Tap Room	13150 N. Dale Mabry Hwy	Tampa	FL	33618	(813) 961-2337	
Beef "O" Bradys	840 South Main Street	Wildwood	FL	34785	(352) 689-0048	www.beefobradys.com
Smith's Olde Bar	1578 Piedmont Ave NE	Atlanta	GA	30324	(404) 875-1522	www.smithsoldebar.com
Hammerhead's Seafood & Sports Grill	415 Peachtree Industrial Boulevard	Suwanee	GA	30024	(770) 945-3570	www.facebook.com/HammerheadsSeafoodSports

INDEX OF THE BARS

Name	Street Address	City	St	Zip	Phone	Website
Prost!	2566 N Lincoln	Chicago	IL	60614	(773) 880-9900	www.prostchicago.com
Durkin's	810 W. Diversey Pkwy.	Chicago	IL	60614	(773) 525-2515	www.bar1events.com/durkins/
Dark Horse Tap & Grill	3443 N. Sheffield Avenue	Chicago	IL	60657	(773) 248-4400	www.darkhorsechicago.com
Nickel Plate Bar & Grill	8654 116th Street	Fishers	IN	46038	(317) 841-2888	www.nickelplatebarandgrill.com
Main Event	7038 Shore Terrace	Indianapolis	IN	46254	(317) 298-4771	www.maineventindy.com
Johnny's Tavern	6765 W 119th Street	Overland Park	KS	66209	(913) 451-4542	www.johnnystavern.com
Buffalo Wild Wings	3434 Veterans Memorial Blvd.	Metarie	LA	70002	(504) 252-4606	www.buffalowildwings.com
Cooter Brown's Tavern & Oyster Bar	509 S. Carrollton Avenue	New Orleans	LA	70118	(504) 866-9104	www.cooterbrowns.com
Fox and Hound	1200 S. Clearwater Parkway	New Orleans	LA	70123	(504) 731-6000	www.foxandhound.com
Lir	903 Boylston Street	Boston	MA	02116	(617) 778-0089	www.lironboylston.com
Roggie's Brew & Grill	356 Chestnut Hill Ave	Brighton	MA	02135	(617) 566-1880	www.roggies.com
Todd Conner's Bar & Restaurant	700 S. Broadway	Baltimore	MD	21231	(410) 537-5005	www.toddconners.com
Buxy's Salty Dog	28th Street Bayside	Ocean City	MD	21842	(410) 289-0973	www.buxys.com
Outta the Way Café	17503 Redland Road	Rockville	MD	20855	(301) 963-6895	www.outta.
Te Roma	24436 Van Dyke Ave	Center Line	MI	48015	(586) 757-7575	
Vivio's Food & Spirits	3601 E. 12 Mile Rd	Warren	MI	48092	(5860 576-0495	www.vivioswarren.com
Patrick McGovern's Pub	225 7th St W	St. Paul	MN	55102	(651) 224-5821	www.patmcgoverns.com
Helen Fitzgerald's Irish Pub & Grill	3650 S. Lindbergh	St. Louis	MO	63127	(314) 984-0026	www.helenfitzgeralds.com
Fitzgerald's Irish Pub	201 East 5th Street	Charlotte	NC	28202	(704) 900-8088	www.fitzgeraldscharlotte.com
The Locker Room Sports Lounge	4809 S. Tryon Street	Charlotte	NC	28217	(704) 523-1050	
Big Al's Pub & Grubberia	631-401 Brawley School Road	Mooresville	NC	28117	(704) 664-0992	www.bigalspubandgrubberia.com
Beckett's Bar & Grill	81 Pearl Street	New York	NY	10004	(212) 269-1001	www.beckettsnyc.com
Reservoir Bar	70 University Place	New York	NY	10003	(212) 475-0770	
The Irish Exit	978 2nd Avenue	New York	NY	10022	(212) 755-8383	www.irishexitnyc.com
Hibernia Bar & Grill	401 W 50th Street	New York	NY	10019	(212) 969-9703	www.hiberniabar.com
Martino's on Vine	2618 Vine Street	Cincinnati	OH	45219	(513) 221-8487	www.martinosonvine.com
O'Malley's in the Alley	25 Odgen Place	Cincinnati	OH	45202	(513) 381-3114	www.omalleysinthealley.com
Winking Lizard Tavern	811 Huron Rd E	Cleveland	OH	44115	(216) 589-0313	www.winkinglizard.com
Lake Effectz	6710 Lake Rd	Madison	OH	44057	(440) 428-5400	
Fox and Hound	5113 Bowen Drive	Mason	OH	45040	(513) 229-7921	www.foxandhound.com
Fox and Hound	1479 Som Center Rd	Mayfield Heights	OH	44124	(440) 646-9078	www.foxandhound.com
Bubba's Gourmet Burghers and Beer	3109 Washington Pike	Bridgeville	PA	15017	(412) 564-5638	www.bubbaspgh.com
Lombardo's Tavern	915 W. 21st Street	Erie	PA	16502	(814) 455-7821	
The Cab Bar & Grill	5442 West Ridge Road	Erie	PA	16506	(814) 838-0507	www.the-cab.com
The Pittsburgh Inn	3725 W. Lake Rd	Erie	PA	16505	(814) 833-0925	www.thepittsburghinn.com

INDEX OF THE BARS

Name	Street Address	City	St	Zip	Phone	Website
Sharky's Café	3960 State Route 30	Latrobe	PA	15650	(724) 532-1620	www.sharkyscafe.com
O'Neal's Pub	611 S. 3rd Street	Philadelphia	PA	19147	(215) 574-9495	www.onealspub.com
Fox and Hound	1501 Spruce Street	Philadelphia	PA	19102	(215) 732-8610	www.foxandhound.com
Tilted Kilt North Shore	353 N Shore Dr	Pittsburgh	PA	15212	(412) 235-7823	www.northshore.tiltedkilt.com
Mullen's Pittsburgh	200 Federal Street	Pittsburgh	PA	15212	(412) 231-1112	www.mullensbarandgrill.com/pittsburgh
Jerome Bettis Grille 36	393 N Shore Drive	Pittsburgh	PA	15212	(412) 224-6287	www.jeromebettisgrille36.g3restaurants.com
The Original Clark Bar	503 Martindale St.	Pittsburgh	PA	15212	(412) 231-1009	www.thepipagroup.com/clarkbarandgrill.html
Sunny Jim's	255 Camp Horne Rd	Pittsburgh	PA	15202	(412) 761-6700	www.sunnyjimstavern.com
Dave and Buster's	500 W. Germantown Pike	Plymouth Meeting	PA	19462	(610) 260-4483	www.daveandbusters.com
Billy's Black and Gold	514 Sharpsville Ave	Sharon	PA	16146	(724) 981-2030	www.billysblackandgold.com
Delaney's Music Pub and Eatery	117 W. Main Street	Spartanburg	SC	29306	(864) 583-3100	www.delaneyspub.com
Piranha's Bar and Grill	113 2nd Ave N	Nashville	TN	37201	(615) 248-4375	www.piranhasbar.com
Spanky's Sports Bar	330 Welch Road	Nashville	TN	37211	(615) 837-3450	www.spankyssportsbar.com
Bobby V's Sports Gallery Café	4301 South Bowen Rd	Arlington	TX	76016	(817) 467-9922	www.bobbyvsports.com
Malarky's Tavern	4460 Trinity Mills Rd	Dallas	TX	75287	(972) 931-7300	www.malarkystavern.com
Eagles Nest Sports Grill	8455 Boat Club Rd	Fort Worth	TX	76179	(817) 236-8881	www.eaglesnestsportsgrill.com
Woody's Tavern	4744 Bryant Irvin Rd #946	Fort Worth	TX	76132	(817) 732-4936	www.woodystaverntexas.com
End Zone Sports Bar & Grill	15209 Westheimer Rd	Houston	TX	77082	(281) 597-0241	www.theendzonesportsbar.com
Austin Avenue	1801 N. Plano Road	Richardson	TX	75081	(972) 907-8003	www.austinavenue.com
Pappa's Ice House	314 Pruitt Road	Spring	TX	77380	(281) 364-8140	www.papasicehousetx.com
Frank 'n' Steins Bar and Grill	9907 Highway 6	Sugar Land	TX	77498	(281) 744-4547	www.franknsteinsgrill.com
Southside 815	815 S. Washington Street	Alexandria	VA	22314	(703) 836-6222	www.southside815.com
Brittany's Restaurant & Sports Bar	12449 Dillingham Square	Woodbridge	VA	22192	(703) 730-0728	www.brittanysrestaurant.com
Fremont Dock Restaurant	1102 N. 34th Street	Seattle	WA	98103	(206) 829-8372	www.fremontdock.com
Fado Irish Pub & Restaurant	801 1st Avenue	Seattle	WA	98104	(206) 264-2700	www.fadoirishpub.com/seattle
Cheers Bar & Grill	2611 Pacific Avenue	Tacoma	WA	98402	(253) 627-4430	www.cheersdowntown.com
Capitol Centre	725 W. Capitol Dr	Appleton	WI	54914	(920) 735-9941	www.capitolcentreonline.com
Wilson's Bar	2144 Atwood Ave	Madison	WI	53704	(608) 241-2226	www.wilsonssportsbarandgrill.com
Quaker Steak & Lube	4900 S Moorland Rd	New Berlin	WI	53151	(262) 754-9090	www.thelube.com

ABOUT THE AUTHORS

JOSH MILLER

Josh played in the NFL for 13 years as a punter, eight of those with the Steelers (1996-2003). He also played for both the New England Patriots, where he won a Super Bowl, and then for the Tennessee Titans. He retired in 2008. He was inducted into the National Jewish Sports Hall of Fame and Museum in 2002. Josh is a nationally recognized drive-time sports radio show host for 93.7 The Fan morning drive in Pittsburgh, a local CBS Radio affiliate. Josh wakes up every day next to his best friend and together they are raising their three beautiful kids.

SHAWN ALLEN

Shawn is a "serial entrepreneur" with a background in industrial and memorabilia auction sites. Shawn managed the auction for the sale of the memorabilia from Three Rivers Stadium and for the Civic Arena. He has a B.A. from Allegheny College, a Master of Arts in Statistics from the University of Pittsburgh and a Master of Business Administration from the University of Pittsburgh. He has entirely too much knowledge concerning beer. He's been a home brewer for more than 15 years, has traveled to beer festivals through-out the United States and has attended "Craft Beer School" sponsored by the Pittsburgh Cultural Trust since its inception in 2006.

Visit us at www.alwaysahomegame.com